WALLABY WARRIOR

WALLABY WARRIOR

The World War I diaries of Australia's only British Lion

TOM RICHARDS

EDITED BY GREG GROWDEN

ALLEN&UNWIN

SYDNEY•MELBOURNE•AUCKLAND•LONDON

First published in Australia in 2013

Allen & Unwin
83 Alexander Street
Crows Nest NSW 2065
Australia
Phone: (61 2) 8425 0100
Email: info@allenandunwin.com
Web: www.allenandunwin.com

Cataloguing-in-Publication details are available from the National Library of
Australia
www.trove.nla.gov.au

ISBN 978 1 74331 661 0

Typeset in 11/15pt Minion by Midland Typesetters, Australia
Printed and bound in Australia by Griffin Press

10 9 8 7 6 5 4 3 2 1

MIX
Paper from
responsible sources
FSC
www.fsc.org   FSC® C009448

The paper in this book is FSC® certified.
FSC® promotes environmentally responsible,
socially beneficial and economically viable
management of the world's forests.

CONTENTS

AUTHOR'S NOTE

While researching *Gold, Mud 'n' Guts: The incredible Tom Richards, footballer, war hero, Olympian*, I discovered that Tom Richards's war diaries were held at the Australian War Memorial in Canberra. After countless Sydney–Canberra trips, I was saved from going completely bonkers when the Richards family provided me with a copy of Tom's diaries so that I could complete the manuscript. I am forever indebted to Richards's niece, Hazel Young, and his daughter, Joan Menck, for giving me permission to use them then and now.

Joan Menck is an inspiration, and I am delighted she has been so enthusiastic in ensuring her father's war diaries were made available to a wider audience. I dedicate this book to her.

Editing the diaries was a difficult task as Richards was such an enthusiastic and relentless writer, often penning more than 1000 words each day during four years of war. As well as his thoroughness in describing everything that was going on around him, he also delved heavily into his feelings and inadequacies. To make the war diaries manageable I focused on the most important events and experiences and the most crucial descriptions. This also meant not sanitising the text, so I have retained Richards's original descriptions such as 'niggers' and 'coons'. While racist and derogatory, this is how the Australian soldier spoke during the First World War.

INTRODUCTION

'If ever the Earth had to select a Rugby Football team to play against Mars, Tom Richards would be the first player chosen', *The Times* of London gushed. The *Yorkshire Post* said that in matches Richards stood out 'like Saul among the prophets', and London's *Evening News* described him as 'the best forward in the world'. What's more, 'he was also certainly (now girls!) the handsomest man in the team'. Newspaper scribes seemed to compete over who could make Richards most resemble an athletic god, which was understandable following his pivotal role in Australian Rugby Union's first serious venture— the tour of the United Kingdom in 1908–09, which lasted for seven and a half months. Richards was the standout player of that tour: an imaginative, fearless, clever forward. He convinced the northern hemisphere snobs that the colonials actually were the best at something. So accomplished were Richards and his fellow troubadours, who included pastoralists, train drivers, plumbers, bank clerks, 'gentlemen of leisure', surgeons, university layabouts and butchers, that following the tour they were chased by those with money to burn who were masterminding the establishment of the Northern Union professional code in Sydney. Almost immediately after arriving home, the core members of that first Wallabies team signed up for the big bucks on offer to play for the Rugby League rebels.

Richards, however, had better things to do. For him, expanding one's horizons was far more important than money; he wanted to broaden his mind, not his pockets. Coming from mining stock, he was self-conscious about his perceived lack of education and decided the best way to be with the world was to embrace the world. He wanted to discover the riches and mysteries of faraway continents. He endlessly pondered how civilisation operated. There were so many questions to be answered. He later explained: 'I aimed at travelling to distant lands, using Rugby as my passport and my ability as an introduction'. He was a born wanderer, an international tourist at a time when travelling anywhere, even within Australia, was a challenge, often near impossible. Heading overseas was beyond the comprehension of virtually all.

Richards's constant drive to improve himself and his inability to keep still were instrumental in his winning an Olympic gold medal and becoming the only Australian-born Rugby Test player to represent the British and Irish Lions. He introduced surfing to France and then coached the French Rugby team for a Test match. Then, with a swag over his shoulder, he discovered the delights of Biarritz, Spain, the Riviera, northern Italy and Switzerland before meandering extensively through South Africa.

For such an active, inquiring man, serving as a soldier in wartime might be thought to have been the ultimate adventure. But Richards found that the long periods of inactivity and uncertainty, the endless waiting for instructions and action, and the bungling of his superiors frustrated his sense of organisation and leadership. When he became a leader, he showed courage, determination and doggedness that galvanised those around him. He won and held enemy positions, leading to his being awarded the Military Cross. Luckily for us, during his years at war he turned to his diary to record these achievements and frustrations.

John Richards, Tom's father, was born and raised in Cornwall but at the age of 21 was off to Australia as soon as he heard about all the people making their fortune on the country's goldfields. He tried Ballarat and Bendigo before convincing himself it was more lucrative to be at a tin settlement called Vegetable Creek, near Tenterfield in northern New South Wales. There, on April 29, 1882, Tom, nicknamed 'Rusty', was born.

When Tom was only one year old his nomadic father headed to the far reaches of Queensland after hearing of the latest strike in Charters Towers. Despite the never-ending boasts that their life was about to change for the best, it remained difficult. The Richardses never became rich. The big gold discovery did not come their way, and there was no alternative but for Tom from his teenage years to follow his father and three brothers into the mines. It was dreadful, soul-destroying, back-breaking work. Richards wrote: 'I worked in places with sweat clogging in my boots and oozing through the lace holes, amidst sickening fumes of exploded gelignite and floating screens of dust. I have often wondered how a human frame could stand such abuse, bullocking and heaving, sweating and swearing.'

He needed an outlet, and it appeared in the form of the New South Wales Rugby Union team that travelled to Charters Towers in 1897, when Richards was fifteen. This visit, he said, 'sowed the seed of Rugby in my heart'.

Playing involved sacrifices, however. As the miners worked Saturdays, all organised sport in Charters Towers, including cricket and Rugby, was played on Sundays. Richards's father, though, was a prominent member of the local Methodist Church and forbade his son from playing Rugby on Sundays. Richards was forced to appear under the assumed name of Brown to avoid his father's notice. It didn't work.

A solution finally appeared. The discovery of gold in South Africa convinced Richards's father to pack up again and leave for the Transvaal. Now the way was clear for Richards and his brothers to enjoy Sunday football. Within a year Richards, with his impressive, angular figure and most piercing of stares, was a representative player, and with his elder brother Bill was selected for Country Week in Brisbane. Talent was scarce, so Bill was fast-tracked into the Queensland team, playing the first of his five Tests for Australia in July 1904 against the visiting team from the United Kingdom.

Tom's progress was considerably slower and involved taking the long route, including thousands of kilometres travelled and countless exotic venues visited, before he could also boast Australian representation. His first major venture was to South Africa. In 1905, he followed his father to the harsh veldt land and, after settling in the Johannesburg suburb of Jeppes-town, ventured back down the deep shafts, mining some of the richest gold deposits in the world. The money was good, but the work perilous.

The football grounds were not friendly either, with games played on dry, dusty, rocky fields. But Richards found appearing for the local mines Rugby team far safer than working hundreds of metres underground, with its constant threat of being buried alive. A stringent fitness routine saw him among the first picked in the mines side, from where he quickly progressed to the Johannesburg representative team for its annual match against Pretoria and then the Transvaal team for the Currie Cup competition. From this team, the international South African team, soon to embark on its first overseas trip with a 29-match tour of the United Kingdom, was to be picked. Despite Transvaal being a South African Rugby powerbase, Richards was among the first picked for the squad. But he then discovered he had not lived in South Africa long enough to be eligible for Springbok selection. Were it not for this, he would have become the first Australian to be picked in the South African team.

Richards wasn't deterred. He refused to be left behind and instead followed the Springboks to the United Kingdom, explaining: 'I always felt that if a team is worth playing with, it is also worth playing against'. He disembarked in Plymouth and headed for Bristol, realising that, with three English internationals in its 1906 line up, the city's team was his best chance of appearing against South Africa in competent company. Within days, he was travelling the country with the illustrious Bristol team and enjoying rave press reviews, described as 'a typical New Zealander in his style of play, handling the ball like a three-quarter and untiring in the open'. This was exactly the type of player the Gloucestershire selectors wanted when the county was called upon to field a team against the Springboks.

At the first lineout, two South African players idly looked across at their opponents and did a double take. There were their old Transvaal teammates 'Opa' Reid and Andrew Morkel, but in different colours. In unison, they asked: 'What are you doing 'ere?'

'Doing my best,' replied the cheeky Australian.

Not surprisingly, Gloucestershire won most of the South African lineout calls, because Richards understood Afrikaans. Due to Richards's involvement, up front it was close; but out wide it was no contest, and the Springboks scored five tries for a conclusive win. 'There was not a happier man on the field than myself', Richards wrote. 'I was proud that I had fulfilled my mission.'

Following this, Richards discovered that the Australian Rugby Union team was planning to follow South Africa and New Zealand north for its first full-scale tour of the Home Nations. By 1907 he was back in the Charters Towers mines, focusing before and after work on the Australian selection trials. During his time in South Africa and the United Kingdom he had developed a lean but still muscular physique, but this wasn't enough. His training included cadging a regular 130-kilometre lift to Townsville, because he believed extensive sprint training along the beach would help his stamina. More importantly, he wanted an adaptable, hardened frame.

> I learnt to fall over fences and obstacles so as not to hurt myself, and thereby toughen my muscles and strengthen my sinews.
>
> I wanted to prepare my body to resist the knocks, bumps and jolts that do so much to break down a player's condition, particularly in the last portion of a vigorously played game. I also put into operation a system of going as long as possible without water, refraining from drinking at meal time so that the salivary glands would be developed to a point that would give a maximum of saliva, which, in preventing a dry mouth, would also aid physical vitality.
>
> Nobody in Charters Towers, not even my closest associates, knew that my objective was that year's Australian team.

The Queensland Country selectors were more in the loop, aware of Richards's ambition and credentials. They made him captain of the northern team for Country Week in Brisbane, after which he was named in the Queensland team to play New South Wales in a four-match selection series. The opponents dominated the series, but that did not diminish Richards's hopes, as he was the standout of the Queenslanders, making his mark when involved in one of the most talked-about tries ever scored at the Sydney Cricket Ground. Forever near the action, he picked up the ball about 5 metres from the New South Wales line, fended off one defender and had only the home fullback Jack D'Alpuget to beat. *The Referee*'s reporter wrote: 'As D'Alpuget bent for the tackle, [Richards] sprang in the air over the fullback and came down with his outstretched hands holding the ball in goal, and his legs in the air on top of the fullback—a beautiful try'. That try sealed it. He was on his way to the United Kingdom.

Before leaving, during a dinner at the Sydney Town Hall the Australian squad discussed what they should call themselves. The name Rabbits was suggested and for a time was popular amongst the players. Thankfully, by the time they arrived in the United Kingdom in late 1908, after 42 days on the RMS *Omrah*, sanity had prevailed. The players, directed by their skipper, Herbert 'Paddy' Moran, a captain who freely admitted to being 'a miserable, stooped, poring, introspective sort of fellow', had voted on the matter, with the winning name being the Wallabies.

But they could have easily called themselves the Reptiles following Richards's strange behaviour when the players disembarked at Plymouth. Around his waist was tied Bertie the carpet snake, the team mascot brought along by the comedian of the team, Bob Craig. To smuggle the snake into the country, Richards had slung Bertie inside his singlet, tied the snake loosely around his stomach, and stuck its head inside a sock and its tail down the front of his pants. A large overcoat hid any bulge. The plan worked, even though Rusty grew exceedingly uncomfortable when Bertie began to wriggle during the official speeches. Sadly, Bertie died after catching a cold from a stiff Irish breeze.

Despite the cuddly moniker, the British press took an immediate dislike to the Wallabies, complaining that they were a vulgar mob of thugs, especially when Australia's illustrious forward Syd Middleton was sent off against Oxford University for punching an opponent in the face. (Middleton took offence at being called a 'convict'.) The tourists' gallivanting off the field also upset their hosts, with the Wallabies even being accused of appearing drunk and disorderly at a midweek race meeting. Not even the achievement of winning an Olympic gold medal at that year's London Games led to any plaudits from the local media. Tom Richards somehow rose above it all and was singled out by the press for his outstanding achievements on the field, scoring the pick of Australia's seven tries in a one-sided Olympic romp. He was underwhelmed by the occasion, describing it as 'forgettable'. He didn't even bother attending the gold medal and certificate presentation.

Richards was certainly more primed for his first Test appearance, which coincided with the most important match of the tour—the international against Wales at Cardiff Arms Park. Within minutes, Richards was on the charge, heading towards the Welsh try line with the ball safely tucked under his arm, until he was called back for an alleged knock-on. There was no dispute a short time later, when an Australian backline overlap gave Richards the room he needed to score the first Wallaby try in an international. Australia then wilted and Wales cruised past to win.

After Australia's Test against Wales, Lawrence Woodhouse of the *Daily Mail* put Richards in his 'World's Greatest XV', selected from those whom he had seen play between 1868 and 1908. Following the Test against England, the same newspaper was so moved that it described Richards as 'the greatest player seen during the season, whose pace, tackling, cross-kicking and resourcefulness stamps him as one of the finest forwards who ever put on football boots. Throughout the tour he was the best man on the field in every match, and how many tries he gained for his side indirectly would be difficult to say.'

The Wallabies eventually travelled on to California and Canada, via New York, for matches against Stanford University, California University and Vancouver, until, 30 weeks after farewelling Sydney, they again sighted Manly and the Heads. After such a long time on the road, many of the team members felt disconnected and succumbed to the Rugby League entrepreneurs' offers. Tom Richards was one of League's chief targets, but he resisted every approach. He had no interest in League, believing many of its players to be uncouth and the game to be lacking in subtlety: too fast, no science—a headless chicken exercise. He also had no interest in staying around or being penned by professionals. His feet always wanted to be somewhere else. In 1910, once again he was convinced by his family that there was a fortune to be made in the South African mines.

During that year, the fourth British team to tour South Africa arrived for a 24-match trip, with Tests against the Springboks in Johannesburg, Port Elizabeth and Cape Town. The combination of a fragile touring party, formidable opposition, unforgiving playing conditions and long train journeys soon saw the British Lions decimated by injuries and illness. One was feared to have typhoid; another had blood poisoning from gravel rash; others were out of shape because they couldn't stop hitting the grog. A Kimberley citizen wrote to the local newspaper complaining about the Lions' behaviour: 'Off the field a good many of the team seem to think they are out on a glorious "beanfest"... I can tell you that we home-growns are disgusted with the team'.

Replacements were desperately needed, and the Lions management was relieved to discover an ideal candidate hovering nearby, supervising a mine in Johannesburg. Due to his involvement with Gloucester football, Richards was also eligible to help out. Adding to the allure was that he was world class, probably better than anyone else they had. By invoking his Bristol club membership, Richards became the first and only Australian-born national player to boast British Lions representation.

Richards tracked the tourists down in Bloemfontein. What followed were two of the more unusual months of his life during which he avoided the drunken binges by his teammates in Kimberley and played on fields where stones as big as the players' fists were dug out of the ground. The squad included players who were so incompetent that they only seemed to know how to satisfy their enormous thirst. Not surprisingly the Brits were given no hope against the Boks. Yet, somehow, they got it together when required, losing by just four points in the first Test. In the words of the *Cape Times*, 'at the lineout and in giving assistance to the backs, [Richards] rendered yeoman service'. Then came an almighty jolt: the Lions won the second Test in Port Elizabeth. The British vigour took the locals by surprise, with Richards 'conspicuous the whole time for consistent work in the scrum and the loose'.

The series decider was in Cape Town, and the Lions continued to astound. Just before running out, they changed their line-up: Richards was no longer in the starting fifteen. The reason was never properly explained, but the *Cape Times*'s reporter, writing before the game, had 'no hesitation in saying that this is a bad tactical error'. His words were prophetic: the Brits were thrashed 21–5. Richards never discussed the moment, but it did nothing to improve his generally low opinion of the Lions contingent. In a letter to a friend, he revealed:

The Britishers did not leave an enviable reputation behind them, either on or off the field. They were loosely managed . . . the team was much too weak for the undertaking, some of the players knew very little about the game at all, and it surprised me how they were even brought on tour. But I was glad to have been playing when Britain won the second Test game in good style.

Richards didn't stay in South Africa for long, finding mining work a 'dangerous calling'. In addition, the local white inhabitants suffered from the 'dreaded disease known as swelled head . . . and they have it in a most chronic form'. The future looked far brighter in Australia, this time in the seaside Sydney village of Manly. Richards moved into the area in 1911, became a foundation member of the Manly Surf Lifesaving Club, took to the sea twice a day and gravitated towards the local Rugby team.

He linked up with the brothers Ralph and William Hill, who apart from being deeply involved in the New South Wales Rugby administration were successful in the garment-knitting industry. Richards worked for them as a salesman travelling throughout the state. This link was beneficial, because when an invitation arrived from the Californian Rugby Union for an Australian team to tour the United States, Richards was able to take time off to satisfy his Wallabies wanderlust. He was named vice-captain.

The touring squad comprised the core of the 1908 team along with some new names. The players set out determined to have a good time. As five-eighth Bob Adamson later recalled: 'We were never in bed. That was the trouble. I never had such a time in all my life'. Bill Hill described the tour as being 'very much of a holiday for these players'. Often they were billeted at university campuses and revelled in the wild student life. They became notorious for playing up. The San Francisco *Examiner* began a match report with: '"Late to bed and early to rise" was the motto of the Australian Rugby players yesterday'. One newspaper cartoon showed a dashing American beauty pulling the petals off a waratah bloom while gazing longingly at an Australian player who bore an uncanny resemblance to Richards. She was saying: 'He loves me, he loves me not, he loves . . .' The caption read: 'All our girls are doin' it, doin' it, doin' it'.

The distractions almost led to a sporting disaster, when in the one-off Test against the United States the little-known Americans were leading 8–0 after 60 minutes. So infuriated were the Australian supporters in the crowd that the call of 'Throw your cigarettes away' rang around the ground. The Wallabies took the hint, and eventually found the points to win 12–8. After losing every game in Canada, where they struggled against oppositions bolstered by quality British imports, the team travelled home—except for Richards, who as usual had more exotic plans.

The Bristol club became aware of Richards's anticipated arrival in the United Kingdom and sent off letters in all directions trying to find him. He was eventually sighted chatting with some old friends in the South African touring team at Twickenham, where he was cornered and coerced into playing for Bristol. He took some convincing, as he had believed his Rugby career to be over—a chronic ankle injury was giving him hell. However, the prospect of a trip through France with the Midlands and East Midlands Counties team was enough incentive to join the party.

Richards revelled in everything French, and did not return to the United Kingdom after the tour. Instead, with a swag, several books, a pair of shoes and two changes of clothes, he embarked on an extensive walking tour. Most nights he slept outdoors or in barns—anywhere he could avoid using his limited savings.

He walked first into Spain, then changed direction to travel along the edge of the Mediterranean, back over the Pyrenees, along the coast of France to Biarritz, Tuscany, through northern Italy and into Switzerland via the Alps. For a short time he lived in Biarritz, using the skills he learnt on Manly Beach to introduce surfing to France. For most of each week he would tramp through the Pyrenees before catching a train back to Biarritz on the Saturday to play Rugby for the local team. He was even seconded by Toulouse to manage the side when they went on tour, including one trip to Bayonne, where he was convinced to put on his boots and add to the long list of illustrious teams for which he had played.

He was occasionally spotted by fellow Australians. In a letter to *The Sydney Mail*, WM Early wrote:

With a party of tourists, I was sitting outside a small cafe in a Spanish village on the Pyrenees Mountains when a lanky individual covered in dust and carrying a swag, strolled up and called for food and wine in a strange mixture of Australian and French.

He had gone for a stroll into Spain . . . and was then making his way back to Paris and to England—all alone on foot and carrying a swag in real Australian fashion.

When Richards returned to Paris, the French Rugby Union authorities asked him to join their coaching staff for a week to prepare the team for a Test match against Wales. He attended the French training sessions, devising tactics to counter a team he had tussled with five years earlier, and almost masterminded an unexpected 8–all draw, until because of a refereeing error the game went into extra time, during which Wales scored the three points required for victory.

Eventually, Richards's money ran out and he had to return to Australia. Such was his fame by this time that the *Sydney Morning Herald* was there to greet him when his ship docked in Sydney Harbour. Aware of Richards's writing skills—he had penned a series of Rugby-related articles for Australian publications—the *Herald* offered him a job that included covering several matches of the 1914 English Rugby League tour. Richards accepted. But his time at Australia's most prominent broadsheet was short: a bigger assignment beckoned.

When the United Kingdom declared war on Germany in August 1914, Richards was, predictably, on the road, managing the Manly Rugby team during a country tour of New South Wales. While far from a passionate enthusiast about the United Kingdom, he believed there was no other option but to enlist immediately. It was the right thing to do; a young nation like Australia needed to show it could be relied upon when support was required by its allies. Besides, enlisting appealed to his unquenchable adventurous instincts.

On the surface, Richards was of course perfectly suited to be part of the daring landing at Gallipoli on the morning of April 25, 1915, and plucky enough to ignore the chaos around him in order to capture the moment on several rolls of film. It comes as no surprise that later in the war he was awarded the Military Cross. But he was, after all, only human, and the physical and mental toll of Gallipoli and his subsequent years of war service remained with him for the rest of his life. In an effort to find some sense in it all, he chronicled virtually every part of his army life, in which he felt himself to be a 'misfit' and a 'strange cove'. He was a talented, observant, often frustrated writer, never more comfortable or at one with himself than when formulating his thoughts on the page. He may have preferred his own company, but never missed anything, fascinated by everything around him.

In his four years of war service, he wrote in his diary virtually every day, the only lapse being during several days of fighting at Bullecourt on the Western Front. Occasionally he wrote in the morning, but mainly in the evening, sometimes jotting down a few hundred words, often becoming immersed in long essays which regularly applied the blowtorch to himself. He wrote hundreds of thousands of words about his time as a soldier, filling diary after diary, chronicling in intricate detail his days on or near the battle line.

While Tom Richards is mostly remembered today as a Rugby player, his war diaries present to us a man of great integrity, unwavering loyalty and strong opinion, giving us insight into the qualities and characteristics that made him not only a great sportsman but also, perhaps against his better judgment, a superb soldier.

Chapter 1

UNDER WAY, 1914

⟶⟩⟨⟵

August 26: The war news on the 9th August prevented me doing any business at all, so I went and enlisted for the front. The authorities seemed so slow that I went down to Sydney by *Wollowaka*, arriving after a rough, seasick passage. I set about volunteering for the Light Horse but after waiting four days found they were full up—so Fritz Schwarz and I signed on with the Army Medical Corps and went into camp in Queen's Park. The first day I drilled with an awkward crowd of fellows and was also awkward myself. The officers did not know their drill either. Most of them are doctors and without much in the way of military knowledge, but are nevertheless a splendid set of men.

September 1: Queen's Park. I have been fitted out with a new uniform, was vaccinated and had a fairly easy day. The Light Horse Ambulance, camped adjoining us, are a reserved crowd of fellows, in fact they are conceited.

September 4: Harold Baker came down to the camp on a lovely horse and took me away to his home in Randwick for dinner.[1] His wife is nice and very young. They were married when she was only 17 years of age. It appears Harold, as

---

1   Harold Baker was the brother of renowned Australian sportsman Reg 'Snowy' Baker. Harold was also a notable athlete: he played Test Rugby for Australia, captained his country at water polo, was a leading surf lifesaver and even refereed some of Australia's most notorious boxing bouts. He worked with his brother in running the Sydney Stadium.

well as the girl's mother, thought she was 19, but when her lawyers in England started to fix up her estate they discovered their mistake. They have one child. We wandered around Coogee in the moonlight and I admired it immensely. I got into camp at 10.45pm after taking off my leggings, boots and socks and leaving them in a tree to return for them as I had to beat the guard.

September 5: We now have a full uniform. General leave was extended until midnight. Bob Miller and I went across to Manly. I went for a walk in the afternoon and down the Corso where the band was playing. It was my first night out in uniform and I felt very uncomfortable. I did not know whether to raise my hat to the number of friends I met or not.

September 6: This is the second Sunday I have been in camp and again went to the English Church service in the open air. The preacher with all his regalia worried me by his one-sided version of British righteousness in taking the part of the weaker nations in the present war. The singing was very poor. The English followers were asked to step forward, also the Methodists and marched off to different parts of Queen's Park.

September 9: Roast mutton for dinner today. Yesterday we had tinned beef, cold for breakfast and made into stew for dinner. The usual bread and jam for tea. The Commander is tightening up all leave. We appear to be sailing in about four days' time. A quantity of gift clothing was distributed today. It seems to me that the average man has, with all his years of civilisation, raised himself but little above an animal, as when those clothes were given out their eyes were as those of a begging and anxious dog.

September 12: Rain. Our tent was in a hell of a mess—all under water. The language one hears in our camp and all around the place is vile and notice-able amongst the empty-headed young fellows mostly.

September 13: I must get my Ambulance work in properly, and as I'm not going to get any fighting, which I so very much regret, I will at least attempt to gain some benefits and go thoroughly into First Aid work. My blankets and clothes are all wet and no chance of drying them just yet.

September 14: I regret more and more the fact that I am not in the real fighting line instead of buggering about with Ambulance work as 'linseed lancers'. There is always that doubt ... with a fellow likely to be termed a 'quitter'.

September 17: This camp life is perhaps not so hard as it is depressing. The grub is passable but though it is plentiful and wholesome there is a miserable sameness about it.

September 21: Fritz arranged a football match against the Light Horse (the conceited party adjoining our camp about 60 strong), which resulted in an easy win for our men. I was captain and our score was 21–0.

September 24: Things are getting very close to sailing. Our daily papers are hardly worth reading as they are all war cables and notes which never seem to agree with one another. I am disappointed at the tone of the press in attempting to belittle the ability of the Germans and accuse them of all kinds of murder and plunder. They even accuse them of cowardice and crime.

September 25: Up at 5am and away to the boat with the transport horses at 8am. One man, one horse and they behaved splendidly going through the city to Dalgety's wharf. The going aboard was accomplished in half an hour. Our horses were under the main deck while there were layers of horses on two decks below, making in all four decks of horses—the lower one being perhaps 40 feet down the hold; they were not lowered down, but walked down along the gangways. It was just wonderful.

October 5: We all marched in good order for about eight miles to Maroubra. The back section had a lot of trouble picking up the correct step, due considerably to the fact that our officers are such bad, short-stepped and rambling marchers. But the average soldier is an arrogant, conceited and boastful person—'superb grandstand players'. Always judging their standard of manhood by the worst man in the squad. The Englishmen mostly are a loud-voiced, empty, inconsiderate lot, and can be easily picked out by their stiff and bound up movements.

October 6: We are this morning preparing for a march through the city. The fellows are keenly looking forward to it and are now bustling round in great expectations. We filed out of Moore Park about 11.45am and the whole route was thickly lined with people. The Army Medical Corps was lost in

the procession but nevertheless they came in for applause and complimentary criticism. Going through Macquarie Street where our doctors are so
well known, we had a great reception particularly from the hospital. Many
of the people provided fruit for the troops—the skins of which covered
Oxford Street.

October 19: The eventful day has at last arrived. The camp was astir at
5.30am with kits packed and handed in by 7am. A damned poor breakfast
and we were on the road by 7.45. Tram cars were used from Charing Cross
to Fort Macquarie where we were aboard the majestic looking *Euripides* by
lights in very quick time. We were put into messes of 20 men and there we
sat for hours until the 3rd Infantry were put aboard. There were few people
out this morning as we passed along Oxford Street—yet there were some
stirring little incidents as we drove by. One aged man holding a stout stick
for support tried with as brave a heart as ever a soldier possessed to stand at
attention. Another old warrior straightened himself by the aid of a verandah
and saluted. Lots of men and women waved a pleasant good-bye but it was
only skin deep; nobody but ignorant persons could treat such a mission as
we are about to undertake so lightly and almost with frivolity. But the men
who have seen service were as the two above mentioned, full of sincerity and
hope knowing there was hard work for us to do. I am no blubber, pain and
distraction harden me, but warm affection with a manly, conscientious face
filled my eyes with tears of joy. Most people are so wrapped up in themselves
they forget even those nearest until something serious happens and brings
home their foolish idea that because they are alright everything and everybody as a matter of course must be also. Many of the hundreds of boatloads
of people that sailed around the *Euripides* today thought of nothing further
or deeper than that a friend or brother was going to war, and as it was a long
voyage they came to wave to him (not the troops) a pleasant and safe return.
     The Coast Artillery with their brass band aboard the SS *Miner* went
around our vessel for one and a half hours playing cheerful tunes, but just
before leaving they struck up 'Auld Lang Syne'. They finally played 'God Save
the King' and I was fighting again to keep back the tears as we stood lined up
at attention on the top deck.

Many of our well-wishers waved flags and shouted frantically. But it was a couple of people on the *Burra Bra* making for Manly that made water come to my eyes. They stood still and held a blue Australian flag outstretched. It was plain to me what was meant. They were cold, level-headed persons and seemed to say: 'keep your end up boys, wherever you're going, for the honour and for the glory of your dear Australia and your love for the mother country'. It fairly thrilled me through and through.

There are six or eight nurses on board. This afternoon I saw them on the promenade deck and amongst so much khaki colour their sky blue dresses with a bright red cap makes a pleasant change. This will be particularly noticeable later on when the dungarees and browns become an eyesore. Midst the hooting of the whistles and the cheering of our boys we slowly steamed down the harbour, but to our astonishment we put into Mosman Bay and hung up for the night. There was a great scramble for bunks or hammocks at 6.15pm. They were hung very close together, so much so that when one man turned over he woke up the man next to him and set a whole line of them swinging. Yet the fellows seemed to favour sleeping on hammocks to the ground at Queen's Park.

Ship's rations
Bread 1 lb per man
Meat ¾ lb
Jam 8 ounces per week
Salt 2 ounces per week
Pickles 6 ounces
Milk Condensed 1 lb tin per week
Sugar 14 ounces per man
Butter 10⅓ ounces
Potatoes 4½ lbs

October 20: The *Euripides* got under way at 5.30am and steamed past Watson's Bay with a high wind and blinding rain. We were running fairly steadily yet before breakfast the decks were covered with prostrated forms. The 'fall in' was sounded at 10am and it was sorrowful to see the fellows dragging themselves and one another up for the parade. No more forlorn a spectacle could be witnessed than a crowded troopship on the first day at sea.

So far we find the conveniences of the *Euripides* somewhat lacking. There are not enough hammocks, and the galley arrangements are inefficient as the poor mess orderlies have to wait a very long time to be served. There is a terrible congestion of men both underneath and on decks. The wet canteen was opened today between 11 and 12. The fellows went past in single file and paid three pence for a mug of beer. Beer was the only beverage dispensed. I was a little surprised that the fellows did not rush it more feverishly as there are some excellent looking beer-loving countenances about the ship. It is surprising the number of sports followers on board, and the present cricket season and the coming football season must suffer in consequence.

When one looks over the troops as they stand around, their height and physique are admirable, their age is thoroughly mature and their faces, though hard and weather-beaten, are very determined and strong looking. I like them immensely.

October 21: Last night the boys were merry, the bagpipes and orchestra keeping them bright. There does not appear to be anything like sufficient accommodation for the 3011-odd men aboard. At 9pm I had some bread, butter and herrings before going to bed. At 2am I felt very bad and vomited freely. The hammocks are placed too close together, yet the fellows like them and sleep well. Through some mismanagement, there was no arrangement made aboard for the Army Medical Corps at all so that we have just to squeeze in and make the best of a bad position. So far I have no regrets at having volunteered but I wish we were at the end of our destination. This ship life does not offer anything novel. The mess orderlies are having a rough time and by the growling that goes on the ship is generally unsatisfactory. The wet canteen has met with general approval and is opened only between the hours of 11 and 12, and it takes the full hour hard going to get finished with the long line of constantly waiting men. The dry canteen is open from 7–8 in the morning, 4–5 in the afternoon, 7–9 at night. The rubber shoes supplied at two and six are scandalous. They fall away from the sole in half an hour's wear. The dry canteen's prices seem far above Sydney prices all round. Tins of coffee costing sixpence in Sydney stores are sold at one shilling.

October 22: There are some really terrible-looking fellows amongst the troops and reports that the Germans have been looting and murdering will not be any worse than what those wretches are capable of. We parade from 9.30 to 11 in the morning and from 2 to 4 in the afternoon. The deck is too small for marching so we have to double mark time and walk or run around in single file circles, some physical exercises and sometimes leap-frog in small parties. The childish behaviour of some of our fellows reminds me of the holiday jaunts to Townsville and Ravenswood when we indulged in horseplay and noisy, disorderly singing, only that now we have jealousy and conceitedness intermingled with it. I have adopted my best air of reservation and do more reading and writing than ever before with very little conversation. Why I don't look more for company I cannot say, as there are many really good fellows amongst our party of 204 men.

October 23: The menu shows up a little better and stronger just now. Yesterday we had porridge and stewed sausages with tea and bread and jam to finish off with. At dinner there was soup, meat with beans and potatoes, followed by plum pudding. The sea is as calm as is possible, and in consequence none of the fellows are sick though if it should blow up a little these crowded decks would be hell with a record roll call as the fellows have to take down their hammocks at 6am, tidy up their odds and ends, and are not allowed inside again hardly until 6pm, when the hammocks are laid out, with lights out at 9pm. The bagpipes and the military brass band with perhaps a short evening Church service help considerably to break the dullness of the day and give the troops a little harmony which is absolutely essential to their brute-like nature. Gambling goes on all over the boat. No attempts are made to prevent it.

October 25: All hands are busy writing, yet there are a number of gambling schools going strong. Many games have been barred such as two up, crown and anchor, under and over 7. One man got 90 hours in the cells for playing crown and anchor. Several new cases of pox in the hospital today.

October 27: To WTB[2] I wrote six pages and confessed much of my longing for her, and at the same time giving her liberty to get another man. If he is a man I won't grumble. I would not say this but how is it possible for me to offer anything in the way of comfort and convenience? Yet it will come hard

2   Little is known of WTB other than Richards sometimes called her Zelda of Manly.

to part with her, and I cannot keep her waiting for what may be a forlorn hope. When I reason coldly, Win is no good to me, but my heart won't agree and seeks her wildly.

October 30: The troops are feeling very despondent at waiting around here jammed in and scantily fed. I seem to be very lovesick indeed just now. My mind flouts back to it and its many problems as soon as I take it off my reading, in fact I am so badly hit that I compare every female character I read of with her. Gambling is now stopped. I don't know how the parson is getting on without the fool game of House. I have seen him at it for days. The war news of the past couple of days seems to be very misleading, viz. the Germans are being defeated all along the line yet they have captured Calais. It seems to me they are just laughing at the Britishers and are working down the Coast with the object of striking at England on the land and waiting an opportunity to smash in on the water. There is no doubt that Germany has applied her scientific brains to war as well as to other sciences and has been brought to such perfection that the Allies are not going to win for a very long time yet.

October 31: Our brass band seems to be improving fast, the evening's program being highly appreciated. The dinner was very sadly complained of. Soup was as thin as water and salty, corned beef as tough and hard as possible. The meals have failed badly from time to time. Whether it is meanness or bad galley work it's difficult to say. The venereal patients are still increasing in number—some 40 now. My age is troubling me considerably of late. I am too old both in years and in mind to be travelling with a crowd of fellows like these.

The censor is getting very particular about our correspondence during the last few days. First we were notified that letters and packets etc must be left unsealed, later only postcards and urgent wires would be received. Now we get printed cards with sentences on and you have to cross out, leaving something to the effect that 'I am quite well and hope you are the same'. Damned nonsense, we all seem to think.

November 1: Every man on the ship stood to attention as we passed several of our own transports and ten waiting New Zealanders. The Maorilanders gave us a haka and many sounds of cheers as we passed quickly by. We, under instructions, had to remain at 'attention' and not with a sound in acknow-ledgment to our Southern comrades' greetings.

It was a mighty solemn procession. Thirty-five transports and a convoy all running in single file, and not a murmur, not a gunshot or whistle. No, not even a bugle call. The low sounding trumpet was used to bring us to 'attention'. The whole business seems almost unbelievable. Thirty-five ships laden with men and weapons, some 30,000 in number, including some of the country's very best men and most valuable assets. There is something wrong with the world. This is how we sailed out from Albany, in mournful procession, for a destination unknown, and enshrouded in mystery, making a course westerly. Church service was held at 11.30 when the Chaplain tried to justify the Allies' position and asked God for protection and deliverance. The irony of it all! What hypocrisy! Surely this great God, if he had the power to influence victory in any particular, would also have the power to prevent it at the very first and before lives were sacrificed.

November 8: I slept on deck last night but could not withstand the tempta-tion of using my hammock and so swung it quite 10 feet from the deck and over the top of the other chaps. The chatter that goes on around both before going to sleep and before getting up in the morning is most vulgar and miserable to listen to. We learnt a private named Kendall, a policeman from Bathurst, had died of pneumonia. Our ship pulled out of the line a little and buried the body off the well deck. It was a silent and impressive ceremony.

November 9: Great excitement prevails. Men are cheering wildly at the news of *Sydney*'s defeat of the *Emden*. The band play 'God Save the King' with all standing at attention amidst perfect silence. Very striking contrast to the fervent joy of a second ago. A man had just this morning died, and another is fighting hard against death in bed—pneumonia. We were given an afternoon off today on account of the *Sydney*'s achievements.

November 10: Rumour has it that there were German warships about, also that mines had been laid, and so many of the fellows were in a very excited state. The decks were crowded with men in every possible corner. Why men were not allowed their blankets to sleep on is beyond me altogether. As I now sit writing it seems hardly like a shipload of Englishmen at all. Their costumes are so remarkably varied. Some have shirts on; others have nothing at all on. The pants vary in both colour and length to a remarkable degree and very few have boots on at all. And the noise! My God! Could anything possibly be worse? Midst the harsh clamour of the card players and the band of arguers, the roars and vivid curses of the practical jokers and their victims can be heard rehearsing a hundred kinds of impromptu choral societies. The gramophone can be heard grinding out its discordant opposition in no unmistakeable manner, while a cornet, mouth organ and an accordion are heaping on the agony from different quarters of the deck.

November 11: There are no matches to be had on board and whenever somebody or other strikes a match to light a weed there are often six men begging for a light off it. Some ingenious fellows are selling cigars, but the best genius is employed by the lemon squash sellers who are increasing in number from day to day.

November 12: I had a glorious swim in the canvas tank before 6am. A hose full of water is running into it the whole time. It is remarkable the number of peddlers of one kind or another who have worked up the ranks. The barbers started doing business immediately the ship left, but the cigar sellers, biscuit and lemon squasher have not been long with us. One of our men told me he sold 14 buckets of 21 mugs at 3d per mug. Squash is two shillings per bottle and sugar nearly nothing. One bottle makes a bucketful.

November 13: Today has been a full day's holiday to celebrate the crossing of the 'line' . . . Equator. There has been much horseplay and many injuries have occurred. I was on guard but nevertheless prepared myself for the ordeal. When they called for me I warned them that I would not go without a struggle. I fought them for 15 minutes and knocked them about like skittles on the wet decks. So heavy did I kick that I felt very sorry after-wards. However they got me in the tank alright. The band has been playing until dark each evening lately and it is a great relief to hear some harmony. Tonight they played 'Rendezvous'. This is the most stirring piece of music I have ever listened to. It seems to cast a spell on me.

November 17: We are at anchor just outside of Colombo. There was a craft composed of six planks laced together without ends near our side this morning. The three natives were a source of much amusement to our fellows, and as they dived in after money and got it so quickly and easily the boys gaped on in amazement, doubly so in fact when they learnt that the water was infested with sharks. Our fellows are rather indignant at not going ashore, but I think the authorities are wise as there would be much stealing at the native stores and generally bad and childish behaviour would be certain to arise.

November 18: We left Colombo last night about 8pm. The band played a fine programme of music. It was most delightful sleeping on deck until 4am when it commenced to rain. We stuck it until the water came along underneath the blankets, then it was compulsory to gather the bed up and go downstairs.

The fellows are dissatisfied at the number of regulations that have to be observed and which look so useless and childish but I really did not find much to complain about other than that we should be encouraged with our baths and washing clothes [more] than we are. If a man washes his shirt he had better stay and keep his eyes on it for fear an order is suddenly issued to the effect that all clothes must not be hung around the deck. Then the military police take them down and they will probably turn up in the 'scram' bag on Thursday. The band is playing again tonight and the fellows dancing around the well deck in a surprisingly orderly style.

Rations per day on the Euripides:
Bread per day 1280 loaves
Sausages (breakfast only) 5120
Tripe (breakfast only) 896 lbs
Meat (dinner time) 1280 lbs
Potatoes, beans or peas per meal 1829 lbs
Butter per day 320 lbs
Plum puddings per meal 1024 lbs.

November 21: With six others we paraded before the Colonel this morning for leaving the guard room without permission. There is tremendous indignation in the mess room owing to short rations and the heavy sour bread. Really the bread is over the odds. It's just terrible. Plum pudding and rice and raisins have disappeared from the menu for the forthcoming week. The weather is still hot but the sky is clear and full of strange, interesting stars. The Southern Cross is gone.

November 22: Quite a lot of gambling has been going on unobserved at cards, but there are also a lot of fellows who play it for interest and enjoyment. I am beginning to think with the other fellows that we are being subjected to unnecessary annoyance. I missed Church parade this morning as I detest listening to prayers for our own puny selves and it grieves me to hear prayers for the defeat and overthrowing of the enemy.

November 26: This morning as the reveille blew we steamed out of the Gulf of Aden and into the Red Sea. We seem to have the whole of our fleet with us and the British cruiser *Yarmouth* at the head. The AMC do not drill in the morning and it is a hell of a job to get somewhere to sit down. This morning I sat down midship on a large pile of potatoes which have been there for six weeks, so you might imagine the stink of diseased potatoes that arose, and to make it 50 times worse the sun beat terribly hot from the awning. It was a sickly heat accelerated by the steam pipes leading to the winches.

November 28: There is quite a lot of ill-feeling in the ranks as to the kingly way the officers are living compared with the roughness of ourselves. There is a two room cabin at the isolation area, half of which is used to treat 44 venereals with two hospital attendants to care for them. In the other half is a young officer who is also a venereal patient and, mark you, he has the same room as the 44 men and three orderlies to wait on him alone. The men sleep all over the deck and get a very rough time. There were 120 men in the hospital or lying around the decks last night with ptomaine poisoning got from the cookhouse. I saw Le Fevre, champion golf player, sweeping decks today.[3]

November 29: There was a hell of a chatter going on yesterday when it was reported we were bound for Egypt but today the fellows are more anxious than excited. We had sausages for breakfast this morning. Just fancy cooking two per man, or 5120 in all. I am writing up a lot each day for WTB. She occupies a lot of my mind. Sometimes I feel very sorry that I ever left Manly,

---

3   Arthur Le Fevre went on to win the 1921 Australian Golf Open and PGA title.

then it dawns upon me that it would be better for both if I never went back there at all.

November 30: Suez is to be seen ahead but where we are going to land is as yet a mystery. We seem to be going to Cairo without doubt but for what purpose I know not, and it worries me as I can see months of garrison duties waiting in the background of all this. If we get fighting here and go on to England about May next it will be indeed delightful. I am not keen on fighting niggers in their own sandy, desolate territory with crude weapons and blood-curdling methods. It would be better and more educational to mix with the scientific genius of the European powers as applied to warfare.

Chapter 2

EGYPT, 1914–15

December 2: We anchored here at Port Said and the fellows have had an after-noon of intense interest. The gangs of niggers on each side running baskets of coal weighing, perhaps, 45 lbs, up planks are novel and cause much merri-ment. All around the ships are boats of traders and musicians. But they have to pass us and go on to the other transports as our sentry are told to keep them off and in doing so several shots have been fired—blanks I think. We are anchored near the landing stage and it is seething with hurrying natives paddling anywhere and everywhere to get in or out with goods. They must be having a golden harvest with 20 to 30 transports crowded with eager young fellows with money to spend on any old thing at all. A few veiled natives are going to and fro in boats. This method of disguising their womenfolk is indeed strange but we must consider they are a very old race of people with a lot of experience in the handling of the female, and this covering up of all but the eyes must be founded on solid and necessary lines. The men dress in all manner and colour of loose-flowing robes and it is difficult to distinguish them from women.

We had boiled rabbit with beans and very old potatoes for dinner. Ptomaine poisoning is rampant again—the fellows are lying everywhere and 'bunny' is accused even though many of the troops solemnly argue that no blame can be attached to our great and natural production.

December 3: I was one of the 900 men to suffer last night. At 11pm I got the axe right enough. My tummy twisted around like a spring mattress and felt as though a violent thunderstorm was raging therein. Boiled rabbit is being blamed for all of the bother but surely poor bunny could not have caused all this commotion. When I came downstairs men were lying in heaps—some had fallen out of their hammocks, others hadn't sufficient strength to get into theirs, so they just lay there, some had slipped under the mess table vomiting and groaning—never have I seen or experienced anything of the kind.

I saw the plainest possible case of bribery this afternoon. A native policeman was detailed to keep all natives, traders or otherwise, back from the ship. He succeeded in driving away all but two conjurers. These two argued and dodged about for an hour, and then they came up to the ship's side and started with their rather clever show of stock in trade. As the collection of three shillings was taken up the policeman came along and drove them away to behind some railway tracks. This little procedure continued some five times so I watched and saw that when the policeman got them away they paid him for the privilege to return. I actually saw the money change hands.

December 4: A stolen day in Alexandria. Set about escaping and paying the city a visit. Had we gone down the usual way—that is the way of the traffic— the military police would have arrested us, so we bribed a nigger boatman to run across to Marine Street for a shilling. Once safely on the streets our hearts beat much lighter. We wandered around the native quarters enjoying the quaint little specialist shops and the tremendous variety of wares traded from the narrow uneven footpaths. The fruit and vegetable stores made a splendid show with the large rich-coloured half-fruit half-vegetable type of things. All manner of peculiar looking and strong smelling eatables were cooked, sold and eaten on the road or in the unwashed gutters. The butcher's shops were most curious. The few pieces of meat were displayed from chains and hung some distance from one another. In all there were never more than seven pieces of strange coloured meat hanging forlornly about. We took a cab down to Pompey's Pillar and the Catacombs and had a terrible row with the cabman over his payment question as usual. Muttering to himself he drove away, while we caught an electric-driven tramcar and went back to the Square. We walked back through the native quarter, through the maze of crooked streets and small smelly shops to the waterfront where we were rushed by boatmen and buffeted some, until, using a little force and looking as savage as is possible, we got away with one boatman, who, when we started out against wind, had tremendous trouble judging by the jabber of the two natives in getting the sail set. We told them a hundred times to take us to the 'Coal Quay No 1 Lighthouse'. We landed and quarrelled about the fare. The fellow going over got a shilling, but this chap hassled us for 1/5 [1 shilling and 5 pence], though he wanted 2 shillings. We got aboard safely, passing the guard on the wharf and gangway in such a business-like way that we were unchallenged.

December 5: When the deck was cleaned up rations were issued—one 6 lb tin of bully beef and some bread. All aboard the train and away at 8am in third class carriages. There were probably 1000 men off the *Euripides* on the train and not any of them looked back with the usual farewell signs at parting with one's ship or home for seven weeks past.

Decided to bolt off and do the Pyramids and Sphinxes. It meant walking three quarters of a mile only. There we were assaulted by several guides and as usual in black tourist countries they would not take 'no', emphasised with a flourish of adjectives, for an answer.

Murphy's legs suffered before reaching the first half of the 450 steps. The nigger gave him a hand. This worried me to see a black man lending aid so I got in and assisted him to the top where we remained for perhaps 40 minutes deeply inspired by the whole scene. The point that bothered me most was the fact that all these huge boulders were brought from miles away taking thousands of labourers years of work just to satisfy the vanity of a king. The moon was well up as we descended and lit up the country like day. The mystic haze was particularly noticeable. We discharged the guide and went off to the Sphinx which was perhaps a mile back over a rough sandy track. It was disappointing as we approached it from the north-western side. It seemed so small and different to what we expected but when we moved around to the east it pleased us and was three times as high. I fancy some excavation work has been done on this side to expose the base more.

It was a wonderful night. The ancient touch was broken by the barking of dogs while we were on the Pyramid top. Murphy thought it desecration to eat tinned plums on this monument—I brought a tin of stolen fruit with me.

December 7: Seven of us went down to the Continental Hotel and had one of the most delightful dinners I've had. With the beer it ran out at 6/3 each but the contrast between camp life and dinner in such style is positively going from the sublime to the ridiculous. Fancy a man having finger bowls and a serviette after fighting with cooks, mess orderlies etc for a feed and washing your own tin and mug out when you're finished. It was only a five-course meal, but from pea soup to dessert it was joyous. The whole meal was like a large ice cream on a hot day—it melted away and left you wondering whether you really had dined or was it a sweet dream.

The taste of the peas served up still lingers longingly with me (20 hours afterwards). The silverware was amazing after the one old rusty knife and fork of camp life. I will never go back to the Grand Continental Hotel again—it holds up too strongly the weakness and poverty of a soldier's life. In the dining room were officers of all ranks and it placed our party of non-coms and privates in rather an awkward position regarding the salute and discipline. After a cigarette and some writing-paper we wandered down the native or poor European quarter, where low-down cabarets were going big guns, brothels of the most horrid type with soldiers walking in and out or laughing and holding the foul slatternly bitches. The lanes and alleyways were as putrid and ugly as the frequenters thereof. We got a two-horse cab at 10.15pm for the camp. The journey was nine miles. After six miles we came upon a number of cabs with Australians getting back to camp. Our driver got warmed up and racing started. We beat several at the trot, and then we took them on at a gallop. The race was terrific for so narrow a road, lined on both sides with large acacia trees closely together. We shook off a pair of good greys. Another go was stopped by some six cabs taking up the road and blocking us. The driver watched every move and with a dare-devil rush got through and past all but the leading cab. This one came at us in great style. We raced both pairs of horses striding like greyhounds. The wheels came together and grated. It looked a certainty of a smash-up but with our horses tiring fast the other cab drew away and won an honourable and exciting race. I never had such dare-devil excitement for years. I do not understand the cabbies racing like this unless our driver was goaded into it, and being an arrogant fellow he was trying to belie our scathing remarks at the outset. We gave him another few bob and both sides were satisfied with an easily won victory.

December 8: The Sphinx grows more imposing and wonderful each time one sees it. The sun was setting about this time and the whole scene stirred me with amazement and wonder. Fancy a poor miner from North Queensland seeing and glorying in the world's great sights such as I have done. It makes me feel something as though there is a screw short somewhere.

Copied from the notice board:
Syphilis and Venereal Diseases
It is well that soldiers should realize that in this country prostitutes are all more or less infected with disease. There is absolutely no control over European prostitutes, and they, unfortunately are the most affected. Soldiers should also realize that in resorting to the company of these women it is not only venereal, syphilis and chancre that is to be feared; many other diseases from which soldiers die abroad are directly attributable to infection from brothels, such as smallpox, enteric and dysentery.

December 10: I have just returned from the Egyptian barber's up near the three large canteen tents. The nigger barber's is absolutely and positively a house of torture. Never did I think there could be anything like it, and I recall being shaved by men-hating women both in Winnipeg and Johannesburg. As I came into the rough square tent building without any floor, a big gaunt fellow got out of the ordinary chair bleeding from several places and feeling his face tenderly, saying: 'I wouldn't sit down there again for a pound.' My turn came; the nigger borrowed the soap brush from his neighbour and filled up my mouth first shot, then worked around into the corner of my eye, and later filled my nostrils when lathering the upper lip.

He slapped the razor across his hand and set about scraping as we used to do in North Queensland with a bit of glass to remove hair, the same as aboriginals do for arms and legs. I felt certain he would slice a piece off, as he was very unsteady and uncertain in his actions. The chair slowly sinking in the sand made the position one of great danger, and the blunt razor and novice operator made one think it was a dentist and every hair cut a tooth extracted. I got away three times to cool my face and get my breath back. Just as I was finished and thanking the gods for my safe deliverance a soldier whom I had been watching squirming and twisting opposite said: 'Go for your life, Laddie, before they get you again.'

December 24: It's Xmas Eve. I had no desire to go amongst the noise and drunkards of Cairo so I got Murphy to explore the interior of the three Pyramids. A ghostly kind of occupation no doubt for Xmas Eve but it seemed fitting to the surroundings. We had our guide book and thank goodness we dodged the native guides. I have a happy knack of shaking these fellows off, but there are so many of them and they just 'come out of the ground', interrupting one's conversation with a nasty jar, especially when one is living and puzzling with 5000 year old problems, which are so common in this weird part of the world. Murphy treated me to a lovely cup of coffee with bread, butter, jam and biscuits at Mena. When we left to return to the camp a sentry stopped us and having no passes we bluffed through as hospital attendants and arrived back in camp just before 'lights out' to find that two bottles of whisky had transformed the tent into a music hall, and there was Hucking without any trousers on, standing and singing: 'When your luck is in, life's all right but when it's out, it's all wrong...' while Sullivan joined in the chorus, and about five other fellows were struggling to keep their heads from drooping and rolling about, so bad were they. When I came in the visitors were sent away and soon all were settled down. It was extremely complimentary of them.

December 25: At a cafe we fought hard for a light meal and a glass of beer, and were pestered by peddlers who wanted to sell razors, cigarettes, silks, sticks, small boxes. It is this kind of bother and interference that makes Cairo a bore to me.

Xmas in camp was only recognised by the extra rations allowed for dinner and the inspection of the messes by the whole outfit of officers who were cheered by the fellows. The extras consisted of a one lb tin of plum pudding to three men, a tin of fruit to four men, two ginger nuts and two soda biscuits per man and four bottles of wine to the mess of 24 men.

Everybody was remarkably happy and the scene mindful of a Sunday picnic. The same spirit was in the air. The usual portion of stew, however, formed the basis of the dinner.

December 26: The New Zealanders are having much fun about town with cars and bagpipes, and other music. They race around the town and very often parade, with hordes of niggers in their wake. Tonight I am told three of them on donkeys went into a cafe and caused a good natured uproar. The Australians are more given to getting drunk than lighter frivolities. Anyway Xmas has started the fellows going in for practical joking and I kind of think they will continue it and Cairo will wish the Colonials were never in Egypt, though at present we are in great demand and considered big fry for all kinds of dealers, particularly in the brothel quarter. The 'Tommy'[1] complains that the prices of everything are now beyond their reach as they are poorly paid. Some married men draw 1/3d per day, half of which is paid to their family. Others draw no more than 2 shillings per week while in this country; therefore it is no wonder that they pal up with the Colonials so that they might have a meal and a wander around the city as guides on the cheap. This unevenness in pay is sure to make the 'Tommies' very discontended; they are risking just as much as the Colonials and getting not a quarter as much pay.

December 29: The women in Cairo have been making enormous sums of money even at as low a figure as five piastres. I have not been inside one of those places but I am told from six to a dozen soldiers are often waiting in the one room for their turn. It also shows a terrible weakness in our educational affairs when young men must run this awful risk to get their knowledge of the world and thereby learn to curb [their] carnal appetite.

December 30: At 7pm Rev Green, Chaplain to the Forces, delivered an interesting lecture on Egypt in the YMCA rooms, which was greatly appreciated by the 300 soldiers present. He said 'that probably here on this very same spot nearly 100 years ago Napoleon camped with his selected troops who were later cut off from their lines of communication by Abercrombie, and his men were left to perish of starvation'. He referred to the many sights

---

1   Tommy was a description for English soldiers.

and scenes which have taken place within the limits of those silent and majestic monuments of age.

December 31: It is 12 o'clock and our tent is in a cranky uproar, we who are sober are having a rotten time. It is now midday on New Year's Eve and many of our tent are ashamed of themselves, and their behaviour of last night warrants the self-conviction disgrace. I rather admire a good drunk at any time providing they have something to celebrate and go about celebrating it in a proper way and a frivolous manner. The wet canteen was closed early in the afternoon, but not before many of the fellows were drunk. After parade and a poor tea there was 'Baulkham Hills' marmalade jam, or really oranges boiled in water. Sixpence a day per man is now allowed on account of proper rations not being procurable. The Quarter Master buys extras to that amount, or is supposed to, but every man in the camp thinks there is something very wrong and graft is getting away with the money.

I had a bottle of lemonade and some biscuits, and wrote a letter to my dear WTB. Oh this woman does make me think of my duties in life. I feel as though I must get her but then how are we going to live in peace and at ease? I should be writing up stuff for the papers[2] but somehow or other I cannot get the time and I never seem to waste a single minute—in fact I seldom join in the camp conversations as I have something always on hand. And again words do not come freely. I seem very worried indeed.

Sir George Reid addressed about half of our 18,000 men yesterday and another half today. Afterwards a review—Sir George accompanied by Lieut-General John Maxwell and Major General Bridges, also Mr McKenzie, High Commissioner of New Zealand. Sir George opened with a nice piece of flattery to Sir John Maxwell and all of the officers of the Expeditionary Force, in which he excelled himself. After throwing away compliments in his wonderful and masterful manner, he asked the troops to remember Lord Kitchener's warning. Do not forget those in your distant homes that love you. Remember Australia's fair, untarnished name and honour. A few wrong ones there are sure to be, and these can easily besmirch the good name of the whole army. Your first and best victories are those of self control. Hearts of

---

2   Richards was sending articles to Sydney newspapers.

solid oak, nerves of flawless steel are made by such victories. Do remember in this bright and peaceful clime which tempts so strongly, the awful risks you are approaching.

On New Year's Eve I lost my peace and tranquillity which I so much love and enjoyed right up to 10.30pm, when I returned to the tent to find the fellows beastly drunk and making an awfully foul and hideous night of it and continuing until 12.40am. Had it been a congenial, light hearted party I could easily have been induced and make merry, but under the circumstances the New Year dawned upon me in my bed of misery.

Chapter 3

ON THE WAY TO GALLIPOLI, 1915

——⟫●⟪——

January 1: We were called as usual this morning and paraded at 7am. I fell with Arthur Searle to cleaning out a stuffed up incinerator, a dirty stinking job, and later levelled off a hospital tent with a shovel and a rake until nearly 12 o'clock. So you can see the New Year did not open in a particularly bright manner, but as my life seems to go by contraries, I am quite cheerful and happy. In the afternoon Fritz Schwarz and I went out to the third Pyramid. About seven of our tent were on guard; the rest went to Cairo and returned for a wonder in a pleasing and sober state without the usual coarseness and tales of brothel experience.

January 2: A letter awaits me from South Africa in which dear Father writes telling most vividly of brother Charlie's death in the Glencairn Mine. I wrote to both Ruth and Mother tonight and tears streamed down my face.[1] It all seems so hard, cruel and unwarranted. Mother must be in a

---

1   Charles Richards was one of Tom's older brothers. He was killed in a mining accident, crushed by groundfall. Ruth was his wife.

terrible state, with Father so bad too, and I playing soldiers, with our lives in danger. It must be hard on elderly people to have reared children and then to be left alone in their older days to their hunger and longing. The first tears that have rolled from my eyes for many years did so when writing to Ruth and thinking of little John asking so plaintively for his Daddy. It's a harder and a more cruel, unaccountable world than ever I have previously accused it of being and I have been very bitter from time to time. I went to bed very despondent.

January 6: On Parade the commanding officer stated that the Corps would have to be reduced to less than half its present strength. Only the best men will be retained, the others being split up amongst the other departments. This is excellent as I want to get into a fighting squad of some sort. This nursing stuff is unworthy of a fighter. All leave is to be stopped for three days to keep as many uniformed men out of Cairo as possible so that the police will have a chance of getting at some of the 122 men who are missing from the Australian and New Zealand ranks.

January 13: Two men Hucking and O'Sullivan (our ship's mess orderlies) have not received any mail as yet. So they have decided to write to one another and the general joking is quite good.

We have been paid today (14 days) one pound and six. Pay day is a matter of great importance with the fellows nowadays as their surplus is spent and times are indeed hard. The borrowing game is about played out. I am perhaps only one pound short of the 4 pounds which I had on leaving Australia but I must spend about three pounds on brooches for Mother and Manly. A letter from Manly today was something to make me think very deeply about as she is waiting and God knows I do not think I would actually keep a girl waiting. A girl's life is so different to a man's and it is a shame to keep one waiting with a chance of nothing ever happening.

January 14: One of our Chaplains inferred, after an interesting lecture in the YMCA shed, that the bushmen in South Africa during the war were commonly called the 'bloody Australians' because of their frequent use of the adjective; and though they swore continually their swearing was clean. This could not be said of our troops at present in Egypt. Their words are of the most filthy possible to use and if not immediately curtailed or stopped the damage to the natives, and the cross against the fair name of Australia, will be most shameful.

We arrived gleefully home . . . the natives gathered around and bartered as only these Arabs can to sell their wares—chocolates, lollies, tomatoes, oranges and even snakes. Fritz, as would be expected, bought a snake for a shilling, and was happy as a schoolboy but he lost it in his tent and there is a big outcry amongst his tent mates. The snake was a thin, prettily marked one about four feet long. Fritz is very much troubled with sores on the legs as though he had some vile skin disease. He is very careless and almost dirty—sleeps in his pants and will not clean up things until the fit takes him.

January 20: Our non-commissioned officers are up against one another like fiends. Sergeant Barnes, the old woman buggeriser, had a difference with Sergeant Bullmer, the disciplinarian, and challenged him to fight in most emphatic terms. Several of our Sergeants—Brown, Smith and Coleman—seek every opportunity to get drunk.

January 26: I tried to throw a rope over the Sphinx so as to climb up, but without success. We went into the Temple of the Sphinx, and then we came up around the Cheops Pyramid and climbed up into the five chambers over the top of the King's after much struggling and crawling amongst bat dung and fine dust.

At the Museum we came in touch with two nurses and I quite enjoyed a few moments' conversation with them, as they are the first women I have spoken to since leaving Sydney some months that seems like years ago. From the Museum we went to Sault's for afternoon tea. It was very fine indeed. Then off to the Mouski where we barracked and bartered with the shop-keepers and bazaar thieves and drank tea at a Turkish cafe which was an excellent and picturesque sight. A donkey ride, or really a race, between Neve, Pido and I. Pido won but not without extending his animal to its fullest along the traffic-strewn narrow street.

I had quite a good day today, though I am just as discontented as when in Queen's Park. All this waiting and hanging about seems such a dreadful waste of time.

January 30: It has been a lovely day. We loafed around in the morning cleaning up stones etc., though I ran away and fixed up with the Fourth Battalion for a game of football in the afternoon. Our side turned up in full strength and ran out winners 11–0. Our Colonel is a poor sport. Although he gave us leave to play, he did it very grudgingly indeed. I took matters very easy and still scored two tries.

February 2: At 5pm a heavy dust storm came along and filled the tents with sand and incidentally our stew at the same time. To evade the dust I proposed to go with Sid Wade and Pidcock to the picture show, paying 2 piastres admission. An American coon was singing, but after a while a fellow wanted to know: 'Why don't they give us some bloody pictures?' and a lot more such questions. So that the coon had to withdraw.

February 5: I called on Ted Larkin tonight.[2] He is a peculiar type of person to be a Member of Parliament. His tales circled round can-can and the lewdness of Cairo in a light jocular manner. He played football the other day and boomed the miserable game in the Cairo press. I can't see how the Australian Government is going to be strengthened or even run on honest lines when this type of man can secure recognition and a seat in the House.

February 6: Boxing is in full swing at the Victorian Stadium twice a week. In several of the Battalion mess rooms at night tournaments are fought off, midst much excitement. There is a good deal of all kinds of football being played but the fellows are not raving about it on account of having so much marching to do on this trying sand. Several of the Victorian Battalions have gone to the Suez. Some of the New Zealanders are already there. Reports of yesterday show that considerable fighting has taken place and some 3000 Turks killed.

---

2   Ted Larkin played in the first Australian trans-Tasman Rugby Test against New Zealand at the Sydney Cricket Ground in 1903 as a forward. A staunch Labor supporter, Larkin left the police force to be the New South Wales Rugby League's paid secretary—the body's first full-time official. He was actively involved in the recruitment of leading Australian Rugby players to the professional League ranks. In 1913 Larkin joined state parliament, winning the seat of Willoughby and becoming the first Labor MLA elected from the north side of Sydney Harbour. Larkin was killed shortly after the landing at Gallipoli on 25 April 1915 when he was hit by Turkish machine gun fire.

February 8: Last night in our mess room the Dean of Sydney, the Chaplain to our Forces, during a service (the first yet held in our room) spoke in very strong terms regarding the foul language and the cases of venereal diseases that are so prevalent amongst our troops. At all of the Church parades yesterday the various Chaplains denounced the same offences and appealed to the men to reason with themselves and look clearer and nearer to the more manly side of life. The Dean said it was a humiliating shame and an everlasting disgrace for any young man to visit the brothels of the large underworld that exists in Cairo and took the awful risk of contracting (such as some hundreds of our troops have done) a disease that is not only filthy and degrading, but is carried in the system and transmitted to and breaks down the health of the innocent wife. It also brands the offspring with ulcerated sores that mark the disgrace of the parents at the first weakness or illness that comes their way. A man that has been wayward enough to contract a dose should never be permitted to marry. Fancy a woman giving a clean and wholesome body to a wrecked and turbulent, diseased body of a soulless man. The horror of it! 'Oh if you men would only look ahead and think of the bright young sweethearts left behind and the lifelong corruption likely to be brought to blight their trusting lives by your visits to the terrible dens of sin and sorrow so plentiful in this country. A man who violates the law of chastity in these dens of infamy should have a harlot for his wife.'

It was a lecture that carried tremendous weight and has given the fellows something to think about. Why this lecture did not take place eight weeks ago before there were so many young and inexperienced fellows dosed with dread venereal troubles is difficult to understand. I think Headquarters have given our Chaplains a bit of a shake up, as they are seldom seen in the camp and just rush carelessly through their services. Anyhow it's better late than never.

February 9: I had a chat with Captain Wessel about football being of such great benefit to the men, which he agreed, but he and the other officers have not attempted to assist in either arranging games or obtaining leave for the players, so unless they move and take some interest I will let it drop, as I have no inclination to play. I don't get much fun out of it and run greater risk of being knocked about as they leave such a lot of work for me to do. Football is a thing of the past absolutely. I have been knocked about sufficiently during my sixteen years of play, though fortunately never very seriously. I have also had my fun and glory out of the game.

February 16: The infantry moved off about this time and headed for Mena Camp. The march back was very pretty and full of rural interest. The infantry men have a very busy time indeed. They seem a good spirited set of men though their home-made songs are a bit thick at times—cursing the officers etc.

> The officers get turkey
> The sergeants they get ham
> But all the poor old privates get
> Is bread and bloody jam.

February 21: We went across to the football grounds and saw NSW beat Queensland at League rules in the intense heat. I would have been playing but for my gravel-rashed knee which is very slow at healing. I don't like the League game though. It's altogether too continuous like a hurried through film at the picture show. The Union game gives more scope for thinking and seeing ahead of movements and also a chance to see them succeed or fail according to the understanding and ability of the players. Yes, the more I see of League brand the more I find in and think of Rugby Union. There was a time when I did give some little thought to playing League for the money there seemed to be in it, but I am now very thankful that I did not do so, as professional sport has not the same honour and enthusiastic achievement. It does not carry the 'hallmark' on it.

February 28: We won the game against the Transport Section yesterday and beat the 3rd Battalion badly today on the ground at Mena flat in a windstorm. WTB is troubling me frightfully. I feel in my heart I must win her but then she does not seem my type and marriage now needs money to make it successful.

March 1: The 3rd Brigade left Cairo last night. We will all follow. Much anxiety prevails in the camp as we may be going to England, France, Turkey or Syria, and will perhaps not know until we arrive there.

March 2: Our camp is all excitement awaiting orders to move off at any moment, but where to is problematic, though to my way of reasoning and the logic of the lecturer on Damascus in the YMCA this night, there is but little doubt but that Turkey will be our objective. I feel pleased with it as the type of fighting will be more suited to the undisciplined and impatient Australia than the trench-to-trench kind of work now going on in France. The lecturer tonight is a doctor with 30 years' residency in Turkey. He spoke very plainly and forcibly of the corrupt and bad Government of the Turks: 'Their small-mindedness, avariciousness and sensuality was certain to destroy them as a nation sooner or later, and the time seems to have arrived and your men will do it.'

March 3: Went into the Mouski to collect some films. The little Italian girl behind the cash register had a pretty voice and her English is so entertaining that I gave her a note requesting her name and address so that I might send her a postcard. It's a treat to hear a woman's voice after the men, men, men around the camp. Things are so bad that it even sounds pleasant when in conversation a fellow is referred to as 'miss', or should our neighbours come to the tent to enquire for anybody they might ask in a weak voice: 'Is Miss O'Sullivan in, please?' It might look stupid in cold ink but it is a relief to hear it nevertheless. There is always something striking about the sound of the word 'miss'.

March 7: Church Parade as usual. There were some nurses present this morning and no doubt they tend to cheer the poor solitary man a great deal. The form of a woman is somewhat of a novelty to us now. The Chaplain lectured the men to keep fit and always prepared to serve their country instead of drinking and abusing themselves. There is a lot of drunkenness and gambling going on about the camp just now. The fellows want to get busy. This desert camp and training is growing sickening, more so as the men will never be any more fit than at present; in fact we seem to be wasting time more than anything else.

March 8: I received the address of Victorine Warschafsky c/ Robena Boss, Nubar Pasha Street, Cairo. This is the Italian girl with a pretty English accent who attends to the cash register at the chemist and photo shop in the Mouski. I may send her a postcard now and again.

March 10: It's high time we shifted out of our desert proceedings. The hawker boys are better than parrots and repeat just what they hear our soldiers say. Last night at the picture show a young coon was shouting and selling 'can-can peanuts' and 'fair dinkum peanuts' but the house gave way when the big lump of a dancer in doing the splits and such like poses turned her bottom to the crowd, who rose like one man and pelted pieces of carrot and other vegetables at her. Talking about niggers I heard while going into Cairo today some terribly bad language from the hawkers. 'Egyptian Mail bum fodder' was being called out everywhere, even in front of the Continental Hotel.

March 13: A letter came to hand from the Italian girl who states that her brother-in-law got the letter I wrote her and would not let her see it even. A woman's lot in this country is the very devil right enough.

I washed a singlet and few socks this afternoon and wrote to WTB tonight. I have a persistent itch all over my body. It's not very noticeable but it's awfully annoying. Many of the other fellows have it also. The sores that broke out on my knee near the gravel rash have appeared on my ankle. I am getting very anxious about it.

March 16: I am getting quite a dodger nowadays and make everything work that is likely to keep me away from those irksome parades. A bit of a sore ankle was the excuse for an easy time today. I will have to show up a bit as we have the most detestable shirkers about and I must not for a moment be classed with them.

I had a look around our Canteen tonight and the beer drinkers were peacefully playing at the 14 or 15 crown and anchor boards. It's a great deal better than other things they might be doing and what's money to these men? By all means let them gamble. Encourage them in fact if they will otherwise keep respectable. Yet I fear the military police will raid them again as they have done before.

The Colonel examined our heads for the length of hair and everybody had to have the clippers over them or be fined. They are afraid of lice evidently but why we don't get shower baths to keep clean with beats me.

March 23: Today is mail day. I was sitting in the Mess Room reading with interest 'With Kitchener to Khartoum' when the bugle blew 'letters' and there was a rush from everywhere in my direction. There were some 200 letters called out and claimed by the anxious and eager crowd. The expression of curiosity, expectation, joy and disappointment was splendid to take note of. My lot turned out to be one postcard but it was good and worth much to me.

March 26: I look and long each mail for Win's letter. It's strange that I should be so hopelessly overcome by this girl, when all hard reasoning sums against having anything to do with her, more so when it means a poverty-stricken existence such as mine seems to hold out. It all seems so hard that a person has oft times to remain single owing to the abnormal cost of living.

March 27: We all attended the funeral of young Pickles this morning. He is the first dead in our AMC Corps to date and to keep up the average number of deaths in the Australian Forces since landing in Egypt to somewhere about one per day. The coffin was taken to Giza Station by tramcar, from there on a gun carriage. The 4th Battalion supplied the firing party of fourteen men and the brass band. The ceremony was strangely and singularly impressive, particularly during the lull between the three volleys and the bugle calls. The 'Last Post' stirred the sympathy in the veins of the lowest man present. Tears entered the eyes of many men but mostly the unthinking foul-minded type of fellow.

March 29: A grand concert was given in the YMCA tonight, which was a huge success. The women were very nervous and I should say that it was very trying for a woman to stand before such a sea of wedged-in healthy male faces and not feel it. The Salvation Army Captain McKenzie was in his crude element and handled the fellows splendidly. This captain is a rough, ill-educated, adventurous type of man. I don't care a rap for the strength of his religion but he is the man for the boys all right and worth a dozen of the other and better Chaplains that we have here. He follows the route marches if the men are camping out and organises concerts etc.

April 2: I've heard that Harold George, Ted Fahey, Twit Tasker, Fred Thompson and others are coming out here on Sunday next.[3] I hope they do as they are good fellows.

April 3: At 8pm last night I got orders to be under way by 6am. Riding in Alexandria by motor 130 miles in four hours or a little less is very good going right enough but there are no turns, curves or gradient along the track. At Alexandria we drove in cabs to the wharf. This city is teeming with all kinds, particularly Englishmen. Our boat the *City of Benares* carries 600 men and some 300 horses, so we are in for a dirty, foul-smelling trip if they don't soon land us somewhere. George Hill, George Flyne and I went into Alexandria last night and felt rather impressed with the English, or rather French, aspect after the real Arabic Cairo. The girls without veils and walking about so freely rather struck me, when in Cairo a girl cannot walk about for the rotten gaze of the street idlers. The underworld here, like all seaports, is bad indeed. There are hundreds and so cheeky in their solicitations. The prevailing price seemed to be two shillings, but, ah God, I don't even get an idea, much less an understanding, of your way of working when such women exist to run and kill by their foul diseases the young, ignorant and unfortunate inexperienced men as they do. It's just awful.

---

3   George, Fahey, Tasker and Thompson were all Australian Rugby Test representatives, and close friends of Richards. Fahey survived the war, but George and Thompson were killed at Gallipoli in May 1915. Tasker died of gunshot wounds suffered at Harbonnières in the battle of Amiens in 1918.

Chapter 4

LANDING, 1915

———⟫●⟪———

April 5: It is so pleasing to be under way again. The idea is that we are going to Lemnos Island some 600 miles up to put down a base hospital, but who knows?[1]

April 8: We were packed up with one blanket and two bags of iron rations (48 hours' supply), water bottles filled and ready to go ashore at a moment's notice. We were told there was no water on the land or, if any, it would probably be poisoned. Therefore we had to drink as much water as possible before landing. My thirty-third birthday turned out one of considerable interest and pleasure (such as pleasures go nowadays).

April 9: On guard at 4 to 8am. The night was magnificent and dawn was greatly intensified by the rising quarter moon and occasional glimmering of the dazzling planet of Venus. My mind was busy thinking and working out what the future would hold for me and the possibilities of Mother's protection and the chance of my marriage. I have told Win much about my love for her and my desires, but where it will end is beyond my solution just now.

---

1 Lemnos Island was used as a base for the naval attack of the Dardanelles and then as a military camp for Allied troops. It later housed large hospitals and convalescent camps.

April 10: I slept splendidly on my plank last night after the sleepless night before on guard. We are still anchored in Lemnos Harbour with a constant wind blowing. It is fairly cold—rather annoying as a swim and some rowing would be lovely.

New troopships arrive here all day long. There must be many thousands of troops waiting now. The Dardanelles are only two hours or so from here and it's really hard to realise that we are so close to the bombardments and danger. Whether we are to storm forts or land on Constantinople is hard to say. Our spare blankets were returned to me yesterday so I expect there is more horrible waiting and loafing to go through yet.

April 13: It has been raining and things generally are depressing. The *Queen Elizabeth* went into the Dardanelles yesterday with the 1st Brigade Officers aboard but what they saw has not been made known to us, though rumour has it that things are all at a standstill there and that the moving field batteries have baffled the warships. Also that we are in for a jolly rough time when landing amongst mines and barbed wire entanglements. But why we don't get some war news beats me—something to keep us alive.

April 14: There are some 300 horses aboard and some of them are real old 'smoodgers'. They love to be massaged and played with, while others are very cranky. At meal time they kick up a terrible row stamping their feet on the boards.

I went on board a French-Greek ship today with some patients, and it was astounding—there were no nurses and no arrangements of any kind have been made. We put our two men into cabins without any bedding other than a mattress. Poor devils, they are in for a dead rough time right enough.

April 16: Pay day yesterday. I am now holding 2 pounds. It will last a long time as I am not smoking and there's not much else for me to spend it on. The canteen is running biscuits and soft drinks only but the 'bum boats' bring nuts, dried figs, chocolates, etc.

April 18: About 16 days ago while in the Dardanelles three warships were sunk, two badly damaged, but the *Queen Elizabeth* escaped with shots through the funnel and one through the porthole. No one was injured. The Turks have beaten off the fleet's attack, chiefly by the use of field batteries and land torpedoes. Now it seems as though we are going to strike from the land side, but again there seems a terrible and costly delay. We are on a very tough proposition I believe.

April 19: Last night I had some hot lime juice and brandy going to bed for my cold. I must get it better at once as I must not miss getting into action fit and well. On guard I had a loaded rifle to challenge all rowing boats and prevent the trading boats from selling nuts of any sort, chiefly I understand on account of the shells being thrown all over the deck.

Lice hunting is now popular sport, although the catches and excitement are not so great as a few days ago. Nevertheless they are large and plentiful. 'You're lousy' is an expression that is no longer offensive as the cleanest fellows are indeed lousy.

April 22: I have taken up all the off time today by putting a waterproof lining in the back of my great coat. These coats do not keep the water out at all, and to make matters worse we have to land any moment now without any blankets at all. There cannot be much time now before landing and attacking the Dardanelles Forts. In a plain talk to the Engineers today Major Croxton warned his men of the grave danger of getting out of hand. On no account must they turn and run. 'If,' he said, 'you are walking along quietly with a pick on your shoulder and a shell should burst nearby, for your very life don't dream of turning round and running, as fear may spread like wildfire and utter confusion as well as a victory turned into defeat will probably result. Stick to your ground, men, no matter what befalls us. A large number are sure to fall and you will have to take your chance and there's honour in dying while still fighting.'

'There is no water on the land,' he continued, 'so you will have to get around as much as it is possible to squeeze into you before leaving the ship, and be as careful with your water bottle as you would be with your ammunition.'

Our officers have told us also that we are in for a very rough time and there may be as many as 2000 men to attend to, but damn the injured man, I wish to glory I was in the firing line somewhere. Anyway, I am in charge of a squad and must play my part right up to the hilt. What knowledge etc of first aid that I have will be worked upon to the fullest possible extent.

A message was read from Ian Hamilton[2] on parade begging the troops to respect the property of the Turks and keep right away from the Moslem quarter and leave the inhabitants absolutely alone, as any interference might spoil the mission of the Allied Forces in Turkey.

April 23: Today has been one of considerable anxiety. We have been worked up to believing that sailing point was at hand a dozen or more times, and then at 4pm today we drew in the anchor and after turning round steamed quickly down the crooked rows of transports and war vessels of many types, large and small. Perhaps a British transport (there were Australians, French and Indians there also) yelled the fine old British call 'Are you downhearted?' to which our men in a body shouted 'No.' This cry has a wonderful effect on all men in a serious moment. I've heard it at football games and other hard contests bringing the crowd around from extreme nastiness to a fine sacrificing and generous body. It would have a splendid effect upon a half-beaten lot of soldiers, I am sure. This I will try and remember too. Anyway the *City of Benares* moved past the *Lizzie* (*Queen Elizabeth*) saluting on all sides, at which of course we had to stand 'at attention' until we passed the long torpedo nets suspended from buoys, then swinging to a sheltered nook to our surprise and dismay, instead of going to Dardanelles, we dropped anchor and here we are now for how long? Personally I am past the age of speculation and just wait patiently by, neither believing nor disbelieving.

On parade this morning it was announced that, along with some others, I had been promoted to the rank of lance corporal. I was not surprised at this, though really I've dodged more work than most others in the Corps, though I used my head carefully. I have such a dread of non-coms. with us, and the rotten way in which the stripes have been given out, and even worse is the fact that the Colonel is a waster at the best. This came hard to me when he told Yank Ives to curse and swear and give the newly arrived person a rough time at Mena. This hurt me very much and summing up all the little points in the proposition I decided to ask Captain Welch to put my case to the Colonel and ask to have my appointment countermanded. Two

---

2   General Ian Hamilton was in command of the Mediterranean Expeditionary Force. He was instructed to prepare a plan to land Australian, New Zealand and British forces on the Gallipoli Peninsula.

or three stripes I would accept, more for the rise in pay than the position, as this is a miserable kind of game to be at and a rotten lot of growlers to work with. If I thought many of us were going to be shot at then I would take it on, as goodness only knows I want a few pounds badly enough. Above all these arguments perhaps is the fact that I've worried so much of late that my nerves would not stand any more. I used to think my nerves were steady and strong but I find they are always fidgety and impatient, and what I want is freedom and nobody but my own little stretcher party to bother about.

All this makes me think that I have led a rather strange life for the past 15 years, or right along my 32 years for that matter, in which, however, nothing in particular has happened other than the close protection of my gods and realisation of a small-minded though stupendous ambition. I have, I believe, a temperament that appreciates achievement and has never known the enjoyment of the 'hour', and as I never strayed far from the path or looked for roses, I have thereby missed the thorns that go with their gathering. Never having given myself up to emotions or feeling, I have never known the usual grip of love. It seems to be something that allures, tempts, defies and then escapes. My future line of life does bother me very much and I often watch the vision of the approaching crisis of my fate, whether it is to be a business life or the existence of a hermit or tramp.

Presentiment follows presentiment until I feel worried and at cross purposes with the whole world in general and myself in particular.

April 24: Tomorrow is the all eventful day. We have our bully beef and biscuits with a full water bottle for two days or more. There is no water on the Gallipoli landing place at all, so we have to take great care of our water and fill ourselves up to the neck before landing.

At 3.30am the first landing parties comprising battalions of the 1st Brigade will face the music which will probably be poured out to them from the trenches only a few hundred yards from the open beach, but it is just possible that the fleet will have cleared the Turks back from their advanced positions.

At 8am the Engineers and 1st Field Ambulance go ashore in small barges and rowing boats. Of course, our landing will be free from rifle fire but there are two huge forts 800 ft and 600 ft high back 2½ miles with a clear range on to the landing place. The fleet which includes the *Queen Elizabeth, London* and *Prince of Wales* may hold these forts up and keep them busy. Let's hope!

I listened to Major Croxton speaking from the bridge deck this afternoon. He gave particulars of the numbers and the battalions landing and what was expected of them. His speech was full of fine humour, dealing chiefly with our likely fear. It was hardly the kind of speech one would expect on the eve of big doings, as there was plenty of ridicule, nonsense, but no hard facts or detailed information. It seemed more as though we were preparing for a pantomime instead of grim warfare. I don't mean for one moment that he should have made us melancholy and miserable but he could have given us something like an idea of what to expect.

Into my overcoat I have sewn a piece of waterproof sheeting as the coats do not keep the water out very well, and added extra pockets to my coats for possible convenience and emergency sake. I also have a waterproof bag to carry my notebook and camera in. I have seven rolls of film (8 exposures in each) which will have to do me for a time, until we reach civilisation I suppose.

Gallipoli has mythology interests as the great warrior of the Siege of Troy, Achilles, is buried here, or at any rate there is a place described as the 'Tomb of Achilles'. Lemnos Island is known also to mythology as it was here that Vulcan landed when he was thrown out of Mount Olympus by Juno.

There was a glorious sunset tonight. It was just like a stage setting with the lovely deep red-coloured orb disappearing between the purple hills and the dainty rose pink sky. I was drawn away from it to get more bully beef and biscuits in my mess tin.

Tonight, although the fellows are naturally a little excited, they are in good spirits. They have shown up splendidly (comparatively speaking) since we left the loafing and waiting ground in the sands of Egypt. There has been a stronger tendency for sacred music also of late, with mouth organ and concertina.

Only a few minutes ago they were playing and singing 'Nearer My God to Thee' and 'Lead Kindly Light'. It's wonderful how religion gets them down when there is danger about. This ordeal should also test and bring my lack of faith home to me and give me a new light in that direction, as I walk blindly and aimlessly now.

I don't feel the coming danger any more than I have felt anxious the night before an international football match.

April 25: No bugle call to wake us this morning, but most of us were astir before the sun rose—a brilliant and pleasing red glow. It was just the same as sunset last night—a stage setting with the flashes and booming of the cannon to enliven matters.

From just before daylight as we approached Gallipoli, there was a wholesale roaring and spitting of big guns, our warships being particularly aggressive. The roar of guns did not bother me much but as we were landing on the torpedo boat *Scourge* at 8.30am a shell came just over No 13 transport and stirred up the water to a height of 60 feet, within 150 yards of us. This brought home to me the grim reality of war, but to my surprise I wasn't troubled and took seven photos before landing over our knees in water from the rowing boats into which we were transferred from the *Scourge*.

As we were landing, a shrapnel shell burst 150 yards away and threw a shower of bullets into the water—rather a pretty display.

Twenty minutes on, with stretcher at the ready, we were climbing the steep, rough hills looking for wounded, but it was about 1pm when I got my first case and from then until 6pm I had fully 20 dressings to do.

The wounded were in splendid spirits, telling me that in landing at 3am the Turks were right down on the beach, but were soon driven back over the terrible ridges for a distance of two miles. But alas! Our fellows got knocked about badly before this.

Seeing that the Turks had been pushed back and three guns taken it was surprising to find only a few dead and wounded Turks, while our officers and men were knocked about.

In a fairly well sheltered valley I waited for an hour within a short distance of the attacking party. The word was continually being sent back that help was badly needed on the left flank. A whole battalion of men were sent in but it was too late.

The Turks had brought about a successful counter-attack and driven our men back through the use of machine guns and shells. Showers of these shell bullets were falling all around our positions and it made us shake. Machine guns were being pushed forward by the New Zealanders. They were only just past our little party when a captain got a bullet through his calf and a lieutenant got a shattered forearm. Both came under my treatment. A fellow came along and asked me to go up and fix up his pal whose foot was shot. With a stretcher, Watts and I went only 100 yards along the valley.

The bush was too thick and the water-worn track so rough that we discarded the stretcher and proceeded on all fours up the firing trenches upon which our fellows had been driven back. Here was a poor devil with his heel and sole blown away, and although in great pain he was what might be considered cheerful. I cut his boot off and dressed the foot. Bleeding was then not heavy. Now the trouble was to get him away with rifle fire pinging overhead and through the bushes within a foot of us. This safely done, the way out was awful but my patient skidded down the steep side on his hands and seat while I went forward holding the limb. In the bottom of the gorge I got him onto my back and made good progress, but as the foot started to bleed heavily, I had to put a ligature onto the artery at the thigh.

Fully two hours had passed before we got back to the boats taking wounded aboard the transports, and he bore up wonderfully well throughout. In his belt was a large sum of money, which he said amounted to 100 pounds. When we got back I was pretty well finished. It was a hard job for me, but truly terrible for the patient. When he was waiting he got out a sovereign and made me take it.

It was a remarkable day right enough and a day in which it was easy to pick out the wasters, also the brave men. I am delighted with our Australian troops; the way they take the gruel is splendid.

At times there was a shortage of ammunition and reinforcements were badly wanted but seeing they had landed everything under shell fire I should say they did very well. The Turks seemed to do most damage with shrapnel shells, not so much damage perhaps as fright. Our warships kept up a steady fire throughout the day but I fear they were missing their marks badly.

It was heart-rending to hear the plaintive, and only too ominous call of 'More ammunition wanted on the left.' What a doleful story these words really unfold. Also the call for reinforcements that came back from mouth to mouth told of dire troubles experienced on the other side of the hill. 'Reinforcements—hung up on the right!' What a significant sentence, especially when uttered by the parched lips of a wounded man. Reinforcements were hurrying forward, sweating and panting, loaded with their equipment and a box of ammunition between them.

April 26: The warships seem to have a monopoly of the firing, some six ships taking part. The Turks are not replying at all. Indians, with a whole line of mules, are ashore and carrying guns and shells up the most difficult slopes with these sure-footed animals.

All last night the rifle fire was terrific. I went up behind the firing line at 3am and the flashes were a bit thrilling to say the least of it. I slept in a bit of a 'dug out' in the hill that runs down almost to the shingle [pebble beach], but it rained and the position was too awkward to sleep much.

9am: Rifle fire is going on along our front to the right of where I am sitting, camera at my feet, and by reports of the terrific firing I should say our men are beating off an attack. At 10am with three stretcher parties we were dodging shrapnel for 1½ hours under the side of the gorge. The rain of lead poured down incessantly and as each whistler was heard overhead we ducked. I am beginning to pick up the sounds of the different guns and to know the bullet pellets. This is indeed a wonderful experience and seeing there is so much slaughter and lead flying about we all take it mightily coolly and joke all the time that we are dodging. Bully beef and biscuits for dinner with a dixie of tea boiled over a pine case fire.

At 2pm we in stretcher parties were away out again and met the very despondent 3rd Brigade going back into the firing line. Two companies out of each battalion of this brigade comprised the landing party on Sunday morning, and although they suffered heavily I cannot yet understand how they came to effect so successful a landing, or any landing at all, in the very teeth of a machine gun in such small parties. The mistake made seems to have been in following the Turks 2½ miles back from the beach, which in this country meant getting away from ammunition and all supports, so that when the Turks stopped the 3rd Brigade got cut to ribbons and were too far away to be assisted. As we got a lot of wounded from there, the cry going along the communication lines was like a lost soul crying: 'For goodness sake hurry along more men and ammunition as we are losing ground like hell.'

Later ... reports are very encouraging and make out that our left and right supports are making wonderful progress capturing 1000 men and nine guns. But around here we seem to be up against it all right and have probably lost 1800 men for the two days. Our Corps were working until 11pm and were out again at 1am, gathering in the wounded, most of whom bear up with wonderful fortitude and patience.

April 27: I got to bed at about 4am but woke at daybreak after 2½ hours' sleep—good sound sleep too—as this carrying work is very hard going. The big guns—chiefly the Turks'—prevented any hope of further sleep. It is now 9am and I expect 40 tons of lead has passed overhead going both ways already, as I lie in this dug-out balcony bedroom. We are told to sleep now as we will be out all night in the moonlight. The Turkish shells are giving our ships that lie in front of the landing stage a very rough time.

It is reported 18,000 Turkish reinforcements were brought in last night. I fancy our 'front' is feeling it at this moment as men are being gathered from all over the hillside camping and resting ground and being hustled away forward to the line of front which extends over a length, as far as I know, of 3½ miles, of which the country is somewhat like the ravines in the Blue Mountains only covered with low thick bush and a natural hiding place.

Yesterday we had several Indian-manned mountain guns in action and they seemed to hold back the opposition fire. It is grand to watch these Indians at work. They are so quick with their guns and remarkably cool. We have some number of mules taking shells and tins of water over the hills handled also by Indians, and bullets never make them flinch in the slightest.

News that the French and British troops have met over on the Dardanelles is good news and might mean that our poor devils in the trenches get assistance, as it must be a perfect hell. Shrapnel is such a strange and mystic stuff to our men; they don't like it and it makes them very shaky.

News has (also) just come through that the Australian submarine has sunk a Turkish battleship in the Narrows but no news would raise any kind of a cheer just now, the fellows have had both nerves and muscle so knocked about during the past 48 hours.

At 6pm we started out to work but the stray bullets and bursting shells drove us into shelter for one hour. At 8pm we reached the right flank first-aid post but to our delight there was only one case which shows our artillery rescued the position that got so badly knocked about yesterday.

Chapter 5

WAR, 1915

April 28: Got to bed about 2am and slept in about nine inches of room until 8 o'clock. We five have spent a lot of time building our home and now there is a road coming through the middle of it. Things seem to have gone fairly well with our boys yesterday. The wounded, though thick enough, were much smaller in number than the two previous days.

I fancy we are beginning to settle down to steady fighting on the front lines and take greater precautions. Now that we have a large number of all kinds of guns in position we have a good, strong hold of things.

A number of transports have just arrived with (so rumour has it) Indian troops aboard. This is pleasing news as some of our men have been in the trenches for 48 hours and the strain there is terrible. I met a party of 3rd Brigade men last night and it was impossible to imagine how worn out they looked—a glassy stare in their eyes and quite a ghastly colour. In shifting around to our new camping ground, I met an officer of the 3rd Brigade, and several of his men. He told me only four officers of the 34 who landed are now left in the field of battle. He states that deeds of marvellous daring and unheard of determination took place all day Sunday [April 25]. One fellow was shot through the heart at short range by a Turk, but so determined was he that he first ran his bayonet through the Turk before falling over dead.

The 9th Battalion did wonders, by all accounts, and it made my heart rejoice to listen to the enthusiasm of these game warriors.

One kangaroo shooter from the north of Queensland wanders along with a small telescope and accounted for eleven snipers in one day. The stories these Queenslanders tell and the easy-going slangy way they explain things is cheerful to hear, more so as they have lost about 2500 men out of the 4000.

April 29: There is very little shelling going on this morning though rifle fire and machine guns are active. I went for a walk this morning right up on the right flank just to have a look at the men and see their trenches. Everything was extremely quiet there. The men were mostly occupied in digging fresh trenches and but for the heavy growth of whiskers on their face they were little worse off for their three days' nerve-wracking work. This flank on Monday night last drove the Turks across the valley for 1½ miles but the Turks came back again and gave them particular hell, driving them (the 4th Battalion mostly) back to the trenches. We hardly know yet what damage was done to each battalion, as the Companies and men got so hopelessly mixed up in the mad rushing attack of Sunday last—an attack which will, I believe, go down in history. The more one looks at the position and the subsequent results the more difficult does the position of our brave men appear.

April 30: It was a very cold night last night but with two pairs of socks and all my clothes, including an overcoat, I managed to keep warm and sleep all right. Most of the fellows complained bitterly, particularly two Tommies I brought out of the Aid Post wounded. They said: 'The night freezes you and the sun roasts you.'

I have been wandering around the trenches out of curiosity for one hour chatting with one and another of the 'Death and Glory Boys' (9th Battalion) when the gunner of No 1 gun (there were three of them) saw a Turkish charge about 1000 yards towards the centre. The gun was trained and fired. What a sight followed! Turks were seen blown up several feet into the air and what of them that were left made back to the trenches on hands and knees but the 18-pounder continued shelling and at such short range must have done terrible execution. Some 30 rounds were fired like clock-work before the bullets began flying in our direction in dozens. It was then Major Hughes ceased firing and ordered the men around him to cover, and shouting to the ammunition carriers: 'No more ammunition.'

Several other fellows took up the cry and it sounded like: 'More ammunition.' Major Hughes turned around from his range-finder and roared: 'This is no bloody chorus; shut up you damned fellows.' General Rosenthal, looking in a moment later, said: 'That is the first time I've ever seen Major Hughes serious.'

When the 3rd Brigade made their gallant landing on Sunday last they threw off their packs on the beach in the rush. These packs were mostly lost and strayed, so yesterday and today boatloads of kits and packs were strewn along the beach for them to open and make good their own kits. These kits belong to the killed and wounded and it did look painful to see them strewn about. Yet even worse was the letters, Xmas greetings and even birthday cards that now remain on the shingle beach. They all speak of sad hearts that the loss of their friend will bring when the news is made known. Rev. Green buried a few men yesterday but away in the front they are buried in holes and no ceremony.

May 1: It is a beautiful day, but with shrapnel falling thickly all along the beach. We are all living like fighting cocks now, as for the first time we have received anything like military rations. We have to cook it ourselves of course but as we work in batches of four men it's not hard. My party— Tom Yeomans, Claude Watts, Andy Elliott and self—get along splendidly. We have a 6 lb tin of stew at midday with bacon, cheese and jam, bully beef and biscuits aplenty. We pinched some onions and potatoes down at the stores and as thyme grows in plenty all round the camp we get up many good meals. This morning we made up a decent mince. Water is not at all plentiful and I've had to wash my underclothes in the sea water.

May 2: Patches of shrapnel fire and rifle bullets have been passing round now and again. A bullet dropped into the fire at which I was cooking the midday meal. It's truly wonderful how accustomed everyone gets to narrow escapes from bullets. A piece of shell landed ten feet away today and the first remark was: 'Who threw that tomato?'

May 3: Poor B Swannell is dead several days ago.[1] A week ago today, I believe, he had a shot through his head. I am really grieved as 'Swanny' with all his faults etc was quite all right, though he is a character seldom met.

The first patient I had this morning had his head terribly blown about. The doctor said we should leave him to die—nothing on earth could save him. We started out for the depot thinking the operation table there may give him a chance but no! He died on the stretcher. Around his neck were charms of several kinds, one a religious charm. Alas, charms, beliefs or creed play no part in man's preservation during war, bloody war.

Something went very wrong with our left flank last night. Our boys attacked, chiefly with the New Zealanders, at about 8pm. I believe we gained 600 yards but the pace was too hot and reinforcements so slow that the ground had to be given over. Whatever happened the fighting line is in the same place today and hundreds of wounded have been taken back to the beach and sent aboard the transports. It has been the heaviest day's wounded since a week ago today. Some of the cases are terrible. This afternoon my squad brought in a fellow shot right through the body penetrating the lungs. He was in agony and asked for something to send him to sleep but like all Australian soldiers he was game and did not grumble.

May 4: These Turks seem to be damned good fighters, regardless of the tales of dissension and lack of spirit. A note from Ian Hamilton read out to us yesterday says the Turks are tired of fighting and prepared to throw in the towel at any moment. But I wonder. Not for a moment am I afraid of them

---

1   Blair Swannell was one of Australian Rugby's most unusual and notorious figures. This English-born forward, who had toured Australia twice with British Isles teams before settling in Sydney at the turn of the century, had the unenviable reputation of being the ugliest man to ever play the game. His face was like a battered prune. Swannell's personal hygiene was also a concern. His prized possession was a once-white pair of football breeches that he wore in every match and refused to wash. An incessant bore who boasted about his military conquests, including fighting among the insurrectionists in the Republic of Uruguay, Swannell would arrive on game day wearing a filthy cream sweater bearing on it the badges and dates of all the countries he had represented. On the field, he was an absolute mongrel, renowned for kicking defenceless players. The Wallabies' first captain Paddy Moran said Swannell was a 'bad influence in Sydney football' whose 'conception of Rugby was one of trained violence'. When Swannell died, at Gallipoli, the suggestion was that because of his domineering English manner he was probably shot by one of his own soldiers. The real story was that Swannell led a charge towards the Turks, forcing them to retreat higher up in the cliffs. While kneeling to show his troops how to take proper aim at the Turks, Swannell was fatally shot in the forehead.

beating us, but I admire a fighter and I feel sure we are not going to have matters as foolishly easy as they try to tell us.

Stories of treachery in our ranks are common.

A low, flat-lying point (Gaba Tepe) of jutting land covered thickly with bush almost to the water's edge has been the scene of several bombardments by our fleet and watched closely at night time by searchlights with light torpedo boats cruising in closely. There is a huge building on the point and also what appears to be a fortress. The Turks presumed we would make our landing there and so put barbed wire entanglements thickly along the beach and dug themselves in with rifles and machine guns with which to oppose our landing, and, ye gods, we've got something to be thankful for that we landed one and a half miles further north. This morning, however, the strength of this Turkish position was tested. One hundred and ten volunteers came forward from our ranks to make a landing at daybreak. They landed right enough but the reception was so hot they turned and made back with six killed and 36 wounded. Not a man would have lived to return had it not been for the rain of lead poured into the Turks by torpedo boats. Later several of our warships gave this point some number of shells, but I understand the Turks have trenched, tunnelled and dug themselves in to such an extent that it will be the devil's own job to get them out of it at all.

Our fellows take their injuries with remarkable fortitude. The last patient I brought in was along the muddy gully, now known as 'Dead Man Gully' on account of the men and animals that are killed there from shrapnel, as anything that bursts on or over the firing line falls along this deep gully. This man was shot through the lungs and had little time to live, but on the way down he said several times: 'By God, that Turk could shoot well. He got me a beauty, didn't he? I thought I had him right enough but he beat me easily. Ah lads, how long is this job going to take to mend? I would like to get back on that damned Turk.'

May 5: A lovely morning. Breakfasted on fried bacon, toasted biscuits, cheese and jam. Yesterday a launch and boat with a Red Cross flying went right under the Turks' guns on the beach to the south and without interference buried the dead and took away the wounded.

May 6: The first call our No 8 squad got was a shattered arm which was later amputated. This fellow—Robertson of the 12th Battalion—was one of the most optimistic men possible. There were five of them in a trench when a Turkish shell broke away the side of the trench and mixed them up all together. Some were blinded by the dust, peppered by the gravel and their clothes were badly shattered and torn away from them. When the smoke and dust had died away Robertson was the only man who could not rise from the debris, his body partly buried. When we got him he was in the best of humour and seemed satisfied that the Turks will get hell when the boys get fairly at them. He consoled himself with the fact it might have been a lot worse. He was indeed a splendid character, small in size but one of the real 'Bulldog Breed'. I am thankful Australia can produce them as well as England.

Our next case was shot through the body and died before we were 100 yards on our journey. We placed the remains on the hillside and went back for a fellow with a shrapnelled leg—an easy injury. One of the 8th Battery fellows with a shrapnel wound in the back came along too. He walked all bent and doubled up, but what a lovely long, lean, raw-boned Australian he was too.

We Ambulance fellows also had some touchy work to do. One shell burst around us. Four of the five were hit in easy places—one chap right through his hat leaving four holes in it.

This morning a Turkish officer came riding along the beach holding a white handkerchief over his head. He is credited with saying his men were short of food and tired of war. He personally was full up of being bullied by German officers and had deserted.

It is now dusk, and waiting for Yeomans to get the stew ready—potatoes, onions, thyme, tinned beef and hard biscuits, also a little bacon. We had no sooner sat down to enjoy this stew to be followed up by cheese, jam and hard oatmeal biscuits, when shrapnel began to fly around. The very first one broke back 20 feet from us and directly overhead. The pellets passed by us and landed fair amongst a party of fellows having dinner 20 feet away. One was seriously shot through the abdomen, one had his hand badly damaged and another his arm smashed about. I took two of them into our doctors but the shells came along more thickly so I got the Maconochie[2] ration tin with my stew in it, three biscuits, some jam and a mug of tea and screwed myself into H Miller's 'dug out' and between eating, watching and ducking from fiercely-bursting shells I had about as exciting a time as ever I want to have.

My squad also got busy with pick and shovel and now we have a good balcony room dug back into the hill where we will be able to view the bombardment with reasonable safety. There is our kitchen and dining room. Our sleeping apartment is lower down. It is not dug more than one foot with bushes at the top and bottom to keep the sun off as it burns during the day and is very cold at night.

May 7: We are going out collecting wounded tonight with shrapnel bursting within inches of us. The contents of one flattened itself against a wall one yard from me. I have gathered about 20 of the battered and torn bullets. This is a damned uncanny business as the brass end of the fuses are coming and dropping around from the east and shells bursting at us from the south side. It's a 'fair dinkum hell'.

May 9: The Turks seem to be very cheeky. One wounded infantry man told me that while the Turks were trench digging 300 yards distant he fired at one and missed. The Turk stood up and clapped his hands at them, 'but,' said my patient, 'my next shot stopped the bugger and he won't clap his hands anymore.'

The Army Service men are having a pretty rough time now taking provisions on pack mules up the gullies and mountain paths. I saw one of them coming along 'Dead Man's Gully' with three mules tethered behind one another. Passing me he said: 'Why they sent those disobedient b— back from Cairo to loaf around Sydney beats me. Why the hell didn't they keep them for this game?'

Came down about 3pm with a shrapnel-shattered patient in a semi-delirious and weak condition, his face and both eyes damaged and a ghastly sight. He's matted and covered with blood. I thought that bleeding men, and

---

2   Maconochie was the name of the maker of a tinned stew supplied to the Services in World War I.

worse dead and dying men, would make me feel sick and dizzy but no, I get amongst all kinds of frightful injuries without any effect. We brought the above case down in haste and through a field of raining lead.

It is a terrible experience to walk slowly with a loaded stretcher across open country with shells bursting all around you. Any of the many reports might mean the end of both patient and four bearers. You have to walk slowly on and let the pellets fly where they will and keep as cool and collected as the circumstances will permit. It's a task that would rattle some of the bravest.

May 10: The crowd of Indians with mules are doing great work in keeping provisions and ammunition up to the front. We never mix with them at all. They just move quickly along all day and seem quite happy, even when the lead is flying thickly. They can do wonders with the damnable mules and donkeys that are bad-mannered when an impatient Australian has the management of them.

May 11: From an 'Egyptian Mail', I learn that many thousands of Turks have been captured on the Gallipoli Peninsula. This is the first time I have heard of it. My squad were out all last night and again I struck some fine gallant Australians. With his back to the wall and fighting he's a dandy right enough but now dreadfully impatient. The other night, for instance, they begged to be allowed to make a charge, which later they did and drove the Turks out of the trench. Regardless of the warnings they had received about the danger of occupying vacated trenches, they went into it and another costly lesson was learned as the trench blew up and put some 70 of them out of action.

Our beach got a terrific racking this afternoon, probably the worst to date. The newly-erected gun drew their fire and as usual the Turks accepted the challenge and gave our right flank and the whole beach a hell of a time. Our stock of provisions piled up high upon the beach got it badly and cases of meat, biscuits, etc were broken and flying in all directions.

May 12: It has been raining slowly on and off for the past 24 hours. We were very little inconvenienced by it, though the soil is of a stiff clay and sticks tightly to one's boots. The shrubs and plants seem to be putting forth their best spring garb just now. I have noticed some strange flowers, though buttercups, tulips and poppies are most common. A shrub bearing fruit like figs is very pretty and the few birds about always shelter in these bushes. Orchids are to be found and are nice but so far not brilliant. Thousands of swallows have passed over us lately, presumably making north for the summer months.

May 13: The Light Horse landed yesterday and went right away into the trenches relieving the English who have gone down to Cape Helles. This morning has been a busy one. I have washed and boiled my clothes (some I 'made' on the beach—a dead man's kit, I expect). I had my hair cut with the clippers, a shave and a delightful swim. The sea is better now that the dead horses and mules have been dragged well out to sea.

May 14: Living extra well as we got a lot of potatoes, onions, peas and other things not allowed as rations, by using our wits down around the provision department. Water at present seems to be a difficult proposition, and we have to get along on hard creek water which runs dry before noon each day.

Had a lovely swim, though it is an uncanny business with shells screaming and bursting overhead. I went 'down town' again at dusk and though fresh water not to be got I made a half kerosene tin full of potatoes, while Watts made some jam, cheese and bacon. Onions, alas, are scarce.

May 15: From what I have seen here it is practically impossible for one army to push another one back when they are 'dug in' and protected by wire entanglements. So I have concluded that neither France nor Britain will have a chance of pushing Germany back. The sacrifice of men would be too great.

Last night I went up into the 9th Battalion trenches and chatted with several of the Queenslanders. Football was much discussed but I did get them to talk a little about their landing on Sunday three weeks ago. Oh what brave men they were and what a hell of a time they had, particularly on the Saturday night when they were so mixed up without any officers or water and very little ammunition. That night was one of horror; wounded men and all had to stand their ground with bayonets fixed and await the oncoming of the Turks. Thank God the Turks were bluffed. The way our fellows dug them out and drove them pell-mell for miles frightened them, yet had they continued the counter-attack on Monday they would have driven us into the sea.

I will never forget one little fellow. He had a flesh wound in the arm and another in the thigh. He came back behind the half-dug trench and asked for a drink. He had lost his water-bottle the day before. There was a lot of equipment lying about. He saw a bottle and asked most innocently if he could take it. I filled it with water and he was so grateful. He said: 'I have not much ammunition and my rifle is broken. I wonder if I could take that one.' He picked it up, opened it and looked for the oil can in the stock. It was full and as happy as a lark he sat down and I helped him to clean the rifle. Immediately afterwards, loaded with water, ammunition and a better rifle than his own, he thanked me most cordially and with the expression of an overjoyed schoolboy hurried back to the trenches. I found out he was in a bank in Queensland and a born fighter.

May 16: I'm afraid our men will be awfully swell headed after this affair. The cables from both England and Australia have been so remarkably complimentary that some of the fellows are noticeably headstrong now. On outpost duty they talk and joke like madmen, so foolhardy have they become. This outpost duty means scouting out ahead of the trenches and as far into the enemy's trenches as possible. It is exceedingly dangerous work and should be done with absolute care as the men are between two firing lines, and yet some of the Australians treat it as a joke, walking about without lifting their feet, talking, sitting down and even smoking.

May 17: I engaged a number of the Victorians (2nd Brigade) who this morning returned from the fighting line south of us in conversation. They were particularly pessimistic. The fighting has been hard and many deaths have occurred, some 400 buried in the one grave. The Turks have a fort on the hilltop and any number of big guns. It seems impossible to take it by storm just now and the warships cannot get the guns' whereabouts. The fellows were blown to fragments by shell today while sunbathing after a swim in the sea.

May 18: At noon today a large flock of Ibis flew overhead, perhaps 500 in number. Some hundreds of rifle shots were fired at them, and it was remarkable only one fell. The bird life seems to become more plentiful as the summer advances, the days grow longer and the twilight lengthens.

May 19: Yesterday's quietness was only the lull before the storm. The storm broke at 2am by a terrible cannonading and rifle fire. It was so bad that I did not dare get up to light a fire to have breakfast until after 8 o'clock so thickly were the tops of shells flying around our dug-out. One piece of steel had hit the side of the 'house' and brought away a lot of earth.

It is now 9am and they are fighting for dear life in the trenches. A party of men have been along the hail-swept beach with boxes of ammunition showing the extravagance of last night's firing. I went up into the trenches this morning to see just how many dead Turks were lying about and instead of hundreds there were only a dozen or so. This disappointed me as I felt certain our men had driven off a strong attack and caused great havoc. Our wounded for the 14 or so hours treated at the beach hospital were 170, some of them badly shattered by shrapnel. Australia is going to be crowded with maimed men after this. Yesterday's battle was no doubt a splendid win for Australia, although the Turkish artillery does such a lot of damage to us. Nowhere is a man safe from them. The shells enter deep dug-outs and kill the occupants. Our camp was riddled with tops of shells and pellets, many narrow escapes being recorded, but it's marvellous how the fellows exaggerate their close shaves and lie about things.

I believe our men are averse to taking prisoners as the tale runs that many parties—one today—with white flag and red cross some forty strong came along but our chaps would not trust them and turned a machine gun amongst them. This kind of thing does not give the Turks a chance to surrender as we are told they really would like to. I know full well that our boys are showing no quarter. It's an all-in fight, no 'beg your pardons' with the Australians. They seek revenge.

May 20: At 2am I walked down with a fellow wounded in the head and going back in the dark alone to be challenged and possibly shot at by our own sentries made it a rather shaky trip. One night the sentry could not have challenged me very loudly as he came running after me with bayonet fixed and kept it level with my chest until he was satisfied I was no spy. So last night being particularly dark I was careful to keep my ears opened.

May 21: The 2nd Brigade and a brigade of New Zealanders have now returned from Cape Helles. Some of them say they were taken there just to lead the attacks upon the Turkish trenches for the Englishmen and the French. They have nothing good to say about the Frenchmen as fighters. I have never heard anybody grumble about fighting and losing men here with us but all these returned men complained bitterly of having to fight down south with the Englishmen and Frenchmen. 'We want to see it out with our own men and for the honour of our own country.'

I have now heard the cause of the sudden outburst of rifle-shooting last night. It seems an armistice was arranged in order to allow the Turks to take away the wounded that lie near the trenches and to bury the dead. The armistice was to expire at 7.15pm. It appears the Turks after taking in the wounded went gathering rifles and ammunition, leaving the dead. This of course was wrong and our fellows were tempted to fire on them. Anyway 7.15 arrived and the Australians went at them hell-for-leather. The dead Turks remain unburied.

I have noticed several cases of lost nerves and strained minds, also a number of fellows accidentally shot through the foot or hand. There were twelve such cases in one battalion of the 3rd Brigade. Enquiries are held as some men shoot themselves to get away from the battle. I did not think it possible men would shoot themselves in the hand or foot so as to get a spell but it has happened several times here.

May 22: At noon today the same 'flag of truce' went on as yesterday and later the same Turkish officer came along the beach blindfolded but this time mounted on horseback. Through the glasses I saw six horses and they were splendid Arab-looking animals. The performance created a big stir.

May 23: I eventually got into the 13th Battalion trenches and found that the fellows had come out for 48 hours. I later found Fred Thompson very well, though Harold George got the axe after a very brave action. It appears he was one of five to go out at midday and attempt to locate a machine gun and Turkish trenches. The sergeant got a rough time and was finally shot. Harold after a while found the corner too hot and taking the sergeant's body he made under a heavy fire back to the trenches. When he was preparing to get into the trench himself a bullet passed through his body low down and it is reported to have injured his spine. This is rotten luck.

May 24: Yesterday an aeroplane dropped a bomb in our lines from a great height. In coming down it made a great whistling, screaming noise and broke with a terrific explosion. One of our men got in the way of it and was killed.

An armistice was agreed to from 7am until 4pm today to allow both sides to bury their dead and it has been a terrible day. At about 9 o'clock the sentries were posted halfway between the lines of trenches and each side had to keep on its own side of halfway and bury their own dead, taking all the enemy's dead to the halfway and leaving them to be buried by their own comrades. The Australian dead had been lying there four weeks—since the first day—and in fair numbers. The Turks, who lay about in heaps, must have numbered 3000 and had been lying there since last Wednesday. It was so strange to see a Turk and an Australian standing together on guard every 70 yards. They tried hard to exchange a few words of conversation too, but it was impossible. The Australians upheld the most noticeable of his characteristics by sitting down with his white flag while the Turks stood up the whole time. At about 5pm rifle shots were being exchanged, and things are now going on as usual—sniping mostly. The bodies were mostly pierced through and through by shot and shell. I helped to dig a few trenches but the smell was awful. The bodies were buried in both narrow and shallow trenches. The burial service was read by Capt. McKenzie. The Turks did not appear to read any service and buried their dead six and eight deep in large trenches.

Chapter 6

DIGGING IN, 1915

May 25: I was sitting in my little dug-out writing room and library when I heard an unusually low kind of a noise or commotion. At this moment I heard someone say the *Triumph* had been hit. I scrambled out instantly and ran to the brow of the hill 20 yards behind our camp and there, sure enough, was the *Triumph* heavily listed to the starboard side, lying out a little more than a mile from Gaba Tepe.

Rowing boats were launched and there was a busy time pulling the sailors into the boats. For 15 minutes the ship floated upside down, then sinking from the bow soon disappeared altogether—25 minutes after the ship was struck. Some vessels went away to the west searching for the submarine. It was a heartbreaking sight to see this mighty iron-clad sink to the bottom without a fighting chance—an unseen stab from an unseen enemy.

Some said it was dastardly cruel and that the submarine crew should be tortured, but I do not agree. It was a fair deal and the *Triumph*'s lookout with the aid of all those torpedo boats and the aeroplane that was around this quarter only half an hour or so before should have detected the submarine.

May 26: A terribly sad affair took place in front of the 12th Battalion trenches yesterday afternoon. Three of our scouts had gone out in front of our own trenches doing dangerous work and were returning to our lines when some of our damned fools opened fire on them killing one and wounding another though the jaw. This was even more sickening than the sinking of the *Triumph*.

May 29: Aeroplanes have been up nearly all day today and making special observations on our left. Shots were fired at them in dozens, the burst of which make extra cloud effects and remain a long time in the clear sky. The 13th were blown out of Quinn's Post and the 15th regained it for them. Major Quinn and Fred Thompson killed.

May 31: There has been nothing but surfing and sunbathing going on down here today. I have been sitting in my private dugout reading and writing, also had two swims.

June 4: A rough mouthed fellow came to Captain Kain's post with toothache. The Lance Corporal got a pair of forceps and after snipping off the stump he got a grip on the next one and after much shaking and wriggling it came out. The fellow jumped up off the kerosene tin holding up his hand as though in appeal and also to keep the operator away, saying: 'That will do. I wanted three out but that will do.' Later he said after feeling his jaw, 'And they told me he was a good man.'

June 5: Hundreds of fellows have been swimming for days past in large groups at all hours. The Turks now lie in wait and send down one or two shells. Yesterday three were killed and about 14 wounded, yet they continue to swim. Wonderful dare-devilry.

Jun 9: An English officer joined the 3rd Brigade and is reported to love the willingness and the dare-devil pretentions of the Australians 'but, oh dear, their language is terrible indeed'.

June 11: Wandered off amongst the miles of travelling ways and communication trenches to Quinn's Post, Courtney's Hill and Pope's Hill. It is remarkable how intricate and mixed up the trenches are up this way. One Turkish trench overlooks one of ours and our men cannot even put up sandbags let alone raise their heads above their trenches. Strange as it may appear our men have the adjoining trench to the Turks covered by Pope's Hill covered in a similar manner. At night time we have several times driven the Turks out but then the place is enfiladed by the Turks' higher and more commanding position. It is just like a game of chess. This Quinn's Post is easily the most dangerous spot on the front, and although our fellows have taken it many times the enfilading machine gun fire has been too much for man to hold out against and they had to leave it again.

There seems to be some nasty feeling between the 14th Battalion and the others of the same brigade. It appears that the 15th (Queensland Battalion) got into trouble and wanted the 14th to cover their retreat but whether it was the officers or the men that refused I don't know but the 14th did not go out to help them.

There are a lot of bush-whackers, copper-gauges from the Cloncurry district in the 15th Battalion and I believe they are the finest of all soldiers, fearing nothing and as full of dash and endurance as man ever was. I am inclined to think they make it too willing bayoneting and killing when mercy should be shown and prisoners taken. Hundreds of Turks, probably thousands, would come in and surrender if they could. But if they leave their own lines without a rifle their own men shoot them and if they approach our trenches with a rifle our men shoot them and in many instances while they've had their hands held over their heads too. There is no doubt our men are hard and even cruel. Then again what else can be expected when so many of our finest men and companions for eight months are shot down beside you and your turn may come at any moment? It makes men restless and revengeful. In the calm, placid atmosphere of the Australian critic's residence or the newspaper editor's den, away from the dying shrieks of your friends and comrades, away from the dust of battle, the splash of bullets and the angry cry of shrapnel shells, such cold shooting and bayoneting may seem unforgivable and wanton, but alas it's war.

It seems to me that war as we read about and glory in, such as honest open hand-to-hand or man-to-man conflicts where the bravest man gets the upper hand, where the strongest arm and the noble heart wins the honour and gratification of the country, is old-fashioned and out of date, like the flint-lock rifles and the broad sword.

Today is long distance fighting with artillery and close fighting between the men with picks and shovels. In short, it is a pick and shovel war, and the men that can dig themselves in and wait patiently by are the men that must also win the day, providing the financial support will hold to them.

I can't see how we are going to progress in this entrenched country without tremendous sacrifice, as the Turks know the value of machine guns and have stocked themselves with them. Nothing on earth can demoralise troops easier than machine gun fire. If we'd had more of them on landing and every man in the trenches schooled to handle them our losses would have been smaller and our enemy's greater.

Alas if the war was carried on out in the open ground as in Napoleon's day I feel certain we Australians would have been in Constantinople by now, also the English and French troops.

It is seven weeks since we arrived here and the miles and miles of travelling ways, trenches and communications, cuttings and tunnels, to say nothing of the dug-outs for sleeping purposes, would make a railway contractor ashamed of his workmen and the poorness of their labours on Australian construction jobs. Yes, it's a pick and shovel war right enough and we can hold our own at this game too, though it has been hard on some of our young city men from offices and easy vocations in life. Australia need never in future fear a shortage of manual labourers.

June 13: Today is Sunday and a church service is announced for 7.15pm. We have not had a church service since Private Andrews, a Christian Brother, held one at Lemnos on board the *City of Benares*. The same good fellow (Oxford graduate and soccer blue) held the service tonight under the unique and ever-to-be-remembered distinction of Turkish shell fire. The commencement was delayed until the sun had set at 7.45. Sinking slowly this huge orb made a pretty showing and a delightfully coloured after effect.

The Turkish artillery usually stop firing at dusk, but tonight they opened out from a new gun position on Gaba Tepe and swept the beach as the 1st Battalion were coming along in platoons to support the right flank overnight. There was a lull of ten minutes and thinking all was over Private Andrews opened the service. Just then a number of water-carriers and supports were knocked over by a shell on the corner of the gully and beach, but as though it was a miracle every man got up in the middle of a cloud of smoke and dust and ran down the hillside into the gully. Here the Army Medical Corps grounded on the back of a steep hill and around their dugout shelters were singing: 'Onward Christian Soldiers'. As if in mockery, the Turks' shells again and again exploded on the opposite side of the narrow gorge as the men passed by. The 'Apostle's Creed' was not finished when the first wounded man came stumbling forward and pitched upon his face down the incline. A soldier with rifle and equipment nearby did not hesitate about his own safety but went and picked the wounded man up. Three medical men were on the spot almost immediately and as the five descended a shell broke with a cruel harsh explosion a few feet over the heads of the party. My heart stopped beating as I rose to go to them. It did not seem likely one of them would come through alive, yet from out of the heart of the explosion, like the mystic production of a pantomime scene where people are produced from a sheet of flame, those brave men came struggling through the low bushes and tangled undergrowth.

The Church services were held spell-bound and silent for the few minutes that the above drama was being enacted, and the prayer concluded they all rose and sang 'Abide with Me'. But as the men continued to come over the brow of the hill, why they did not wait a few minutes for darkness will never be understood, other than the Australians' contempt for the enemy. Another wounded man was followed by still another, carried in the arms of their trusty comrades. Parson Andrews went on explaining the beauty of St Paul's letter to the misbelieving people of Corinth, punctuated here and there by the callous bursting of shrapnel shells. Before we rose for the final hymn 'Nearer my God to Thee' the casualties numbered five.

Whether a testimony to Brother Andrews or not, he at least has conducted a service under circumstances seldom heard of, much less experienced by many wearers of the 'cloth'.

June 15: In the 'Sunday Times' April 25 there are great pictures and descriptions of over 5000 soldiers marching through the dense crowds that lined the streets of Sydney. It is a splendid testimony to the fine sons of Australia. Yet if those soldiers and, more so, the interested cheering multitude could only realise what this soldiering business really meant their hearts would bleed in anguish.

The fighting for one's King and country is fine and spurs us all on to do deeds of noble daring, but it's the other side that troubles me—the buffeting and robbing of just rights and the mean overriding of unscrupulous superiors. For instance, those conscientious young warriors will probably experience as soon as they get aboard the transports that the canteen prices are all out of decent reasoning and they will be driven by the poorness of the ship's food to deal with these monopolists and to pay the prices asked. They will probably find also gifts of food, clothing and all variety of comforts, given by a faithful and unwitting public, will be retained at exorbitant prices to them, and then have to wait in the hot galleries adjoining the engine room for from ten minutes to two hours before their turn comes to get served, such is the crowd. (This at least was my experience on the *Euripides*.)

The men will see at once they are being plundered and exploited but if they raise their voices and explain matters to the officers they may sneer at them or promise to 'see into matters'. But still the thievery goes on and if the men kick over the traces a little they are given extra duties, their water supply curtailed, strict confinement to certain decks, and several other restrainers. Empty cases by the dozen will be thrown overboard branded: 'For the use of troops with the compliments of . . .'

This business shows that the Quartermaster or officers are working in conjunction with the Canteen at the expense of the men. In Egypt we experienced matters even worse and never once had rations or enough to eat until landing on Gallipoli. If these feted soldiers should do the sights of Cairo, their characters will be mauled through the Australian press and their good names tainted in the eyes of their mothers and sisters, as we have experienced. What a crime! What low-principled patriotism! Those soldiers may have to fight from within their own camp as well as against an armed foe. These fine men will also find on arrival at the front that their fighting and very life depends more upon the pick and shovel than feats of arms.

War such as we read about and fostered in our mind's eye is entirely absent. There seems to be nothing left for the human part of a soldier to do. He digs a deep fortification, so does the enemy. They each put up loopholes and erect machine guns. Each position is almost impregnable to the other, and although the trenches are only 20 yards apart, you have nothing to see or shoot, still you keep on shooting. The side that dares to take the offensive is going to lose thousands of men and if not the captured trench is exploded by machine guns or blown up so that headway seems practically impossible.

It's not war—it's a display of uncanny mechanical contrivances in which the initiative and valour of men is taken away by the pick and shovel. So those expectant soldiers are in for shocks and disappointments.

June 16: A large barrel of claret was washed up on our beach today. The fellows broke it open. The men were in great delight. I secured about three parts of a kerosene tin full and have bottled a lot of it for a rainy day, as well as supplied some of our friends with whom we trade or get presents of eatables from. Seven casks were washed upon the shore but an officer with an armed guard broke the ends in, although the men were swarming around like bees, each one with a can or tin. A party of four swam out and towed a barrel in 200 yards and alas, the guard prevented them from even getting a drink out of it.

The wine is unsweetened and a little tart but when water is added, and sugar, it's lovely and reminds me of my sojourn in France. The barrels are very large, probably holding 100 gallons. It was a red letter day with our Corps.

This afternoon George Hill and party were taking a patient around to the beach when a shrapnel pellet hit him in the chest. He walked into the dressing station 30 yards away and dropped. He was sent aboard the hospital ship at once. From the reports and symptoms of the men who were with him, it is indeed a serious case. Poor George, he's been down in the dumps for some time now, but what a sterling fellow he is. This miserable war business is enough to make any person morbid.

June 23: I have written letters to Mr Harrison, Ruth and Win. I have just finished a roll of toilet paper which makes good writing material. It is over 40 days since I heard from Manly. I suspect I have just gone right out of the betting to the extent of being forgotten.

June 26: There is a lot of movement at present amongst our Headquarters staff. Whether it is caused by the Turks' preparation or our getting ready to attack I don't know, but I hope so.

June 28: I am recommended for Award by Staff Captain Pollock, 7th Light Horse. Mentioned in Despatches.

At 1pm about 120 of our men were seen to come out of our most southerly communication trenches. Later with bayonets fixed they were seen amongst the bushes in front of the old Turkish trenches. Scenting a lot of trouble and some excitement, I took my bandage bag and went away up, but to my surprise they asked me if I would go in along the trenches and see what Captain Dods was going to do with his wounded. I went in, had a look round and could see that no arrangements of any kind had been made to get the wounded away, who were walking about in half bandages and no bandages at all, without knowing where to go. I went back to our Captains and asked them to come in with eight men and give Capt Dods a hand.

Three of us went right into the trenches. It was now about 4pm and the 5th Light Horse were retiring, bringing back some of their wounded with them without stretchers and mostly without sheets. Two fellows threw one man out of a trench who had been struck by a shell and taken away the whole of his right leg. He was quite conscious and spoke to several of his mates. I have never seen anything like this fellow in my life—as calm as ever a man was—nor have I seen a more gruesome sight. What was left of the leg would not have weighed three lbs, but for the boot and the foot inside it. The other leg was uninjured. After getting him down amongst the rough brambles and trees, I came back and by glory, the bullets and shrapnel were thicker than ever. Six men came along with a comrade who showed a gaping wound on the thigh, a coat covering the remainder of the leg. I stopped them and covered the wound from the flies, then I saw that the shin-bone was smashed to a pulp. I covered it up also when in lifting the coat to cover the leg again I saw that the foot on the same leg was blown clean away altogether. What a dreadful case. A great shock even to myself.

We left on retiring a number of dead. I hit them with stones from the trenches to make sure they were not conscious. The wounded were probably 15 very badly and 30 mediums, but it is difficult to tell. Much as I enjoyed or rather valued the experience, I have no desire, if only for the sake of others, to expose myself to such a hail of bullets and showers of shrapnel again.

The killed amounted to 70 odd for this day's 'demonstration'. It was this morning that the Turks sent in an invitation for all Australians to come and stay with them. They had plenty of food and entertainment, etc.

June 30: Yesterday I saw 15 men and three officers of the 11th Battalion buried—a pitiful sight. Yet there are others that are not likely to be buried for some time.

July 9: Captain Welch returned a letter to Father as being too big. I went and asked him what the damnable regulations say on the matter. He maintained that Major Stokes' orders were 'one page only' and that he was sorry but would put it through the 4th Field Ambulance for me. I declined with thanks and told him that Major Stokes was inconsiderate, mean and acted as though he was a demi-god. We who in civil life were his equal were treated as low conscripts instead of free volunteers and men of reason. Seeing we have nothing to read and amidst such monotony we grow livery and dull-witted so that it was in the interest of the Corps to encourage the fellows to write and exercise their minds in other ways than gossiping, cursing and swearing. I feel much hurt over this matter. If we were moving on and the censor officers had some work to do, I would be the last to complain, but they are all actually loafing and it does hurt me to think we who are exposing ourselves to danger every day cannot get a decent letter through to our friends and relations regardless of the subject dealt with. The gun enfilading us on the right flank is now called 'Beachy Bill'. It has done a lot of damage too. On the left flank there is a nasty gun too. It is more silent than ours. The fellows call it 'Lonely Liz'.

July 12: WTB stated her intention nicely of marrying Basil, which I cannot complain of and I do wish her luck.

July 17: At 6.25am a Turkish aeroplane dropped two bombs—one in the water near our camp and I have heard since there were a lot of fish blown up and we are cursing at not going down to see at the time. I am writing these notes by lamplight—a home made lamp from a 2 oz tobacco tin with a lint bandage for a wick, candles being so very difficult to get hold of. One soon gets used to the smell of the lamp, but the smoke that arises if one blows it out is strong enough to drive one out of the dug-out for hours. So I use the lid of the tin to snuff it out and there's no smell.

July 21: At Dr Butler's there was a fellow who complained several times of weak, nervous attacks. But the doctor only grumbled and called him a shirker.

This evidently bothered the patient very much and it was a very unfair accusation also. The outcome was the fellow blowing his head off with his rifle today. It seems a shame as this man was a good worker and perfectly honest. But it is the damnable malingerer to be found amongst all soldiers that leads doctors to distrust anyone with an invisible complaint. I wish medical men would take a man's character into consideration and reason more.

July 25: I wonder that the big dogs at the head of affairs don't pay more personal attention to the wants of the men in the firing line. They have worked like slaves for three months now and by the weakened appearance of them and the long sick parades, I have come to the conclusion the men are worked and starved almost to death. Better and more food would keep them fit and well. It is truly cruel, and the military head should above all else in warfare see his fighting line might be decently kept alive. If there was a dry canteen where the men could buy food to pull themselves together with, all would be well, but nothing can be bought. A Light Horse man paid one pound for a piece of chocolate yesterday and often five shillings for a tin of condensed milk is paid. It's a damnable shame and a matter so very easily overcome.

The rumour we are to be relieved by Kitchener's new army is indeed comforting as every man here is worn out and tired of this constant strain without any comforts or change of food.

July 29: Rules and regulations are being strictly enforced in the trenches which seem extremely unfair. The men were doing hard digging all day and went into the trenches (firing line) the same night and because one leaned against the side walls, another had his hands off his rifle which was leaning by his side, and as the third had the top box covering of his rifle muzzle, the whole three were paraded and punished. This is not fair play where there is so much sickness and so much fatigue work to be done on the absolute minimum of food, hard, badly cooked stuff at that.

August 1: The ghastly reality of war lies in front of me now as I sit writing at the Dressing Station at 4pm and there are ten bodies lying in line. Yesterday these were fine specimens of Australian manhood. Men that any nation in the world would be proud to claim. It is a sickly sight if one is willing to permit the mind to dwell on the humane side of life but this we must not allow as there is so much blood and slaughter about to face that one cannot be sentimental. The bodies of two Turks also lie nearby. These are the smallest I have yet seen and very puny specimens. Their boots were badly worn and crudely repaired in one case, while the other had on a pair of light open-topped shoes. All the Turks I have yet seen wear underclothes and about ten rolls of a long cloth around their middle, while as a comparison our men are wearing mostly shorts and only a thin singlet under their tunics. This garb though not picturesque keeps the troublesome lice down effectively. The fact that they died well is no answer to the question as to why they should die at all but alas! It's Hell.

August 3: The most important happening up to 5pm was the miserable complaints of our fatigue party who were commissioned to bring up some poles, iron and sandbags, about 30 altogether, and of all the petty growlers I've heard in my life, I heard today. We as a body, in comparison with the infantry, have not done ten good days' work out of the fourteen weeks that we have been here and naturally when there is a bit to do there is more cursing and swearing than one would expect from a lot of over-worked and ill-treated men. If there is stretcher-bearing work to do they are not so bad, although even here there is bitter jealousy as to which section is doing the work. I am sick of all this squeaking and pettiness. It makes me so wretched.

August 4: Beachy Bill did a lot of work last evening and night. He fired from 8 till 11pm along the beach and must have done considerable damage as the supply depot is crowded with men and mules. Our guns exchanged shots with him, but if our gunners are no better shots than theirs it will take a long time to knock 'Beachy Bill' out of position. One of our guns is on a ledge close to the skyline at the top of our highest hill and the Turks have fired 3000 shots at it over the past 14 weeks but it still exists. It is a queer feeling to hear a shell approaching in your immediate direction, not knowing where it is likely to burst, and because a dozen others passed safely over, one hates to pay John Turk the compliment of ducking.

Down at the beach this morning a sharpshooter was playing along the front. I changed (by taking off the shirt I sleep in) and ran into the water. Above me were some newly-arrived Scotsmen washing their clothes. A number of bullets passed within a short distance of them and others struck the water not ten yards away. Still on their haunches they went on with their washing. An Australian water carrier went by and forgetting entirely he was in the narrow strip of firing area between the walls of the hills and the ocean, told the three Scotsmen they would be getting shot through the guts if they did not get out. The lads said: 'What? Are the b— shooting at us?' 'My b— oath,' said the Australian, at which all three scattered over the shingle beach in an exasperating hurry, and the Australian angrily said: 'Strike me dead! There's no need for such a b— rush. You'll let the b—tard see he's on the right spot.'

I was up at the 9th Battalion last night talking to George Barr. The men here are wild, to think that 37 men were killed and 70 wounded the other night to take a trench that we could have had simply for the digging of it weeks ago. This whole ridge was idle for weeks and while we were putting in time digging in behind the present lines we could have built up this trench for nothing, whereas it cost us weeks of digging and 37 good men. Our old miners laugh at the engineering section's attempts at survey work or tunnelling. They are often three yards out in a distance of ten yards. This department is a laughing stock amongst those who know anything of mining affairs.

August 6: So many troops were landing this morning and overnight that the small launches did not appear to be available to take the wounded aboard the hospital ship. The landing Ghurka Indians looked very frightened as they scrambled one over the other out of the barge and raced along the beach for shelter, where they immediately regained their composure and wore a bright, harmless expression of a child. I like their loose supple limbs and their general physique. They reminded me of Japanese both by their short stature and the features, only a little darker in colour. At the moment we are on the eve of a monster engagement. Each soldier and man have white armbands and a square patch of white material sewn on the back. It's going to be a rough-house tonight and our poor men will get knocked about and battered over and over again.

This morning early I went out through the tunnel under the original firing line to the advanced aid post where there were 21 seriously wounded lying about in all weird heartbreaking positions. We took a brief of a fellow with an arm practically blown off at the shoulder, and after scrambling over the bodies of some eight Turks, we reached the way out. It's uncanny walking on dead bodies!

August 7: War with a vengeance. There is no word or, for that matter, series of words that can convey any realistic idea as to what war actually means. Dante's vivid description of the inferno—a Hindo idea of Hell are as nothing compared to it.

I feel confident we have taken Mr John Turk by surprise this time as at 9am we had 2000 prisoners and to do them justice they were a rather good physical type of man. Their boots were worn and their clothes patched a bit but this can be understood as they have been in the field a long time.

Our General put up a good stunt by bombarding Gaba Tepe beach as if preparing to land troops there last night, but behold when daylight broke there were transports, warships and dozens of ships standing off Suvla Bay on the salt lake. We landed thousands of men there and these seem to have had very little trouble in making ground, and though the hill commanding the whole of the Peninsula has not yet fallen into our hands it must surely do so and then the Turks' fate is sealed once and for all. And God what a relief it will be to get away from this truly bloody awful place. The reality of war I have been through—it is relentlessly cruel and does not give a brave man a dog's chance.

August 8: It is 39 hours since we commenced the attack and it seems as unsettled as ever. The 1st Brigade made some 300 yards of ground and drove the Turks out of three lines of trenches but they are still holding the fourth and knocking fair hell out of our poor men with bombs. A stream of stretcher and walking cases still continue to come down but, thank goodness, the ambulance units and dressing stations are able to avoid congestion. Yesterday morning the poor fellows were lying in hundreds around the beach—a truly terrible sight. I have been working from 12 until 7 this morning without hardly a break and feel perfectly done up. It is now 8am, I am going to try and sleep but those fine fellows being cut and battered to fragments (our men are walking over the bodies of their comrades) keeps me awake, more so as I know that the 16 weeks here of awfully hard digging and fatigue with an average daily sleep of six hours on the poorest class of food has weakened the men to such an extent I fear nature will not stand to them in a long stubborn engagement. Sick parade each morning for weeks past has been up to 126 from our battalion and I understand this is a fair average all round. Even then, the double issues of rum that have been dealt out lately will have a lowering effect on the system as it wears off, and with matters at such a high tension as they have been for the last 38 hours I fear for our men. They should have been fed better or at least have had the advantages of a canteen. Tired and languid they take all unnecessary risks. It's the devil!

Information as to our exact position and what our fortune is scarce. We don't know at all. The warships are crowded in Suvla Bay and doing quite a lot of firing. The Turk is not doing much with his artillery. It's essentially a bomb fight with him. Bombs make terrible wounds too. We should get Hill 971 all right. I don't know how the Turk sticks out against our huge guns at all. He must be a great fighter.

This battle has now been raging 48 hours, and though I still feel confident of a complete victory the news leaking through from all kinds of sources is not so glowing as it was yesterday. One pleasing feature is the fact that very few wounded are now coming down from the 1st Brigade and very little rifle fire can be heard nearby, though on the left there are occasional rallies that sound quite a long way off. I am feverish today and not up to much or I certainly would go up to the firing line and have a look around.

The stories one gets from the wounded are at times interesting, but usually they don't know much of things outside of their own little environment and then most of them are so wrapped up in their business that they see but little of what is going on. I met the first 'squeaker' of the battle this morning. He was a bomb thrower and was only slightly wounded for which he should have been thankful. Instead he pleaded: 'This is what a man gets for volunteering to throw bombs. They rush you up into the trench in the dark and let you go without knowing where to throw or how far to throw. No more bloody war for me, not if the Germs do rule the world.'

This, thank goodness, is an exceptional case and both his spirit and his mind can be gauged from his lack of knowledge as to the contents of the bombs he was throwing. When we are working night and day to succour the wounded it jars to get one waster like this one.

August 9: My head is burning and my body shivering. Fever of some kind, I presume, but nothing very serious nevertheless.

August 11: It is surprising the disrespect the old hands have for all new arrivals. Up in the firing line the reinforcements are cursed as useless. They stop at every shot and squeal at even light work, yet talk with the tone of superiority. Of course they soon come to their level and knuckle down.

August 13: News is very hard to get still concerning our new landing party on the left or north but we have good reason to suspect our success has been very limited, if it exists at all. Several times I've heard the Tommies broke and came back upon the reinforcements in a demoralised state. We have had a lot of East Lancashire, Warwickshire, King's Own and others. Some of them looked loose and solid but taking them generally we Australians have not much faith in them.

August 14: I am sitting at the Clearing Station waiting for a boat for Mudros where I am to have a rest. Major Welch gave me the clearance last night. I don't really want to go but they tell me I'd better. My spleen or some such thing has gone wrong. Anyway I've had nothing to eat worth mentioning for eight days now. I waited on the beach all day long and until 9pm before getting aboard. A boatload went at 1pm but as they asked for the worst cases I missed getting aboard. Well this time there were 160 scattered about a huge barge and away we went wondering how long the journey would take to Mudros but alas, they pulled up at the hospital ship and we all climbed up there and spent the night.

Chapter 7

SICK PARADE, 1915

⸺⸙⸺

August 15: Landed at Imbros and put on milk diet under a RAMC [Royal Army Medical Corps] blighter. I don't like to have anything to do with Englishmen. The brogue seems to prevent any understanding and they also seem so arrogant when placed in charge of everything. Against the warder's threat I did procure some biscuits and grapes. The latter was extremely fine.

August 17: Arrived at Mudros (Lemnos) in early morning. Steamed in between the torpedo nets along the mouth and anchored. It is evident that there is no room at the large canvas hospitals here either as no arrangements have been made for our removal. It is four months since we left this lovely land-locked harbour for the attack on Gallipoli but many changes have come about in the landscape. Instead of it being green and happy looking, it is now dreary and desolate, so bare.

August 18: Rumour hath it that there is no hospital accommodation either here at Alexandria or Malta. This information cheers me along a little but yet it seems altogether too good to be true. We had about 1400 patients on this ship. Some 500 were transferred today so now I expect matters to go along better.

August 21: At dusk a troopship crowded with Australians passed out of the harbour. They were in a very cheerful mood and 'hoorayed' everything and everybody en route. It's truly wonderful how these Australians go gloriously satisfied to their death. These lads must know the hell that they are going into and yet they went bright and gleefully. I wonder if any country on earth possesses men so willing to make sacrifices. I am certain England does not possess the same spirit and not within 40 per cent of the physique. It's a shame to see some of the weakly, undersized, premature-looking English-men we have aboard. They are earnest and willing enough to fight but are not of the same material as the Australians. Their minds seem dull and their actions hobbled. They have neither initiative nor resource in comparison with Australians. The more I see and mix with these Englishmen the more I think of Australia and the independent, quick-witted fighting men they breed. The self-assurance and confidence of the Australian stands out. The shipload of Canadian nurses had not been alongside of us many minutes when several Australians were climbing over the side and chatting freely with the girls. One fellow comes from an out of the way place like Hughenden and he struts the deck as if he were part owner of the ship. He pushes himself in anywhere too and all the way from Hughenden. It's no wonder the world at large cannot understand the Australian.

August 24: I have meals on the deck with a rather decent little Englishman. He is keen on getting back to fight but most of the Englishmen around me want to throw in the towel and are praying that they will go back to England. They are poor spirited and have no inclination to even up their own score with John Turk, nor to their everlasting discredit have they the honour to avenge the death of their own comrades killed by their sides when making for Hill 971 from the new landing at Suvla Bay. I am exceedingly disap-pointed with most of the Englishmen I have come in contact with. I try to evade talking with them now as we seem to have the greatest difficulty in understanding one another, and to my annoyance I can follow them with greater ease than they can understand me, which makes me think I have a hell of a twang. A fellow was buried at sea today. There was no ceremony and the ship did not even ease up.

August 25: We were safely installed in the Gezira Palace Hotel, known at present as the No 2 General Hospital. There is one thing that pleases me very much and that is the long-looked-for privilege of sleeping in a bed with linen sheets and a place to put my clothes. This hospital is situated in what I consider is the prettiest part of Cairo and in the season this hotel is frequented by sporting folk mostly, it being surrounded by the sporting grounds of the country—a racecourse, golf links and dozens of tennis courts as well as croquet lawns. The Fisk gardens and flower gardens abound on all sides, while the present discoloured waters of the mighty Nile run past the back of the whole grounds and severs us from Cairo proper.

I feel as though I am going to be quite happy here and well again very soon and returning to the Peninsula. Most of our men though don't want to go back there anymore and make no secret of it.

August 26: It is twelve months ago today since I went into camp at Queen's Park and learnt the right and left turn. It has been a remarkable twelve months in many respects. The experience and adventure I have gained are most valued but the time it cost and the rottenness and robbery that undermines this military business makes me very bitter and I fear overruns the glory of my experience at military work. The fact that I am not in the fighting line worries me very much and distracts from my conscience the feelings of war achievements, so taking matters all round I perhaps should be well satisfied considering the type and methods of warfare. But there is the feeling that I have not been much of a warrior. I have seen and stood against all the dangers of war and had narrow escapes with the best of them but I have not been one of the fighting line.

September 1: They say the 4th Brigade lost hundreds in getting a trench which they held with ease for 48 hours just lately in the advance on 971 Hill. The Tommy relieved them and in two hours time the Turk drove them pell mell out of it. It was an English regiment that lost Quinn's Post in the early part of our campaign to the Turks while relieving our men, and so we have no confidence in anything English at present. It would not take much to rise a feud between the two here now. The Australian is a cheeky, dominant kind of a cuss.

September 2: I got off the sofa and went down to my bed also on a very wide veranda and in a few moments the arrival of General Sir John Maxwell was announced.[1] He came into the ward with his eyes wide open and smilingly took stock of everything. His staff of seven men had all manner of stars and shoulder ornaments. The General in passing stopped and spoke to me, asking what I belonged to etc. 'I suppose,' he said, 'that you are pleased to be over here away from it and having a rest.' I replied: 'Yes, Sir, but I wish the rest of the 1st Division were away from Gallipoli also, and although this is a splendid convalescence hospital with beautiful surrounds I would prefer to be with the rest of the Division.' To which he said: 'Don't let that worry you. Just settle down and be comfortable. I have sent the 5th Brigade over and the 6th are en route, so that the 1st will get a much needed rest.' He continued: 'By jove, you boys have done remarkably well.' I ventured, 'They delight in fighting, Sir. It seems instinctive.'

'Well bye bye, and good luck to you,' were his parting words as he moved on with a lot of 'big guns' in his wake.

September 9: There is no doubt we have some badly brought up young fellows in Australia. In the barber's today quite a youngster said he's only had one day in Alexandria and it was a good one too. 'When I go into Cairo I do just the same thing,' he said, quite seriously, 'and come home pleased and relieved. On arrival in the city I get around a few drinks, have a feed, go down to the brothel, put in a couple of hours there, and go to the picture show, taking the 9 o'clock tram home.' This, alas, is an ideal day for many.

September 13: Two Australian fellows went into Alexandria last night and did not return. It is very mean and wayward of them. They should consider the doctors and women who are running this place alone without military assistance.

It is remarkable how ill and lame some of the patients are when the doctors are anywhere about and then jumping, racing and pillow fighting on the quiet. It's hard to blame them for not wanting to go back to Gallipoli and such horror as goes on there. I feel anxious for our 5th and 6th Australian

---

1   Sir John Maxwell was a British Army officer, best known for his involvement in the suppression of the 1916 Easter Rising in Ireland and the execution of the rebellion leaders.

Brigades. They went out of Lemnos Harbour singing and cheering, and I am sure they will do the same going up to meet death but the loss of companions and dear mates, without an enemy to be seen, will silence and steel their hearts as it has done to the 1st Division.

September 14: Some of the English nurses in this building fairly hate the Australians and do not fail to show their feelings in the matter. Naturally they are people who can never see from other than one narrow and dimmed pair of glasses lacking decent focus.

September 21: A notice appears on the board that strict discipline is going to be enforced to prevent patients from going away from the grounds without leave. I don't know who these men are but it is easy to guess they are Australians. I am afraid the doctors are going to give themselves a lot of trouble to hold them down. In fact, they can't hold them back. The Australian is too independent and high-spirited, and anyway should the military folk succeed in breaking that spirit the Australian will no longer be the fearless fighting man that he is now. A man without spirit and plenty of self-reliance and willpower is absolutely useless as a fighting unit in a place like Gallipoli at any rate. What call there has been in past wars for discipline and obedience I don't know, but now soldiers must, in order to be successful, have initiative and resource to be of any use at all as the officers are shot down and the troops scattered. Therefore the Australian initiative is so invaluable and yet these officers would kill it all for a matter of obeying useless and thoughtlessly laid down rules. These men have faced death recklessly and it must be very hard to have to submit quietly to the military rules of a hospital, particularly after being allowed practically a free hand to wander where they wished during their convalescence in Cairo under Australian management. The seclusion and loneliness hereabouts only tend to make them fret. It brings back vivid memories of the agonising death of their many comrades, particularly to those who in the last attack had to walk over the fallen—dead and wounded—that lay in the bottom of the trench, and they go into Alexandria against the will of those in charge.

Heart and soul these men are volunteers and are here to fight, not simply to obey fruitless orders issued only for the sake of enforcing authority, just as a self-opinionated and high-minded referee will spoil a game of footer—

asserting authority instead of justice and fair play. Australians are only
allowed to draw seven shillings a week while in this hospital, which does not
give them much liberty to be wild, so leave could be granted without fear.

September 22: Some of the English men and women say the Australian is
wickedly bad-mannered. Well, I agree that even in our quiet home lives
we are not so absurdly and artificially polite as the better class English. But
consideration must be made of the twelve months of wretched camp life
we have undergone and the five months we have been away out of civilisation and living that awful dugout life at Gallipoli, to make light of the
cruel sights, and the preparedness to be killed at any moment of the day or
night and perhaps lie out unburied to rot like a drought-stricken sheep, or
living in the support trenches where in several places the maggots crawled
away from their human prey and wriggled over the supports, blankets and
climbed over the sleeping form, over their bare legs and into the face. Can a
person preserve his manners with the terrible cries of a comrade in death's
grip ringing in his ears, even though it did occur some weeks ago? Oh, if
people could only understand the misery and the hell tortures of a soldier's
life in Gallipoli week after week for months on end, they would overlook a
few mannerisms and the failure of a man to say 'thank you' whenever it is
theoretically correct for him to do so.

September 23: I meet the doctor each morning with the look of an imposter
and can hardly speak to him. Yet I can't say that I actually want to leave here
now. It's perhaps not playing the game and all the rest of it but when such
terrible muddling goes on day after day to the extent of wasting so many lives
as happens at Gallipoli, I feel a kind of contentment in staying here. Man's
life is no more than the life of a louse in value.

I read that the Australians charged and took Hill 72 and held to it while
the English attack was repulsed with great loss at 3.30pm. At 5pm a fresh
attack was made and by dusk Hill 60 was taken and the troops commenced
arranging the captured trenches, when it was discovered that the Turks held
a knoll of ground from which it was possible to enfilade the trenches at
daylight. It was accordingly decided to leave the trenches at once, which they
did and so daylight found the Englishmen in exactly the same position as

they were the previous day only with some 2 to 5 thousand men less and the ambulance men working for dear life.

Meanwhile, the whole of the Turkish guns would be concentrated upon the Australian and New Zealanders' position. We Australians have found to our cost that it is impossible to retire from a position once taken and our men have gone as far as to refuse to obey orders when a retreat has been ordered because they know full well that the ground will have to be advanced over again sooner or later, and in face of the experience gained and the slaughter resulting from retiring at Achi Baba by the English troops, the damned fools still leave positions won at so great a cost. If the hill was so difficult to hold, why not send up reinforcements and remove the sources of annoyance, or dig fresh trenches if there were no reinforcements available? The commander should have been openly hanged for wilful murder. A soldier is often shot for less short-sightedness than is at times displayed by commanders and it's a damned shame that they cannot be got at and hanged instead of being 'honourably invalided home'—more British pigheadedness and hypocrisy to mislead the public and preserve the reputation of a worthless waster of an officer.

October 8: An operation assistant at Gezira Hospital told me that they had taken out a total of eight eyes that very morning from seven different men. One case was where a man was shot through the temple and had the optic nerve severed. The wound healed quickly and now there is nothing wrong with the fellow who is a fine strapping man but the awful part is that he cannot see. It is these things that scare a man from returning to Gallipoli. The dead and maimed while in action I take but little notice of and seldom fret about, but here in civilisation once again my memories fairly haunt me.

A good deal of jesting and joking goes on between the first arrivals (1st, 2nd, 3rd and 4th Brigades) and the newly arrived (5th and 6th Brigades). This is usually done in the best of spirits but there is an occasional row nevertheless. The old hands say the new ones were driven to enlist for shame sake. The new ones accuse the old ones of coming for a holiday, not knowing what was in store for them; also that they are an ill-behaved lot and poxed. The new brigades wear their shoulder colours in diamond shape so that there is no difficulty in identifying them. Now the old hands—and I tell you a few weeks on the Peninsula make an old soldier of any young man—usually refer, with a certain amount of scorn in their words, to them as the 'dinkums'.

On parade yesterday there was a brilliant incident in connection with the casualness of the men from the Dardanelles. The Sergeant whilst calling the roll called a lad's name who was in the adjoining section so he came slouching over to the Sergeant, saying: 'Strike me dead, I didn't know I was in your — lines.'

'Your name is here,' was the abrupt reply of the sergeant.

'Well,' said the rough 'un, 'I expect I'd better — fall in here eh?'

None of the returned men will salute officers about the camp or the lines, although the Tommies make a habit of it. Our men have seen so much and worked so hard at Gallipoli that they care nothing for military law or anybody at all. Many of them are partly dismantled and would take many months to get back to their normal state again. It is pathetic to hear and see them carrying on.

October 14: After early parade I altered the date on a pass, making 11 into 14, and with another chap (passless) we wandered along the beach towards Alexandria, playing here and there with the children at the bathing beaches that run all the way along for miles and are splendidly fitted up with little box-like houses in which to change and dress. The seashore is fine for children, as the sand is firm and the reefs outside break up the waves so that shallow water and calm makes it pleasant and perfectly safe for the youngsters.

The usual officious Tommy MP policeman was bumped into but got through with ease. These English policemen are detested all round by we Australians as they attempt to carry on their duties to the letter and therefore get mixed up in a whole lot of trouble. The Australian policemen always give and take a yard or two and as long as a fellow is reasonable he can get by them. For instance, I have often shown them a blank piece of paper for a pass and they don't say a word. Show them something in case an officer may be out and it's all right but don't give them cheek or be offensive.

The girls here bathe in a similar way to our Manly girls but all wear the skirt costume. We passed several who were not at all embarrassed but there was another damsel who rushed into the dressing house and closed the door in great haste.

October 19: It is one year ago today (365 days) since I sailed down Sydney Harbour in the drizzle of early morning, with my eyes fixed on beautiful Sydney and wondering if I would ever again race across the bay in the Manly boat. The two prominent pine trees on Sydney Road towards the Spit marked a spot nearby where lived the girl who entangled me in her coils—and today that is forgotten by her. She could not go the distance, she was no stayer, and is now the promised wife of another man and good luck to them. May she make him happy and be happy in so doing. A whole year under active service conditions is a long spell, and to go through the horrors of Gallipoli Peninsula is more adventure and novelty than I again want to see but alas, I suppose I will be there again not before long. I hope and pray that it will be Greece.

Yesterday afternoon I pinched out of camp and went out to Montazah, where I met by appointment Miss Bannister and spent a very pleasant hour in her company. The companionship of a woman is a wonderful tonic to a man who has had such twelve months as I have been through. The trouble is that my money will not permit me to entertain this bright little woman as I would like to.

October 22: On the oiling and greasing of the bikes again today, but we got away and back to camp by 2pm where I draw 2 pounds 1/2 which I am not really entitled to as we are only allowed 1 pound and 7 a week, but knowing the pay corporal means everything. Some of our soldiers have gone as far as to give ten shillings to the pay clerk to put their names through for five pounds, and one pound is given for ten pounds, and so the corruptness of the Army is again manifest. The whole system is rotten.

October 24: On the early morning parade a whole batch of fellows were warned to be ready at 7.30am on the following day to proceed 'overseas'. I was called amongst the party and felt almost glad to have another run across to the front, be it either Greece or Gallipoli.

October 25: I got up before daylight to pack up and go on early parade. I got this nicely done by the 'fall in' at 7.30 and we were soon making for the wharf in tram cars, a party of some 140 strong. After some little delay we were lined up and checked like cattle. Then the lieutenant (a splendid young fellow) announced that ten men would have to remain behind and called for anyone wishing to do so. Nobody would volunteer to stand down, so they decided to count out every fifth man in the line and without being pleased or otherwise I was the first five. So here I am tonight in Alexandria for an unknown length of time while the other fellows are dodging submarines at sea.

November 3: Went aboard the *Transylvania* a 16,000 tonner. There are aboard all told 1700 men including 115 Australians and 65 New Zealanders. Our berthing accommodation is right down at the bottom of the ship and in consequence is stuffy and smelly.

November 8: At 1pm we 'A' class men transhipped into a smaller craft from the *Transylvania* while the 'B' class men went ashore. We hung around the harbour and at 4pm steamed outside and headed full steam for the east—Anzac Cove—where we arrived at 10pm without any adventure to recall other than an interesting chat with a Victorian artilleryman and a few biscuits washed down with a small but good bottle of beer.

There were some 115 Australians aboard and sad though it is to relate there were several cases of venereal disease broke out, and I believe there are hundreds of cases of the worst possible kind in the Cairo Isolation area. There is something wrong with the upbringing of our youth when they are not taught to take care of themselves against so dread a disease. It is sheer ignorance that causes the trouble in most cases.

Chapter 8

EVACUATION, 1915

———›»•«‹———

November 9: We came ashore at Anzac at 2am and camped in an infernally cold dugout until 7am, when I set off in search of my unit and discovered they were still at Lemnos Island. I then gave myself up to the DADMS [Deputy Assistant Director Medical Services] and he signed me up temporarily with 2nd Light Horse Field Ambulance. After dinner I was taken up to a dressing station and put in charge of it. There are two stretcher bearers with me. They are changed every 24 hours but I am expected to remain here all the time. To my surprise there is no decent canteen here as yet and such essentials as chocolate, milk, blankets etc are very difficult to procure. This is a miserable matter. Give the fellows something like they are used to in camp at least and they will work with a better heart and die happier.

November 15: In reading from papers the diaries of other men it makes me rather ashamed of my own book and the value of my own work. It is strange too that although I write a number of long letters which the press are glad to publish, still I never have any remarks, advice or criticism mentioned in my letters from friends. I sometimes think I am doing wonders considering my lack of schooling etc, and I know full well there is much room for improvement. That is why I feel annoyed at times to think my friends do not attempt to assist me, or at least encourage me.

November 18: Beachy Bill has had a regular gala day today. He started early and has racked the beach from end to end. The beach is strewn with all kinds of craft and debris from yesterday's storm.

November 19: There is a fatigue party going around clearing up the graves and putting numbered crosses thereon. So now we have little cemeteries all over the place and the fellows returning from their resting camp on Lemnos got a fair amount of interest in reading the names on the crosses and discussing the individual. I have been writing in the dressing station until now and find it very comfortable. The two Victorian fellows I have with me have not sufficient intelligence to read or write so they sit around singing, whistling or walking up and down stamping their feet.

November 23: The excitement is intense as you hear a big bomb coming through the air in your direction. Where is it going to fall? You listen all agape, your heart swelling to breaking pressure. The sound will betray the bomb's height in the air, the sizzling pace of the infernal death-dealing monster, some of which weigh 25 lbs, filled with a terrific charge of explosive and a thousand and more pieces of iron of varying sizes, mostly the disc punching of sheet iron and steel from the engineering workshops. The bomb is whirling itself slowly towards the trench in which you eagerly await all alert and ready to dive into cover of a funk hole. Where, oh where is this one going to pitch and scatter its load of destruction? Wait and wait, it is still approaching. Soldiers' lives seem made up of waiting. Lots of strange things come over the soldier while he is waiting for the bomb that never seems to come, but suddenly he breathes quickly and freely—the bomb with its broom-stick driving attachment has passed overhead into the support trenches. A moment later there is a deafening crash and for another moment you wonder how many, if any, are killed or wounded. Then with a bitter curse you turn to your own duty and concentrate all your forces upon it and wait for another bomb which may come in a minute or half a day. One must collect and subdue his shattered nerves immediately. It would be a slow kind of torture to allow your mind to wander from your own primeval surroundings. In order to stick this nerve-wracking business of dodging bombs a man must live just a breath of air at a time and think also in the same narrow proportions.

November 27: Jim Healy and Bully Ryan came to see me this morning. Like most of the men here they are fed up with the wretched confinement and monotony of the place. I went into the artillery observation post with Lieut. Fred Arons. It was very interesting to see all the Gaba Tepe country through a decent glass and, by jove, it's very difficult country for the attacking party. I used to think South Africa was the ideal country for a defending army but here with so many abrupt hills and ranges of valleys and hollows, nothing but Howitzer guns are of any use. The lines and lines of false ridges do not give the artillery fellows a chance to locate the rival guns. Beachy Bill is still going strong with some four to eight guns and we can't get at them.

November 28: I got into bed composed of a water sheet and a double blanket on the stretcher and two blankets, a water sheet and two overcoats as well as my tunic and pants between the blankets. I was wrapped in two pairs of socks, two underpants, a singlet, two flannel shirts and my big blue sweater with the comforter over my head. I slept but still I had to put my head under the blankets too.

On waking up this morning I peered out and saw the whole of the hill-sides were covered with snow. I woke the 'Brunswick lambs' who had never seen snow before and they were greatly elated. The roadside and hills were completely covered by three inches of snow and you can well imagine how the water-carriers, dismal and cold, swore some as they slithered along up and down the greasy track with a frozen grip on the water-cans. None of our men as yet have their winter clothing and naturally there were complaints to be heard all along the line from the fatigue parties. One chap cleverly remarked: 'Australia soon finish now, I think.'

Around Pope's, Quinn's and Courtney's the slush is fairly bad but yet the terraced quarters on the hillside are waterproof and very comfortable.

November 29: When the stretcher stopped at the door this morning I saw a form so covered with dirt and dust that I could not recognise him. I made his head comfortable and he was staring at me the whole time. His face was a bad colour and as his nostrils were choked with dirt he was gasping for breath. He saw I did not know him and he said, after several attempts, 'It's Griff, Richy. Don't you know me, Griff? And they've got me damned badly. I'm done Richy. I'm done this time.'

I got such a shock. Words failed me. I could only say: 'Stick it Griff my boy. You'll be alright again. Good luck!!' and poor Griffiths passed on. I have been sorry ever since that I did not talk further with him all day long. He may have had a message of some kind for his wife or parents, or his brother Jack is due here.

Strange, last night when he looked out of the station and saw the hospital ship all aglow with green lights he remarked how glorious it would be sailing back to Egypt again out of this cold and distress. Poor Griff, he's gone now ...

All our water was frozen this morning—in fact all day long. They could not get any water out of the tanks until they lit fires under the pipes and taps so that the poor trench men got nothing to drink. They have been on half, or less, rations ever since I have been here—four weeks now.

December 2: I think it must be this hard food and exposure, without any training, that is breaking up our newly arrived brigades and reinforcements. The old hands of the 1st Division just scoff at these later divisions who are going out sick in droves. I fancy it was the severe training on low food and no food at all that the 1st Division got at Mena Camp and aboard ship coming from Australia that built them up to a physical state of hardiness sufficiently strong enough to withstand the ordeals of warfare. We used to complain and the Australian papers fight against this hard and harsh method of training, often referring to the number of deaths that occurred in Egypt, but had these same men been brought across here after a good and easy time they would have died or made a terrible hole in our lines by their weakness and physical unfitness. However, glory be to the hard, rough nature of the 1st Division's training, they landed on Gallipoli's heights fit to a man. There were no sick parades in those early days but now there are ten sick to every one who is wounded, so that the hospital accommodation is taxed to its uttermost. But again, if these new men only had something like their ordinary diets perhaps there would be very few cases of sickness, loss of spirit and self-inflicted injuries, accidental or otherwise. Why shouldn't the men get better food? We know that the quartermaster robbed us at Mena, but here it's mighty different.

December 4: General Bridges in his message before leaving to join the Army Staff thanks all and sundry for their good work, concluding by telling all to be patient and stick tight as the war is a long, long way from its end. There is a wag of a fellow in here at the dressing station talking in an illiterate strain with a good deal of humour. When asked what he would do if he were in Melbourne this night (Saturday), he answered: 'Get a decent feed, my oath, and eat a double quality tea.' One of the Brunswick fellows added: 'And take on a woman after.' 'Well no,' said the wag. 'I might see about that tomorrow night.' This is just typical of the average conversation that goes on at Anzac. The minds of half the fellows never soar any higher.

December 5: I hear splendid accounts of Arthur Buckley, the Manly footballer. He is a great soldier and has done good work on the left. He is at present mending sandbags in the front line of trenches—night work of course and extremely dangerous but Bucks doesn't care a jot and often stands up on the parapet having an argument with his mate. This sandbag job is considered the most dangerous on the Peninsula.

In the afternoon I got down and photographed a 'two-up' school who were talking big money—'A quid I head 'em' or 'Ten bob I head 'em' being the usual cry. I am not sure whether gambling is permitted or not but it goes on just the same and it must draw the fellows' mind right away from the war and it therefore does them a huge amount of good.

December 6: I went round to Ordnance Stores and exchanged a pair of boots. They are all Tommies in charge and miserably strict all round. I am of the opinion the Englishmen make better guardsmen, policeman and storemen, the Australian being so irresponsible and careless—so generous in fact that they give away too much of the goods they are supposed to be guarding. I have heard the police and guards over the potatoes and foodstuffs say to the fellows filling their shirts: 'For Christ's sake give us a chance to get out of your bloody way.' As guards over prisoners they are just the same careless men. At Mustapha the guards bought beer out of their own pockets for the prisoners and they got a bit 'tipsy', kicking up a devil of a noise.

It was a magnificent day. At 11am a wounded man was brought around from the 1st Battalion. Rowley was his name. He was out in front laying down barbed wire when a bullet passed through his body. The night was dark and the road rough, so naturally the stretchers bounced a little. God knows we were steady and careful enough but with each movement he groaned. He asked 'Whereabouts are we now?' I told him we were passing the water tanks in the gully and that we would not be long in getting him to the ship. 'Oh I'm not complaining for myself. It's you fellows I'm thinking of.' Later he asked: 'Will they put me on board tonight? My feet are terrible.' He died 30 minutes later. The bullet had cut into his spine.

December 8: The only case we have had today was a Light Horse man who accidentally shot himself in the foot, making a bad wound. He said he was ready to mount guard and stood his rifle up by the dug-out when he, by some means or other, knocked it down and it went off. These 'accidental injuries' are treated with the greatest suspicion. Self-inflicted wounds in the hands and feet have been common amongst the new brigades and all reinforcements. Some are deliberately self-inflicted, others are downright carelessness due no doubt to not having had sufficient training and being taught how to keep the safety catch down and cartridges out of the barrel. Several men have been shot dead this way and I think it's up to the officers to fine each man with a cartridge in and the safety catch up very heavily. It's the devil to think that the old soldiers have to risk their lives both from inside and outside of the trenches.

December 10: Yesterday afternoon I went over to Pope's Post and found Lieut Heath, Captain Walker and my much respected friend, Capt SA Middleton. Like Lieut Dos Wallach, they all looked worn out and badly in need of a rest.[1]

---

1   Syd Middleton was one of Australian Rugby's most notable players. He was a teammate of Richards's in the first Wallabies tour, in 1908, earning notoriety when he was sent off in the match against Oxford University for punching an opponent during a lineout. He captained Australia in 1910 against New Zealand, and after the war returned to rowing. He was a member of the Australian eight which won the Henley Regatta in 1920.

Clarence 'Dos' Wallach, a notable Rugby forward, played five Tests for Australia in 1913–14, and in 1916 was awarded the Military Cross for gallantry at Pozières. In 1918, he suffered severe wounds to his legs at Hangard Wood, France. He was evacuated and died of his wounds in hospital. The Wallach family suffered badly during World War I. Dos had four brothers who also served. Neville was killed in action in May 1918, Henry suffered shell shock, Arthur was wounded, and Rupert was captured at Bullecourt in May 1917.

SAM sums up this war in very few words that get well to the bottom of the foolish miserable bother. I spent a very pleasant two hours with them and battled off quite refreshed as a chat with 'Middy' does a man a world of good at any time.

I read in our local bulletins that the Turks had suffered terribly from the cold during the recent storm, some of them being drowned and many washed out of their trenches. It is awful damned nonsense for our people to tell us that Turks were drowned because it hardly rained at all. The rain we got dried up the next day. No doubt the Turks suffered from the cold, being, like ourselves, unprepared for it but it's terrible to think that they would dare tell us that any of them were washed up and drowned. This morning we took a fellow down with bad feet. They had been frozen and this is eleven days since the snow fell. Beachy Bill is still a nasty customer on the beach but he is not firing quite as regularly as a week ago.

December 11–12: At 2pm yesterday some 3rd Field Ambulance fellows came along and relieved the five of us. We got away loaded up like mules back to the camp, where nobody had the slightest idea where we were bound for. The feeling was in favour of a new landing, as we had been included in a complete party of about 2000 men comprising Infantry, Light Horse, Engineers, ASC, Artillery with eight guns and an Army Medical Corps. As far as appearances go we were designed as a regular fighting unit that might have been under orders to go into action anywhere. But where on this weird burdened earth could we be going? Up into Greece was impossible from the size of our party. To make another landing on the Peninsula was unreasonable, as we have landings for sale now, more than are ever likely to be of any use to us. Someone said that the natives north of Egypt were troublesome (in Tripoli). Well, if this were so it would be a matter for the Italians, not us. Then there was Mesopotamia. This I was more inclined to follow but then why such a small body unless for garrison work in a small district? Anyway, when we got aboard ship last night and I saw the scraggy appearances of the troops I was quite satisfied that Lemnos was to be our destination, and within the next few days the evacuation of the whole of the 1st Division, or probably of the Anzac zone entirely, was the most likely thing to be expected.

Entering the splendid harbour is always interesting as there are so many different kinds and shapes of vessels lying about, from cumbersome French warships, the awkward oil boats from America, to the clean, agile ships of the British Navy.

On landing we left our blankets on a wagon and battled on foot around an inlet for three miles until we came to the camp sites of the 1st and 2nd Field Ambulance and a large Howitzer battery party, all of whom were 1st Division men including the whole of the 3rd Brigade. There is a large fleet here and football matches take place every afternoon. It is hard ground but what does that matter to our men now?

It is like a regular homecoming to get amongst one's old mates again. All hands say they are living a miserable kind of uninteresting life. And although they naturally have complaints, they are all looking splendid and are sort of contented to be out of Gallipoli. On arriving here this afternoon I went straight across to the Howitzer Battery and tried to attach myself to them as I understand I am privileged to do so after being three months away from your own unit. But, alas, they are now over strength. Had I known I was free I certainly would have stuck myself on to Major Gus Hughes at Anzac but now I'm done again, I suppose.

December 14: This afternoon a football match between two teams from our Corps took place on the hard flat nearby. I padded myself up a lot as usual, and though we won by 23 to nil I kept well out of the way and finished up unmarked while many of the fellows were badly rashed and bleeding. There are some very decent players in our corps.

December 15: The Australian troops are still pouring in and the idea is that a general evacuation of Anzac is about to commence. If this is so, I reckon there will be a terrible feeling of depression and some hard words from Australia. It is hard to do, but being messed up and insufficiently equipped as the all-too-few troops have been on this Peninsula, nothing else can now be done but leave it, or give us some hundreds of Howitzers and thousands of tons of ammunition. If this latter cannot be done, we will be better at Mudros doing nothing than remaining on the Peninsula mere practice for the Turks to train and feast upon. It's just scandalous the weak manner in which Britain, or rather the Allies, are handling this Balkan problem and the relief of Russia from her miserable plight.

December 18: There was a shock in store for me when on calling for Harry Jose I found he died and was buried weeks ago. He was a splendid fellow. I travelled with him from Capetown to Plymouth years ago. He discovered I was on the Peninsula and wrote to me at Anzac, and when I called today I found he had died a long time ago, presumably a few days after he cheerfully wrote to me. The sudden change of diet plays up with these Englishmen. In this particular case I understand that the small party that came over with Harry had first class food—four courses for lunch and eight courses for dinner, without any work. So when they arrived at Lemnos and went on to bully beef and biscuits with twelve hours' work in open sunshine, they broke up badly and many even died.

The womenfolk here are wonderfully moral and I am told there is not one harlot on the Island. This is astonishing, and I doubt if anywhere in the world the morality of so many people could be equalled, particularly with the inducement that our soldiers offer with their over-supply of cash and a longing for female intercourse.

I have not heard any Australian soldier sing or play any instrument on Anzac and seldom smile even. Now I hope they will cheer up but I fear they cannot with Anzac back again in the hands of the Turks. What an awful bungling mess these short sighted damned fool Englishmen have made of this business. Sing, why I doubt if our good Australian soldiers will ever sing again after this terrible Peninsula setback through no fault of their own.

Our fellows are very anxious about the welfare of the evacuation party that will be last to make good the retreat from Anzac. We commenced the evacuation last Sunday so the final rush should take place tonight or tomorrow night.

December 19: At Church Service, the preacher got up against the 'Australia for Australians' mob by telling them they were awfully swell-headed and thought of only their own achievements, belittling, foolishly, those of the Tommy. I am not in the humour to deal in detail with this remarkable service but that it raised considerable discussion amongst the boys. It will do them quite a lot of good as we are hardly broad-minded and fair enough to our opponents or even our friends.

This afternoon there was a splendid game of footer between the Light Horse and the No 3 Stationary Hospital. The game was hardly a scientific or classical one. This however was easily overcome by the energy and vigour of the players. The Light Horse won by a try to nothing after an even game. Capt Matthews played very well but had no support. Jimmy Clarken came down to the tent and I enjoyed an hour with him.[2]

December 21: The last of the Anzac evacuation parties arrived here today. There was not the slightest hitch. It was a comprehensive and elaborate scheme and one that might easily have gone wrong, but, no, it went through without a flaw—no single mistake occurring and not a man is missing. Beachy Bill's shrapnel fire was taken every precaution with and a number of AMC men were told to remain behind and attend to the wounded should any trouble arise. Bandages as well as water and food were left in all the dressing stations. Mines made of bombs and all kinds of materials were laid both in the trench communication way and down along the valley paths and hill tracks. To make sure no one could miss the track or go astray, lights were placed in biscuit tins with letters perforated thereon so that men would find an officer there to direct them. The paths were also white-washed so they could be easily followed in any rush or hurry that may have taken place. Even the boots of every man were muffled by pieces of blanket tied around them and so successfully was the tread silenced that some 600 could walk within 30 yards of a person on the hard path without being heard. If there had been a spy in our camp, for instance, the Turks could have made matters particularly warm, knowing the moment the last men would leave the trench . . . The trench lines were drawn from at 6 o'clock in small batches until about 12 o'clock when only a few men were left in the trenches to run from one loophole to another and fire as many shots as possible while the rest of the men got well down the track.

The fellows tell me the last few hours and especially the last few minutes seemed like so many days to them waiting and waiting, not knowing the minute John Turk would discover our weakness and come through. Even

2   Jimmy Clarken, who was with the 3rd General Hospital and 1st Australian Division Supply Column, played four Tests for Australia.

Tom Richards, the proud Australian Test rugby representative.

Tom Richards (top row, third from left) on the boat from South Africa to England in pursuit of the first Springbok team in 1906.

The 1908 Wallaby team that played against Wales in the first Test of the tour. Tom is fifth from the left in the back row.

Tom's Olympic gold medal certificate.

During the first Wallaby tour of 1908

Tom Richards (fourth from left, third row) with the British Lions team in South Africa.

Tom on first arriving in Egypt, 1914.

In front of the Sphinx before heading to Gallipoli.

Tom's photograph of Australian soldiers on the beach at Anzac Cove, 25 April 1915.

The Gallipoli Landing 25 April 1915

1st Field Ambulance going ashore at Gallipoli landing at 6.45 am 25th April 1915   Photo taken by T.J. Richards

Tom's photograph, taken from the beach at Gallipoli, shows the 1st Field Ambulance going ashore at 6.45 am on 25 April 1915.

The serious military man.

Tom flirting with a nurse after being wounded and sent to hospital behind the lines.

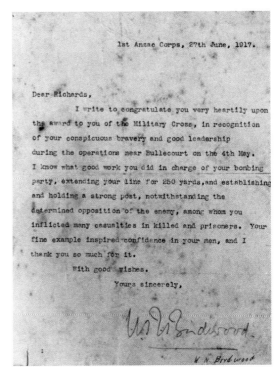

1st Anzac Corps, 27th June, 1917.

Dear Richards,

    I write to congratulate you very heartily upon the award to you of the Military Cross, in recognition of your conspicuous bravery and good leadership during the operations near Bullecourt on the 4th May. I know what good work you did in charge of your bombing party, extending your line for 250 yards, and establishing and holding a strong post, notwithstanding the determined opposition of the enemy, among whom you inflicted many casualties in killed and prisoners. Your fine example inspired confidence in your men, and I thank you so much for it.

    With good wishes.

        Yours sincerely,

W N Birdwood

The official letter from the commander of the Australian forces, Field Marshall William Birdwood, telling Tom he had won the Military Cross.

A studio portrait shortly after winning the Military Cross.

A proud member of the Australian and New Zealand Army Corps.

About to go underground on the
Western Front.

The last photograph of Tom Richards, nursing
his nephew John, in the 1930s.

when the last party was leaving they were anxious as the Turk might miss them at any moment.

It was a splendidly planned move and wonderfully well carried out. If we (or those English devils of Generals) could only plan and carry out an attack as thoroughly as this evacuation, Turkey would have long since been at our mercy. Instead of that, each succeeding month of this war has brought defeat and devastation with it to the Allies' cause, and at the moment matters look so blue that we don't know which way to turn to now.

In the guard tent today we have a prisoner under close observation. He has complained of dysentery and we have to see how many times he uses the pan and call the officer to inspect same. This man Biggs is a liar and not sick at all. The charge against him is refusing to obey General Forsyth when asked to hand over the gambling machine he was playing with. He was one of the eight or ten lowdown rotters we have in the Corps, most of whom seem to obtain more privileges than the decent fellows and we have many of these.

December 23: Today our Corps have received orders to be ready to move off in a few hours, so our 60 patients have gone and the big tents are packed up. But to where other than the Suez Canal or the Persian Gulf, I can't think, but firstly our 1st Division must be organised and brought up to something like proper strength.

Plum puddings and gift billy cans were issued today and the fellows had a great blow out. It is strange that there were only billies enough for one between two men. I tossed and lost my interest in one. I got a set of pyjamas and any number of socks now. It seems a shame to see so many pairs of lovely home-made socks lying about. I could have had dozens of them. I feel sorry we are going away so soon as there are villages and a hot spring bath nearby that I wanted to visit.

December 25: Some of our fellows have been out scouting last night and again this morning for something to drink. But alas it's a dry country and we have not had anything at all to drink for Xmas. I don't want to get drunk but I think a good bottle of wine would brighten up matters considerably. Dinner today was much the same as usual, though we did have a small Xmas cake after a meal of roast meat and potatoes with onions followed up by a 2 lb 3 oz plum pudding and tinned fruit. There are four of us eating together—Reynolds, Elliott and Yeomans, two of whom were orderlies in the hospital and they brought sago, corn flour, but today there was nothing as the hospital had been cleared out. At tea time we had some chocolate with bread, cheese, jam, so you can see we have not been living very high over Xmas.

December 26: Coming home we watched some Indians cooking flat, pancake-like bread. I had some with a curried dish. They made us very welcome after satisfying themselves we were Australians. They just love our men and in return our men love them, they are so clean and trustworthy. For instance, at the 'two-up' school there are many about but gambling is disallowed, a rolling penny hit the foot of an Indian and a fellow turned and swore savagely at him for not getting out of the way. A Sergeant standing nearby jumped in and threatened to punch this soldier for treating the Indian harshly. He said, and I agree with him, that 'these men were the only friends we had at Anzac and we should be grateful to them all our lives. I don't care who you are or what battalion you belong to—you're a — rotter. We would have gone thirsty many a time without these hardworking and fearless fellows and I'm not going to allow you or any man three times as good as you to treat them so while I've got a pair of hands. You're a damned reinforcement or a waster or you would know of the way they worked those mountain guns and saved our own positions time and again with their shrapnel.' The soldier apologised.

December 27: At night I went with others to the No 3 General Hospital to see some of our Corps. The Sister therein is an angel and I was just as surprised as I was delighted to get an opening and 'invite myself' to walk out with her after duty—8.30pm. It was indeed a pleasant walk though dark. I met her again tonight at 7pm. Our Sisters are lonely.

December 29: At 5.20am I heard a rattle at our tucker box and bounded out in my bare feet to see two Greeks getting away with a bag each full of our provisions. I hit one on the jaw and followed up the other with one on the short ribs. Dropped them both but allowed them to escape without taking their bags and they seemed satisfied to get away with their lives. These Greeks in large numbers, from small boys and girls to old men but mostly women, come around the camps in early morning and beg or steal whenever and whatever they can.

Our men have stolen hundreds of fowls from the villages and the Greeks are now stealing in return. Five shillings is the price of a fowl and as our men think it is too much they steal them.

December 31: The last day of the old and troublesome year. It sets one thinking just what the incoming year is going to bring but though I face it with the greatest calm and unconcern, it looks very bad for the new year. Last New Year's Day from the sands of the Egyptian Desert held out stronger and clearer views of peace than does the present moment. The enemy has during the year strengthened their position and gained ground in a startling manner and our hope of winning the war on the strength of our arms seems somewhat out of reason entirely unless we can get better artillery equipment very soon.

I accepted an invitation to spend tonight at the Sisters' Mess where a concert and supper is being arranged. The concert did not please me over much and Maude Darling Soden and I went for a little walk and it was quite nice. She was not in the best of health although her spirit was splendid. The girl is probably 35 years of age and in a quiet way bemoans the fact that she is on the 'shelf'. I fancy she had led a delightfully calm and chaste life as her ideas of what is right and what is wrong strike me as charming. I left her about 10.45pm and caught a Greek boat back to 'Sarpi' where all was in peace and quietness until midnight when all the ship's whistles and bells went off like mad for 15 minutes. None of our tent got out of bed or cheered. They were just miserably sober. Last night there was some wine and gin about but tonight was a dead blank and the fellows so very sorrowful.

Chapter 9

RETURN TO EGYPT, 1916

January 2: Very early this morning orders came through that we were to move off at 10am for embarkation.

January 3: We have been aboard the *Empress of Britain* all day in fitful and uncertain weather. There must be some 4500 men aboard and really everything is remarkably quiet considering. I looked back over Mudros many times but I can recall all too vividly the grand fellows who lay aboard here last April and are, alas, no more. We have left their graves at Anzac but I cannot grieve at leaving Mudros. No, I am glad.

January 5: We have had a quiet and calm day. General Forsyth is running the ship and has issued yards of perplexing contradictory orders. Nobody can understand them at all. One thing is clear: 'No smoking after 5pm and 7am'. The striking of matches is an absolute crime as there must be darkness to avoid the submarines. The latrines are choked with smoke tonight as the fellows will smoke somewhere or other.

January 7: We left the *Empress of Britain* at 7pm last night and were on the train speeding along the rich Delta until arriving at Tel-el-Kebir about 2am. By 4pm the camp was in decent order, some ten large tents and seven small bell tents having gone up, which meant the driving in of some 2000 hard pegs into hard stony ground.

January 9: The evacuation of Anzac has not as yet been published in Egypt. This seems folly and may tend to break the faith (that is if any faith remains) in Britain's most solid adherent as they are sure to hear it now that our thousands of men are scattered around Egypt.

January 21: The most serious matter at the moment is the cutting out of our allowance of 8d per man for rations. There are 14 in the mess and we should have had 48 pasties under the old rule but all we got today extra was three tins of jam amongst 13 men. At the canteen nearby we are openly robbed. This unbusinesslike, insensible way of running things is capable of a military camp only. It's an awful mess.

January 25: Our rations are at present scandalous. Short issues of bread, three tins of jam and hard, dirty figs are all we have received outside of beef for breakfast, with meat and vegetables for dinner and tea three times a day. It seems that the authorities want the men to spend up all of their money so as to keep them from breaking camp or going on passes to Cairo and getting drunk and playing up generally. This matter is the devil of a proposition. The men are entitled to a bit of a blowout but then there is the effect that such behaviour has on unthinking Egyptians. It's a problem that has me beaten. The men want relaxation but it is not in the interests of the Empire to allow them to have it and so only two per cent of troops are allowed on leave at one time and then only for 12 hours now.

January 26: Rumours are afloat that Anthony Hordern is going to pay the expenses of the First Division's fare back to Australia.[1] This I cannot possibly believe at all and have settled myself down here for an indefinite period. Most particularly do I say indefinitely after reading General Hamilton's reports on the Suvla landing each morning in the 'Egyptian Mail'. Mistakes, absolutely inexcusable, took place—all around the British Officers were incapable of

---

1   Anthony Hordern and Sons was one of Australia's largest retailers. It owned the largest department store in Sydney.

handling the business and I fear the troops (English) were unfit to go ahead at all, no physique, nothing but dismal failure.

January 27: The fact that yesterday was Australia's great national holiday made no difference at Tel-el-Kebir Camp—work went on just the same, and those who expected an extra issue of rations were badly disappointed as the grub was practically nil. But money seems to be plentiful as the beer supply at six piaster (1/3) a bottle still goes strong and our tent have felt the worry and annoyance of it these three nights with childish, noisy and damn fool drunks. A good drunk I can always tolerate and sometimes entertain, but a fool drunk is always an abhorrence.

February 3: I had a whisky and milk with Biggs and Denton—they are two of our outlaws. Biggs was sentenced to 90 days' confinement for gambling and disobeying General Forsyth but he escaped from our guard tent and 'jumped the rattler' into Cairo. Denton, Armfield and Croker broke away from camp and have been enjoying themselves in Cairo for the past ten days. Of course they will be confined for some time when they are caught or return when their money is spent. This penalty, however, they are prepared to pay—in fact they weighed the proposition well before leaving camp and concluded it was worthwhile.

February 7: I have been told on the quiet today I have been made a full Corporal. This news does not excite me a little bit, in fact it only bothers me and brings home soundly the fact I should be in the firing line fighting. Anyway it increases my pay 4 shillings per day and that's something I suppose.

February 14: Last night an order came through that we had to be at the railway station by 8am, so all hands were at once busy pulling down tents and packing up generally. It was a busy night for all of us, the lucky few getting three or four hours' sleep.

After unloading from the train we were compelled to wait until 5pm before the pontoon bridge was swung across the Canal for us to pass over to the Asia-Minor side. While waiting on the Canal bank a lot of little vessels passed along, then came a very large ship full of British troops, bound so they stated for Bombay. It was a pretty sight, but rather galling for the Tommies I think because their cheering of the Australians did not raise any demonstration at all from our men. Why, I don't really know, but believe that our men think as little of the English soldiers that they did not consider this boatload worthy of a demonstration of any kind. It seems to show up plainly the Australians' value of an Englishman as a soldier. Had this boatload been Indians and, more particularly, Gurkhas, I feel certain there would have been a whole lot of cheering.

February 17: The 1st Brigade is being cut up and I believe the whole of the 1st Division will be broken up. Naturally this hurts the fellows immensely as they want to stay with the old comrades and in good Australian style the fellows have petitions out for everybody to sign so that the order might be countermanded and they be allowed to remain just where they are. But I can imagine the hearing the petitioner will get by the god who controls our military destiny.

February 23: After tea I went for a walk down to the Canal and saw two vessels steam by going to Port Said. On our side—Asia Minor—were a lot of 2nd Brigade men, while on the other side was a crowd of the 8th Brigade. Our side commenced calling them cold footed b— and telling them across the Canal that they were driven away from Australia by shame. The late arrivals resented this very much and the insults and bad language that passed across the water was terrible. When the feeling is so strong I think the best plan is to break up the old brigades and stop this sickening cry, 'we're old hands and done our bit at Gallipoli'. The only excuse I have for the old hands is that they are all dopey and weak minded owing to the effects of Anzac life.

February 26: It is Saturday and my thoughts run back to the Australian Saturday night when the streets are crowded with men and women strolling aimlessly about. It is a week's form of recreation to many. Even in Cloncurry and Mount Elliott the practice is well carried out, and the men all get well boozed before the pubs close. They never close at Cloncurry or Mount Elliott. But they are not like the American saloons—these have no locks or chains on and cannot close. It is such towns as Cloncurry that breeds a remarkable type of man. A man incomparable with any other on account of the strange environment.

February 27: Perhaps I should have gone to Church if only in keeping with father's views on the subject. By not going, I missed a good address to the men by General Birdwood, in which he stated it was the opinion of those in high circles at home that the Australians, although glorious fighting men, were too ragged and undisciplined to be taken to France. Our Colonel in addressing the NCOs of this unit on the necessity for tightening up discipline said that the Home authorities considered the Australian men were too fond of beer and women to be allowed near the big centres of the French trench lines. This was all that prevented us from going there at once. So at present the training of the troops is more of a ceremonial nature, such as saluting. Great stress is laid on saluting and it seems that it is going to be hammered into the men this time. I fancy the Home authorities have hit it pretty right too when they say the Australian is hard to control and that he is likely to be a danger in France. It is this same high-spirited, don't care a damn tempera-ment that makes them such glorious fighters and naturally if they lose the former rashness, they will also lose the latter virtue. The Australian is a queer bird right enough.

March 10: We must be nearing the date of our departure from the Suez Canal zone, but where we are going to is yet shrouded in mystery. Of course it has been long hinted at that we go to France, but there is nothing definite about this even now.

March 12: Tonight with Tom Yeomans, I went over to the 1st Brigade lines beyond which a Monte Carlo was going strong. Probably there were 14 crown and anchor boards in full swing, and two 'two up' schools also. We hardly had time to look around thoroughly when Tommy saw a number of mounted men draw up some 150 yards away. There was a hurried rush with Tom and I going across the sand for dear life over to the rows of tents 200 yards away. Finding all was safe we came back to the scene of destruction and fellows were scratching in the sand for lost money. The names of twenty men were taken and by this time a fair crowd had collected around again and very nasty names were called out to the policemen. So a charge was made to disperse the mob while a couple of fellows were taken away to the guard tent—one refused to go without being carried, and in screwing his ankle to make him walk it was broken. A couple of men were chased in and around the tents, and bottles were thrown a few minutes later. In 20 minutes all was peace and quietness again. This is the second raid during the past week. It may have an effect of steadying the gamblers but will not stop them, as the men have a gambling instinct or they never would make such fine soldiers.

March 15: General Chauvel, in leaving his command of the 1st Division, met the whole division this morning to speak to them. All of the three brigades squared up splendidly and in rode the General. He got under way at once, and dealt with the much worn necessity for better discipline. Saluting was so strongly enforced in the European theatres of war that by neglecting it we would appear a rabble and so shoddy a soldier that very little decent work or any responsible position would be assigned to Australians.

An English general seeing the troops wandering so haplessly and undisciplined about Alexandria and Cairo reported to the English authorities that the Australians were unfit to go to France and mix with the villagers and soldiers there. Generals Birdwood, Chauvel and others worked hard to overcome this idea. And now, said General Chauvel, that you have got your chance of testing your mettle beside the continental troops, it is up to you to stand by us, and play the game.

The most disgraceful thing that has come under notice, continued he, is the digging up and the tampering with dead Turks that lie buried over there on the desert by the Canal side. 'It is a curse and a crime that Australia will never live down, and to try and divest the blame from the whole Division and the blot from Australia, the men who knew the guilty persons should come forward and expose them. We wrote to Turkey asking that the graves on Gallipoli Peninsula be respected and in no way molested. They, the Turks, gave us that assurance. And now we find you men digging up Turkish graves. How can you expect the Turks to be honest with you and look after the graves of your brothers and comrades?'

I think General Chauvel must take a whole lot of blame for not burying these bodies months ago. I have been here eight weeks and bodies lay about up to a few days ago when they were buried. The rumoured finds that were being made on the corpses no doubt encouraged the men to interfere with the half buried Turks. The General, however, should have seen that these men were properly buried.

March 19: I have a bit of a stomach ache today, the result of eating all sorts of rubbish in Alexandria. But as the Prince of Wales came around our camp with a whole crowd of 'big guns' I forgot my trouble and bustled about getting photographs. The Prince seemed very young, not more than 17 years, with a soft rose and white colour and sat on his horse very well indeed. The men were surprised to see the Prince—they thought it was General Birdwood only, so they ran around to get another look at him and cheered lustily all the time. There was no ceremony at all and the visit was all over in 25 minutes.

I feel a little envious today. The name of HW Stroud appears amongst the Honours and as I was there on the 28th June with him and Harry Bladin, and was the only one to be recommended by the Staff Captain Pollock, I know that this honour should have been mine. Stroud had his leg broken by shrapnel and I suppose sentimental reasons won the honour for him. Our — officers must have pushed his name, but the honours are mine.

March 21: For days past the infantry have had kit inspections and their personal belongings reduced to almost nothing. These poor fellows are the most bullied and worst treated section in the army. In ration matters, they always fare badly. At Anzac for instance, it was shameful to notice how the food stuff diminished before reaching the trenches. 'Every man for himself, and the devil takes the hindermost' is the motto of the Army.

At 4pm the 1st, 2nd and 3rd Battalions marched out of camp with full marching order and bands playing. Their 1st Brigade is 80 per cent new men, men mostly who were never at Anzac. Yet they looked very well indeed, a number of short men spoilt the uniformity of the ranks, but they will do well as a fighting force, even now. I watched them go by in the column and although I liked their appearance, the men of the original 1st Brigade as at Mena Camp 12 months ago were infinitely a better set of men, better physique, hardier and more determined.

March 22: I have read the book 'The Kangaroo Marines' and feel almost annoyed to think that the author did not portray the Australians more distinctly, yet I am sure this book will make reasonable reading for English people and do the Australians a whole lot of good in their eyes. I sat reading on an Arab sailing boat and after a swim returned to camp at dinner time, learning that our unit were to leave for Alexandria in the afternoon. In an open truck we made for Alexandria. Twenty men in a low sided truck does not give one much protection from the wind nor does it give sufficient room for the men to lay down with straight legs.

We went straight aboard the *Simla*, not a particularly inviting looking craft. It was remarkable to see the number of Egyptian hawkers that assailed our train on arrival at the wharf. There must have been 400 of them and they had for sale all manner of goods, even packs of cards and a crown and anchor, as well as eatables of all kinds with dozens of money changers. All this lot shouting their wares made a terrible din.

On board, I with seven others fell in with a storeman and commenced issuing mess tins and pans. These were all in a very dirty condition. We then issued butter, sugar and jam to a line of 115 mess orderlies, a trying sort of business.

At 7 o'clock Bill Drummond told me that Tom Yeomans, who had gone into Alexandria without a pass, had been taken prisoner by a Tommy picket. At once I got a note from the Colonel asking for his relief and as an escort Sgt Clifton and myself went into town to have him released, but those mean and stubborn Englishmen would not hand Tom over as the note should have come from the OC of the ship. Yeomans is a splendid lad, neither smoking, drinking or even swearing and to get caught like this was damn hard luck indeed.

Clifton on failing to get him released, raced back to the ship, three miles away, thinking to get another order written out and go back again. But alas, when we got to the ship's side it was pulling out. Fear ran through both of us and we thought all was lost, the gangway being drawn up full beyond our reach. From on board my attention was drawn to a finder rope hanging over the side. The police advised me not to attempt to climb, but there was nothing else for it, so I set off up the rope, and got aboard. Clifton had some trouble and I had to reach over and help him up. The colonel and a whole lot of others were watching and applauded. I was jolly tired as well as annoyed and disappointed and slept in the only available space, viz. on the greasy floor under a table in the mess room.

March 24: The whistle to get out of bed blew at 6am. Fifteen minutes later our party were busy handing out rations. A hurried breakfast and then to work pulling up stores from the hold. Eighteen bags of flour, 12 cases of milk, two barrels of sugar, two of peas, 12 cases of mineral waters (of which we bagged a couple each) and sundry other stores. This was jolly hard work and knocked us all about considerably. The storeroom is low down and working hard there makes one sweat wholesale in the smelly atmosphere. Rats are very pronounced.

March 25: It is astounding what news one hears from time to time. That Peter Flanagan was in financial trouble and thrown out of the Opera House Hotel was told me for certain. Now I am told Paddy McCue was a whisky and gin traveller in Sydney and has gone to the dogs entirely.[2] I doubt both of these 'facts' and I mention them here to show myself one day just the atmosphere of lies, doubt and ignorance I now live in.

It is surprising the number of men missing from this ship. Also the number of men aboard that previously missed their ship and are now hoping to get through and join up with their own units when we get to France.

March 26: Rats overrun this 24-year-old craft, but other vermin I have not yet seen. A cook sets his traps each day down in our hold and catches as many as 15 in four traps; he saves the tails for which the shipping companies give 1d a tail. I get busy serving out the sugar and jam, sugar 2 ozs a man per day and jam 1½ ozs a man a day. Butter 2 ozs a day. This ration is not enough for the men. 21 tins of jam, 7 lbs must go around and we can't do any better than that. Our party live a little better than the other fellows naturally as everything is at hand for us to get and as there is golden syrup in the store, all goes well as far as I am concerned.

March 27: I have been sleeping on a narrow table in the mess room for two nights, but last night I got past the guard and slept on the lower hatchway, and in consequence of having better air and not so many hundreds of men all around hanging to the roof in hammocks and all over the decks and floors, I was up fresh and went on deck before Reveille, where to my surprise I found we were steaming into the Harbour at Malta. I was delighted at the probability of having a look at a place that is considered so pretty. But alas we only hung off for orders and by 8am were well away to sea again, bound, so

---

2   Flanagan and McCue were teammates of Richards's during the 1908–09 Wallabies tour.

I believe, for Marseilles. I really wish now that I had taken a greater interest in the French language when I had an opportunity some three years ago and then, of course, I would have missed many of the little episodes that I am now so proud of.

March 28: Some say it is Easter Monday today, but nobody is sure of that either. I am more interested in Easter than in other holidays, as my birthday falls about that period. I don't think that I ever did look with any great enthusiasm towards my birthday; it seems altogether too conventional a matter for me to take much notice of it, and to advertise it always sounded arrogant to me. But for some time now Easter seems to remind me so harshly and almost cruelly that I am now another year older and still wandering on and on, no nearer to any settled project, or a future home.

We have been passing along the coast of Sardinia all day and should arrive at Marseilles or Toulon wherever we are going sometime tomorrow.

March 29: I have been following my maps closely to locate the different towns mentioned as being the likely place for which we are now destined. First Rouen, then Amiens and now Abbeville. As these three places are close together right up in the North Western corner of France, I fancy we are in for a very long ride in the train at any rate and that we must pass right through Paris in transit. If they don't jam us into those dark enclosed carriages, the journey will be fine. I am sure if our men could get a real good look at the land en route with its almost continuous villages and closely cultivated fields, it would do them a whole lot of good. It would probably bring home to them more plainly than anything else the fact that people brought up in such a closely settled and thickly gardened country must be a different class of people in their manners and grooves of thought than we Australians are. The Australian is an awfully arrogant individual; this naturally follows with his isolation from the rest of the world. To be considered impudent and small minded by the folk we come into contact with is bad and we Australians should change our ways to meet the ideas of these people we find ourselves thrown amongst. And there is no better way than to first study the country. Our men have heard such stories of Paris high life, commonly called French life, that they must think the Frenchmen live only for wine and sensuality. This may apply to Paris, but it certainly does not apply to France proper.

So our men are labouring, I feel sure, under the impression that morality is unknown in France and that a fellow is at liberty to accost any woman, invite her to wine and then sleep with her. Therefore, I expect quite a lot of trouble to come about with our men over here. Surely our men cannot be altogether to blame, due to want of enlightenment. The weakness of our education systems over and over again. The British are the only people who have any honour, or high morals, so we are always taught, but alas, this theory got a severe shock and our men a sad awakening on their return from England just recently. One man was so impressed by the number of prostitutes he saw, and the amount of venereal disease, that he concluded there was hardly a virtuous woman in Great Britain and that 70 per cent of British soldiers have the pox. Soldiers returning from the trenches to their own homes have been diseased by their own wives, who, during the husband's absence, had to find money to meet the household expenses, go on to the streets, and in many cases take their daughters with them. I don't for a moment think this story to be correct.

Chapter 10

FRANCE, 1916

—————

March 30: We weighed anchor at daylight and entered the Harbour at once. Marseilles is only an artificial harbour; at the same time it is well protected by a curve in the mainland and the islands of Monte Cristo. The bluffs and highlands about seem very bare and desolate; there is nothing pretty or attractive to be seen, even though the history of the surroundings is exciting. The one great satisfaction now is that a man can walk about without having to take a life belt around with him.

Since leaving Alexandria nobody was allowed to move about without a life belt. A good rule, no doubt, but an awful bally nuisance. This precaution has just been borne out too by the news that the *Minneapolis* was torpedoed and sunk near Malta within a few minutes of our passing them. I remember seeing the *Minneapolis*, and can see that we had a very narrow escape indeed. This news is official given out this morning, it must have been picked up at the time, but was held back from us, and just as well too, as it would have caused much fear amongst the men—landlubbers that we Australians are.

The boat—1500 aboard all told—drew up to the wharf about 7am. At 1pm all hands were ashore. A march of one mile brought us to the railway station where we were soon ushered into 3rd class carriages, eight to a compartment, and made off for our still unknown destination. When marching to the station, the 4th Battalion leading then the AMC and Engineers, the Frenchmen stood interestedly but unmoved along the route; they were for the most part a very poor looking people, ill clad and slovenly, particularly the womenfolk; of course this is an inferior quarter of even an inferior town like Marseilles. One woman of excellent appearance stood on the roadside watching the march past when she seemed suddenly moved and, taking a bunch of pansies from her belt, walked unhesitatingly across holding out the flowers towards myself. I stepped out of the column, took the bouquet, saluted and picked up place again, while the lady was saying: 'Good luck Englishman' and something in French I could not follow. It was a very pretty little incident and pleased me very much. Poor as she was, she came forward so earnestly and with such a glorious expression of sympathy and good wishes.

We reached the town of Arles by nightfall and saw the splendid Rhone River. Up at Arles the scenery was very interesting but of a somewhat poor quality. From Arles to Tarascon (a clean military hospital town) the country opened out to one of extreme beauty. Rich in colour and production of all manner of fruit and vegetables. Along the Rhone there were very tall elm and poplar trees just breaking into leaf and making charming little pictures. Over this last stretch, the soft lights of the lowering and then setting sun, as well as the twilight glow before darkness set in, was distinctly different to the evening shades of Egypt, Anzac or Australia. There was a greater charm of soft shades and lingering reflections.

At 6.30, almost dark, we came on to more olive country, it seemed poor land, unsuited for anything but olive trees. The white ribbon-lake roads were pretty and so attractive. German prisoners worked about in large numbers and seemed quite happy.

March 31: At Les Laumes, we had a big break in the afternoon. Immediately the train stopped I got out over the fence to a hotel across the way and after purchasing bread, I looked around and saw amongst a number of French people two soldiers wearing steel shrapnel helmets. I made them have a bottle of beer with me and with pencil and paper found they were artillery men from the Ypres front. I tried on the helmet and found it heavy and uncomfortable although it was well lined and the Frenchmen said they got comfortable after a little while.

April 1: This morning about 8am we drew into Versailles where bread and tea was served up by Red Cross sisters (French). The excitement was now high as to whether we were to go through Paris or not. Fate was against us. Now, was Amiens or Abbeville to be our destination?

We breakfasted a few minutes after passing the Seine River on tea, bread, butter, jam and bully beef. By 10.30 we were moving along through rural eye soothing country. Since starting our journey, we have seen very few men at all and a whole lot of women working in the fields.

April 2: We detrained at a small station 4½ miles west of Hazebrouck at 4.20am and in fours marched along the hard, rough, stone-paved road through Hazebrouck and three miles further on to Strazeele where we are quartered in an old barn. The officers and sergeants are quartered some little distance away and much scattered. Even before 5 o'clock the church bells were ringing. It is Sunday of course and we are now mingling with the most devout people on the earth. Both outside and inside the homes are religious emblems of the Saviour and Virgin Mary; while out on many street corners are life size crucifixes.

Hazebrouck is a fairly large town. Strazeele is a small village only—there are three or four bars and a small shop or two. Wine is cheap—1d a glass— while good champagne is got at 5 francs a bottle. Beer and stout, both very poor, are sold at 1d. The people about are purely peasant, big at the waist and heavy at the ankle—there are very few men about at all, but the womenfolk seem to be taking the war and the troubles they have experienced quietly and patiently. The Germans overran this district in October 1914 and on being compelled to retire took all the men as prisoners.

I have heard that the type of folk about here are not altogether pure French and, in fact, that there are a whole lot of German sympathisers amongst them. On speaking to several girls and young women today, they made no complaint about the behaviour of the German soldiers while in possession of these parts for four days.

There are two Belgian girls here selling eggs and chips. They speak English very well, as do most people about here now—these girls speak very bitterly of Germany and seem to have given up hope of returning there. In fact, the eldest went so far as to hope that some Australian will take her back to Australia with him as her heart was burning to serve a man now and get away from all her terrible memories. There is no water recommended for drinking in this area, so we will have to drink 1d beers, as we are forbidden to drink wine or spirits.

April 3: Our billet is wet and musty and was until recently the residence of huge, fat, white coloured pigs. So you can well imagine we are not pleased with our abode, and there are 47 men sleeping in it. It is about nine feet high to the floor of the hay loft. I slept in a farmer's wagon with Bill Drummond on our arrival home at 9pm. All troops are supposed to be indoors by 7pm. Anyhow, on putting out the candle I could not go to sleep; there was a suspicion of fowl lice crawling over my face. On laying down my blankets, I looked over the side of the wagon and saw a whole lot of fowls on the wheels and rails. I lay there rubbing and scratching—this feeling travelled further, and I thought there were big horse lice moving in my knitted garments. I got very little sleep and was wakened at early dawn and kept awake by the roar of an artillery bombardment all over the front. These explosions continued throughout the day and have a tendency to make a person anxious, but I suppose we must fret and wait until we are sent for.

In the afternoon I cleared away intending to go to Hazebrouck, but not getting a motor wagon that way, Bob Miller and I went to a village three miles away. Here there were estaminets[1] in every other house, and smiling girls in others, but I doubt if there is any immorality practised in the district. These estaminets might in some cases be viewed with suspicion, but I think they're alright. The number of them is perplexing—I fancy the farmers' wives attend to them: it's part of their housework.

April 4: Tonight I had some fried eggs at the cheeky Belgian girls' place. I could hear high explosions all night but now that I am walking in the direction of the firing line I can see hundreds of flashes from bombs and guns. This din continued until bedtime—10pm—at which time I went to

---

1   Estaminets were French public houses.

sleep. Star shells lit up the sky showing the layout of the trenches around the district. It was an inspiring sight and an anxious one.

April 5: Small pox has claimed a case from the 4th Light Horse camped right near to us, so we were all again vaccinated today. I hope it will not spread as we Australians will get the blame of it, and again it is a very severe matter indeed. If small pox should break out amongst our forces, the war would be as good as lost to us.

April 6: We have not been getting nearly enough to eat since arriving in this country, and today we are on half rations, quarter loaf of bread, a bit of cheese and a few sultanas, no jam, while the cook gave us boiled mutton in a limited quantity. At dinner time I went with two others up town and got some soup, eggs and a tin of fruit, it was jolly good. At one of the pubs, I got along very pleasantly with the girls—one is a fine figure with a pretty coloured face, dark eyes full of life and a pretty mouth with good teeth. She, however, is not receiving any compliments from me—most of the fellows do, and I fear the girl is getting badly spoilt. But of course when the war is over she will come down to earth again. Her elder sister is nice too, but old enough to swallow harmlessly what flattery falls her way. The sister 12 years of age is my favourite and I often bring chocolates in for her.

April 8: With a party of 26 men I walked eight kilometres from Strazeele through Merris to the Divisional Baths. We found there four long sheds, 50 by 15 feet, the first one had 24 shower baths with small spaces at each end to change in; behind were two furnaces for heating the water and a fine little pump to fill the overhead tanks. The next shed is used for washing clothes and there are 16 girls working therein. Sixteen girls, but all the beauty they possess, if made up into one woman, she would not have much to sport but a beautiful complexion. Yes, the colour and clear softness of their rural skins are wonderful but their faces and figures spoil them. They are too lumpy.

The idea of these baths is to give the men from the trenches a good hot bath and clean underwear and socks once a week or so. It must be a wonderful institution. Yet, it seems to me the baths must do a whole lot of damage as the men come out of the hot water into the cold winter wind, there being no cold water available to close the pores of the skin.

Outside the bath house I can hear the fellows talking to the girls and the girls laughing. The better English these girls can talk, the more indecent they are. The soldiers have taught them their English and naturally it is very rough indeed. Say what they like about the Australian and his morals, he is more careful, yes, a thousand times, than the Englishman. All around these villages and farmhouses we find the same thing. The girls have been shockingly taught by the English soldiers.

April 9: For some days now we have not been allowed to go outside the billet without having any gas helmets slung over the shoulder in their little bags. The Germans have not used gas since last October on any of the fronts, but still we have got to be ready and waiting for it. These helmets are made of a kind of flannelette to come down over the head and tuck in deeply under the collar of your coat. It is fitted with a pair of large eye glasses, and has a mouth valve of tin with rubber on the outside and rubber over the mouth piece to breathe out through only. The air you breathe comes through the cloth which is impregnated with a chemical solution which will last for four hours, then the helmet needs replacing. These helmets are much better than the lot we had issued to use over on the Peninsula which had no exhale mouth pieces, and consequently soon got clogged with moisture, the helmet unbearably hot and suffocating. Another kind was simply a covering to place over the mouth and nose. It did not make one so hot, but it was jolly hard to breathe in.

Some of the fellows came home drunk again tonight and made a devil of a row. I had some rum and then champagne and listened to the willy nilly discussions before going to bed amongst the corn husks.

April 13: The stores in Hazebrouck are very decent for a village town and anything a soldier is likely to require can be obtained. Yet, like all the villages I have seen, no attempt is made to supply troops with meals. Eggs and chipped potatoes can be got here and there. Yesterday Ned and I had quite a long discussion before an estaminet keeper condescended to build us an omelette with coffee cake. These 'pubs' are only open between 11am and 1pm and from 6 to 8pm for soldiers. I suppose there has been little demand for meals from the English soldier and to a great extent the Australian only wants something to eat chiefly because he has money to spend. And, by jove, he does spend it recklessly too. I met Josh Stevenson this evening (of Wallaby fame); we had two bottles of champagne (six francs) and talked of old times. We then passed on up the road and dropped into another pub, and had two more bottles of champagne, this time the wine came from Epernay '1822' and it was glorious compared with the awful Reims stuff of 20 minutes before. This 'shouting' business is a miserable, yet an elegant, sort of game. If one fellow buys a bottle the others consider they must do so also. And so fellows are enticed to spend more than they otherwise would.

April 18: Wet and windy, our men are getting 'fed up' with it. The sunshine and showers of some days ago was reasonable. We pack and leave for the outside of the firing line tomorrow. Our transport section arrived this afternoon. As we have our five or six fine Sunbeam cars, our horses have been reduced to 47. Some of our transport horses were considered too small, so some big English ones were given to us in place of them. They are indeed big fellows and great workers.

April 20: Bombardment. The day opened as usual, but at lunch time a rumour came along that the 9th Battalion had been battered about and we were prepared for a whole lot of cases to come along. At 3pm, sure enough, the first lot came in the ambulance cars, in 40 minutes the total of wounded reached 38 and they were still coming in. We unloaded the cars, took the patients in, dressed the wounds, injected anti-tetanus and sent them into the hospital across the yard. Another 15 minutes and the total of cases rose to 49. Some of the wounded were then put back into the cars and taken away. But only seven of the 49 cases remained behind and these cases were the worst, two of which are sure to die. It was a big rush ably met by our doctors and men. In fact, it was a great credit to them all round.

April 21: Good Friday and we would not have the slightest knowledge of it had it not been for the ringing of the Church bells and the good folk in their best clothes, all black, coming and going. The day turned out to be miserably wet and downcast, and we are getting quite fed up with the regularity of it.

The sounds of big guns have been common all day and tonight the 'flares' and rifle fire are lighting up the sky and rattling. The aeroplanes had a busy time this morning. There were five of our planes up at one time and the

Germans fired hundreds of shells at them. The sky was painted with white smoke puffs. I was surprised to see how badly some of the shots missed.

April 22: I had the job of attending to the burial of one of yesterday's victims. It is so quick and impressive a service that the fellow is buried before one has time to realise anything of the sadness that surrounds such circumstances. Today, another fellow died; he will probably be buried tomorrow.

April 25 Anzac Day: The weather today was about the finest imaginable. The sun shone brilliantly, but not fiercely the whole day long. The birds are returning from their winter migration and are chirping and fluttering around the hedges and the eaves of the house busily as well as noisily preparing their homes for the summer months.

How different were my thoughts 12 months ago today. On that occasion there was no time to admire Nature's kaleidoscopic wonders and yet there was a similarity about the weather. At Lemnos Island while waiting for the Gallipoli venture, the weather was cold, as cold probably as it was here in France as we were slowly moving towards the firing line. A swim over the ship's side at Lemnos was chilly enough to remember, also the early morning bath in this country only a matter of days ago. The sun shines brightly and keeps us comfortably warm today just as it did this time last year.

The roar of cannon is heavy and there are wounded coming through our hands today. One man with a gaping wound in his skull through which his brains bulged persisted in getting into the ambulance car without assistance. Another fine specimen of Australian manhood is lying in the dressing station on his side in a very awkward position. He has lain there now forbidden to move or ease himself one degree. He was shot through the shoulder, the bullet passing through his lungs and out again at his lower ribs on the opposite side to the shoulder at which it entered. His only hope of recovery is to remain perfectly still. Two heroes also lay nearby, one totally blind and the other with his nose and one eye taken away. Terrible sights to see, but Oh, how proud these unperturbed, battered and uncomplaining warriors make one feel for his own homeland.

A country young or old that can breed such diehards might justly be proud of it and need have no fear for its future safety or prosperity politically or industrially. Men who can fight so gallantly bear their pain unflinchingly and die so ungrudgingly for their flag and country are possessed of the mettle that will raise their young nation to a plane amongst nations that has no superior.

Our men are taking their pains and afflictions as well today as they did on those lead-littered slopes at Anzac; but it is gratifying today to find the number of sufferers far less and the facilities to relieve their agony superior. Great philosophers have said it is suffering and hard setbacks that prove the man and bring out the finer qualities that are in him.

However it is not the brave manner in which men suffer that appeals to one as does the wondrous spirit and physical attainment that enabled our born fighters to hang on to the exposed tops of these steep ridges day after day against a formidable and refreshed foe, with the day's heat and the night's cold chill to counteract. These men never for a moment took their minds off their task. They beat off attack after attack and then dug long holes and scratched away with a trenching tool between spells to protect themselves from rifle and shrapnel fire.

They were fighting for their country's honour and had no time to think of their own hunger and thirst. They were men to the core. All that long 25th day of April 1915, cries came down the paths, over the rough virgin scrub and along the winding gorges wet and deep in mud from every part of our front, firstly for ammunition and later for reinforcements. That every part of our front was weakening seemed obvious. The significance of each call for ammunition and help grew more plaintive and even sorrowful. As the stretcher bearers returned from the firing zone they were plied with questions from the wounded as to how the fight was going; I saw many men rise up from the narrow rubbly beach with haggard faces pale from the loss of blood and attempt to go back to the assistance of their hard-pressed comrades. Yet, through all the anxiety and fear, there was a whole crowd of fresh soldiers waiting for orders to move up and lend a hand. With their instincts roused and their hearts burning for revenge, those men waited hour after hour for orders to move. They shouted, swore, cursed and even prayed to be allowed to join in the fray and as each depressing cry came back for reinforcements, their blood boiled and their mouths dried up with anger at their own inactivity. Late in the afternoon, the order came to 'move up'. This body of tall, gaunt cornstalks came in broken columns over the uneven and bushy country, each man stalking along with tense features, they knew full well what they were going to face, but there was no faltering, their comrades were in need of assistance and no power on earth would hold them back one moment. The hillsides tried their breathing; their feet sometimes slipped, some swore, some remained silent. Their time had come to prove their merit and to test their valour. The land they so proudly represented called them forward. The call for help from their line of comrades steeled their determination and forward they went: shrapnel and bullets held no fear for them. They had heard their comrades' cry and felt their country's call.

These giant cornstalks were our last line, our one hope; we had no reserves in hand now. If the line gave way all was lost, what remained would be driven into the sea and the cherished name of Australia doomed. There was no time to consider pros and cons. It was fight, and keep fighting. Hang on! What it meant to keep fighting and digging in, this terrible business of hanging on over those first three days, only those who were actually there can ever realise. And it was to the honour of these men amongst men, that with a party of four, I went into a hotel tonight and, in the corner, quietly and thoughtfully, toasted 'Our Comrades' of April 25, 1915.

Chapter 11

SHELLS AND SPORT, 1916

———⊱⊶⊰———

April 27: I went home to the pub billet after writing until 11pm and on laying my bed on the floor the guns started a vigorous fire all around us and kept going for an hour; we wondered what on earth was going on and sat at the window expectantly. I could not see any German shells bursting to speak of, while the flares were plain and close. I then concluded it was something distinctly and entirely English.

April 28: I have not learnt the strength of last night's rumpus at all. As only four wounded came through today, I take it that the Germans did not bother to return our fire. I am firmly of the opinion neither the enemy nor the Allies are strong enough to make an attack and that the war will end, whenever it does, with the trenches in about the same position as at the present. I still maintain that to advance is a practical impossibility.

April 30: We walked 1½ miles from Sailly when we came abruptly upon a line of bushes built right across the road, to obstruct the artillery observers' view of the road. Here we met a sentry and turning to the left were warned to walk in single file and at least ten yards apart from one another. The hotel at this corner had been badly blown about but it was still occupied and drinks being sold. At the dressing station where my companions were to go on duty, there were long hessian screens to obstruct the German vision. The dressing station was in a mud battered old farmhouse, a place few men would expect to find peace or even safety. Here I picked up the tramline and led away up to a trench. This trench I followed until I came to VC Avenue. Here I met a 1st Bn man on duty. He told me that around here Michael O'Leary won his Victoria Cross.[1]

He pointed out some German positions and remarked that they had some good sniping positions. Along VC Avenue I continued. It twisted about at intervals of ten yards, leaving a numbered position 'safe from enfilading fire. Sometimes the boarded pathway covered with wire netting that is in the bottom of the trench was under water. Here and there a hand pump. At Pinny's Avenue there was a straight run up to the foremost fire trenches. Here I got a great setback and felt almost indignant to find 1st Battalion men slouching about carelessly. I asked where I was, thinking that there was another firing line in front. But no there wasn't. I got a pair of glasses and in looking between two bags on the top of the parapet, saw the German line some 350 yards away. I had not time to take note of things when several bullets came along and I was told to come down. I put on a steel helmet covered with a piece of sandbag and saw the scene of desolation that existed between the two trenches. It was indeed 'no man's land'. Rusted masses of barbed wire lay before our trench, then a clean space with miles of twisted wire before the enemy line. Their trenches, like our own, were more built up than dug down. After seeing the solidarity and safety of our Anzac trenches, these made me feel annoyed as one field piece could blow away miles of these trenches and kill all the men in them in a few minutes—there were a few bags and a mass of earth thrown up on the surface. Of course the trenches are not heavily manned on either side. It's not like our limited room on the Peninsula. One old soldier told me that it's child's play here and as long as they left Fritz alone he would not give them any trouble. It is said we are starting trench mortars soon; if so, I fear for our own safety if the Germans return the fire as we have no

---

1   Irishman Michael O'Leary won the Victoria Cross for singlehandedly charging and destroying two German barricades defended by machine guns near Cuinchy in February 1915.

sheltered positions from booms, the whole place is so open and kind of unprotected.

The Germans have remarkable glasses, the men tell me that, and I also found it out when they picked me up twice in a very few minutes. On my way out I met Jim Randell, the Manly footballer and cricketer, and learnt that all the trenches and positions around here were German and they lost them. On getting back 600 yards to the open road, I saw a battered house named VC House. This I at last connected with Michael O'Leary. There was a notice forbidding anyone entering or I might have explored the house. Along the road I picked up AG Murphy and slowly we walked admiring the trees and wayside flowers back ¾ miles. Everything was very peaceful indeed; a few shots were fired from our own guns. Yet there was an undercurrent flowing beneath our pretty evening walk. A kind of feeling that a shower of shrapnel might at any moment cover us. It is my first time under fire now for four months.

May 1: Yesterday I heard that the Germans sent across information that General Townshend had suffered at Kut and today our paper verifies it.[2] General Townshend's failure to hold out comes as a foregone conclusion to me. I have predicted it right along. The Turks seem to have right from the commencement laid a trap for this British expedition and Townshend walked into it like a possum into a snare. I have but little sympathy for a soldier who belittles and understands his foe so woefully. And if General Nixon is lucky enough to get himself out of this hole, what on earth they sent him along there for with only half of a relief force beats me. Poor, damn fool English.

May 3: This afternoon I obtained a pass for Estaires. I heard that Capt Johnnie Williams, the Cardiff wing three quarter was about—I called on his men, he was absent, but the five Welsh officers compelled me to sit down and wait

---

2   Richards is referring to the Siege of Kut. Major General Charles Townshend was in charge of the 6th (Poona) Division of the Indian Army. Townshend had been ordered by his commander, General Nixon, to advance up to the Tigris River with the aim of capturing Baghdad. The army came within 40 kilometres of the city but was overwhelmed by a larger Ottoman force. Townshend was forced to retreat back to Kut, where he surrendered to the enemy some months later. He died in disgrace in 1924.

for his coming, and at the same time produced wine, whisky, cigarettes and Perrier. They were not long in finding out my name and my footer performances and a cheery welcome followed right through until I left at 9.20pm. The conversation drifted all over the world and in all topics, mostly more or less interesting to all hands. Football was not much dwelt upon as Williams has retired and Welsh football having gone back so much of late years. I had but little to say as Australian rugby is professionalised and dead. My pass was only to be out until 8pm and it was 9.20pm when I left the mess. The night was rather dark, but to prevent unnecessary risks in meeting the military police, I had to turn in and follow a rough track along the River bank to avoid going through the village of Estaires. It was dark and lonely with a picket every now and then shouting: 'Halt, who goes there?' It was easy to pass them. I usually swore at them and one at least apologised for interfering. I got home safely but the flare shells and roar of bombs, cannons, rifle and machine guns was thick and continuous.

May 5: One hears strange stories of spies and their systems of work every day. No doubt there is a whole lot of German sympathy amongst the people living around here in the villages and right up to the firing line. But at the same time, they can't give any information to the enemy. As far as I can see there is no information to give. Movements of troops and that sort of thing is done in such small parties that if I wanted to give the Germans information that would be reliable or of value, it would be hard because nobody knows what is going on.

We came on up to Laventie and stopped at an estaminet for a while; the girls are clever and attractive, but lacking in English. A group of Maoris took charge of the place and were breaking their hospitable necks to shout for all hands and particularly the Australians. Drummond would only drink coffee and several of the men looked at him in dismay, saying: 'the only bloody Kangaroo I've ever seen that wouldn't drink beer.'

May 6: An artillery man told me today that a corporal of their battery was tampering with an unexploded shell when it went off and blew his head away. This makes a whole lot of such careless incidents that have come to hand of late.

May 7: It is fairly cold today and trying jolly hard to rain, but as the Maori were playing a team from the Welsh engineers this afternoon, I had to go over to Laventie and see it. The Maoris were in the field waiting quite a long time for the Welshmen. While they were waiting the Colonials looked physical giants compared to the lean and wiry Welsh. There were other features in the appearance of the two teams that bothered me quite a while—the great self-possession and confidence of the Maoris, also their straight built bodies and big limbs; while their opponents seemed stage frightened and their awkwardly put together forms bent with hard work and cramped by confinement at the workshop benches.

The contrast was very marked indeed. The more notice I took of it the greater and greater was my love of the Colonial and my mind refreshed as to the difference in appearance of African and English athletes as they stood facing one another in both South Africa and in England. Also the Australians when they faced the Englishmen and Welshmen in 1908. The Englishman, though, always stands up better and finer than the Welshman, but the Colonial is vastly superior to any of them.

The ground was short, narrow and uneven. I did not expect to see much decent football, there being no room to move about on, but I certainly expected to see the Maoris be winners by at least 20 points. My prediction was wrong as the game ended five-all. I should have been more careful in underrating the Welshmen as I have always a great regard for their football powers: they stick a game right out to the very end. Of course, the smallness of the playing area prevented large scoring. In fact, one hardly understands how any scoring took place on so small a ground.

May 10: Chaplain McKenzie was at our billet giving out letters, mostly from schoolgirls, for 'lonely soldiers' and he denounced all Australians for being swell headed and small minded.

May 13: I was told only a few days ago by O'Sullivan that I was a damn fool to take the war and the doings of our fool Government so much to heart. It is making an old and serious man of me. He said: 'They are treating the whole thing at home as if it were a huge burlesque, so why do you not join it and treat the whole thing in a like manner?' Laugh, he said, and b— the world!! This I believe is the correct manner, but then, no sooner do I adopt the lighter frame of mind than in comes a rush of wounded and dying men, men as brave as anything that ever breathed the breath of life. This brings back the murder on Gallipoli. Men lying on stretchers aboard a tramp ship en route for Alexandria went green and rotten for want of medical attention, and had to be cut away from the stretcher. 650 patients with two medical men and a dozen orderlies to attend them left Anzac on one ship. From Cape Helles came similar reports, so can you dear reader think hard of me, or think for a moment that I don't know what I say, when I condemn the British Government (not the British nation) for their terrible crimes? I must, however, treat the whole sordid thing in a lighter vein and would also too, but for the loss of blood and valuable lives that goes on around me.

May 23: Bill and I went down to the estaminet where the school teacher and several other fine girls hold out. They all had a drink with us while the room full of Tommies sang very pleasantly. These women were indeed glad to see us. There was no mistaking their good feeling and kindly interest. I promised to call back one day and have a chat with them when they were not so busy. It was pleasing to see the way the people of this village recognised we were Australians and looked after us with an expression on their faces that seemed to say they were glad to see us and would be pleased if we came back again. I asked the school teacher how the Australian fellows compared with the Tommy for behaviour. She replied: 'Oh well, there's not much difference, only when the Australian is sober, he's better than the Englishman, but when he is drunk he's awful.'

May 24: The non drinker gets a rough time here in France, as there is nothing to drink: the water is bad and is not allowed to be drunk unless chlorinated, and then it is too distasteful to drink. The pubs don't cater for the non drinker at all. Some of them carry citron and water.

May 28: The Third Field Ambulance came along today with a good team and played us a very pleasant game of football on the cow field next door. The grass was lovely and soft, but so slippery that one could not venture to move sharply, this brought forth some funny incidents. We won by four tries and a penalty goal to nothing. There was a good crowd present and they enjoyed the game immensely.

June 1: Today was a big day for the 1st Brigade as Billy Hughes, Andy Fisher, General Birdwood received the men.[3] I regret not being there; only the men we could spare were sent. I hear that General Birdwood must have warned and restricted Hughes considerably in his speech as he was brief, and labouring. He said Australia realised full well that you are fighting and dying for her, and when you come home rest assured that Australia will welcome and look after you for the rest of your days. Good stuff, yes, but how useless for the general welfare of the coming generation of Australians, the fathers of whom will be medical rejects and cold footed malingerers who kidded sick and returned to their homes 'heroes'.

No! If Australia does not want to reduce the size and courage of the coming generation, it's up to them to pick out of the battalions men with clean sheets and free from venereal disease and return them to Australia at once. It's the men whose constitutions are sufficiently strong enough to withstand the past two years that the First Contingent has withstood to be fathers of our young nation. Then by enforcing conscription would the ranks be kept up to full strength? France with its revolution and wars has lowered the strength and physique to such an ebb that it was never regained. France will never recover from this war; I venture to think that as a nation they cannot ever again protect themselves from an action. Germany will have much trouble to regain her former strength, but I believe she will do it considerably quicker than any other nation as she has a sturdy foundation, and modern teachers and scientific ways with her that can regulate and protect the coming generation. Australia should take the lesson from France, and not allow her bravest and her best to be killed off; take them home, they have proved themselves, and replace them with untried men. We have plenty of them.

It was strange Andy Fisher did not say a few words to the boys. More so strange, as he seemed entirely out of his element and just moped along behind Hughes and Birdwood. The review was held in a paddock that may or may not have been out of range of the enemy's gun range, but to give every possible protection there were some eight or ten aeroplanes flying around to keep off the enemy bomb droppers. The Germans would have had a glorious

3   Billy Hughes was the Australian prime minister. Andrew Fisher, a former Australian prime minister, was Australia's High Commissioner in London.

time had they got amongst this body of probably 4000 men. Mr Hughes and party came around and shook hands with all of the OCs. The brass band played its best and when Mr Hughes said that General Birdwood had allowed him to call for three cheers for Australia, they were so heartily given that they could be heard all the way to Berlin. Then one cheer for 'Birdy' was called, and by way of expressing his popularity, the men cheered four or five times. Andy Fisher, also, seemed lost at having to play second fiddle; he was out of it and to our boys it was rather pathetic.

June 5: I note that our old colonel 'Dr' Newmarch has been mentioned in the birthday honours list, and been made a Knight of something or other.[4] This comes as a great shock as Newmarch is a man of mean principle and a lover of a filthy story. This man was in the DTs from drink when we landed at Anzac and when hundreds of wounded men were groaning and dying, he was in a cabin with a guard over him to prevent him from getting out on deck. So much for an Honourable Knight.

June 6: One of the most astounding things that ever happened in the way of bad judgment on the part of a body of men. It seems two war medals were given to the unit for distribution to the men for the best record and it was left to the NCOs to choose the two men. Bladin was one and after some discussion the Warrant Officer Atkin was given the second place in honours. Now, I don't so much mind Bladin, but seeing the WO was not in our unit up to three weeks before leaving Serapeum, or less than three months ago, it seems like an insult to the corps. To think that we haven't got a man capable of wearing a war medal is over the odds.

June 7: This giving away of two war medals as though they were packets of cigarettes keeps me awake at night. Not so much perhaps in my own interests as in the interest of the Corps. It means that the 2nd Field Ambulance have three medals to the 1st Field Ambulance's one, and to think our own NCOs are responsible is my sore side. I went so far as to see Major Dods, the assistant ADMS, and give him my letters to Staff Captain Pollock and his

---

4   Dr Bernard Newmarch, a Sydney general practitioner, formed and commanded the 1st Field Ambulance of the Australian Imperial Force, sailing with that unit on the *Euripides* in 1914. He died in Sydney in 1929.

letter in reply, to read. He told me that I can only sit down and look on as the Colonel's decision is final. I showed my correspondence to our Captain Taylor and he likewise tells me he can do nothing in preventing the WO from receiving our medal.

June 8: Rumours about peace are still prevalent. It is said that in Divisional orders if peace should be proclaimed at any moment, the men are warned not to make a demonstration and a fuss. Take it quietly! What it means is hard to say, probably just a line to prepare our men for an attack or to inspire them for some purpose or other, as there is really no sign of peace in the air as far as we poor deluded devils are concerned. Amen.

The Germans in front of the Australian trenches have said by notices posted up over their trenches that peace will come very soon. Men on leave are notified that in the event of peace being declared, they must report at once to the nearest headquarters. Anyhow, we old hands have drifted into a kind of hopeless groove and don't much worry now as to the duration of the war. We just live on and do so as best we can, that's all.

In concluding another book [diary], I must say that it has been a friend to me. Every day I make up some entry or other without fail, although the time I spend at it may be better occupied in bustling round and spending more leisure time. I keep too much to myself, perhaps, and thereby grow a little reserved and in a small unit like ours it's not good to become reserved—the fellows take it as an unruly kind of superior bearing. Anyway I must keep my book up to date each day; I only trust it will one day be worth reading and sufficiently well written to be not only interesting but of some value.

June 10: The great adventure of today was a football match against the 3rd Field Ambulance on their ground at Neuvea Monde. Four wagons left Doulieu at 1.30pm and bumped and banged along over the metal roads and cobble stone roads for the 5½ miles. We had to cross the River Lys in a clumsy raft which wet everybody up to their knees—this, however, added greatly to the enjoyment of the afternoon. There were football posts on the ground which were perfectly level, but no other marks, neither goal lines nor side lines as the grass was two feet long in patches. Of course, good football on such a ground was out of the question, but it was nevertheless very interesting. We led by one try to nil at halftime, and finished up with four tries to nothing. Some of the tries were very well scored, passing and interpassing a dozen times or more on one occasion. But the strange part was that the ball could not be seen in the long grass and the men kicked yards away from the ball and fell down where he thought it was. I played fullback and enjoyed it, but when it came to dribbling rushes and I could not see the ball, there were anxious moments. A fellow was laid out and none of our players noticed it. He was practically lost in the long grass; the spectators fixed him up after finding him. One big fellow sat down to fix his boot laces and he could hardly be seen over the top of the grass. A jolly good experience second only to the first football match I saw in England when a hailstorm stopped the play and a ball went into a scrum alright and burst therein; the players could not make anything out of it.

June 15: Today is the anniversary of the wine coming ashore at Anzac. It was about 3pm that some saw in the breakers bobbing about what looked like a cask. Later it was found to be a cask driven by the southerly wind up from Cape Helles. It was soon rolled ashore and up into Victoria Gully where it would be safe from the observation of the police or prying officials. Here an axe was procured, the barrel broken open and what a rush: the fellows came tumbling down from all the dugouts and camps all around with receptacles of all kinds and descriptions. With wild shouts of joy they bailed the precious liquid out and drank deeply. I first came down the hillside with a 6 lb bully beef tin, filled it and went back up, returning with ¾ of a kerosene tin and after a melee I got it full and triumphantly returned to my dugout where I carefully labelled and bottled it, burying some of it for the dry days that would surely follow.

I was right, too, as that wine was a blessing after a few weeks. Some of the men got stupidly drunk and possibly the whole of Anzac would have along the right wing. Also as many casks came ashore but were emptied into the sand by an officer. At 9pm, a party of fellows saw another barrel floating in off Hell's Spit pontoon wharf; they went into the water and helped it along perhaps 100 yards and after a big struggle to get it ashore, an officer came along and tipped the wine into the sea. Never was there such disappointment and swearing amongst a party of men. For weeks afterwards four barrels were standing down on the beach towards No Man's Land, Gaba Tepe. The

Turks might have been able to get it at night time although there was a risk of our destroyer turning a searchlight onto them. Yet I believe some of our men did venture down the beach to get at this wine. In all there were probably eight casks of wine; about only two were successfully opened and smuggled away. It was a great and glorious day. Beachy Bill shot some of the fellows around a cask but this did not interfere with them in their attempt to get the wine away.

June 17: Since I received my date for leave to visit England and learnt that the Warrant Officer cannot hold a military medal, I am more light-hearted and free. Today our football team went to Steenwerck and played the 5th Field Ambulance. After quite a good game we won by five tries to nothing. Our backs are by far too good for most teams around here. I played at fullback and did fairly well; the ball, being a new one, was good to handle and kick.

June 18: A church service was held in the mess room at 2.30pm. I enjoyed the singing alright, but alas, the preacher was poor. He went to a University to be made into a parson and that's all there was about him: he had neither command of language nor the slightest bit of dramatic force, nor had he the brains God had possibly blessed him with in seeking information throughout the world for himself. In short, he was a weak legged parrot. They must be short of parsons to push this guy on to we poor suffering Australians.

June 21: At last night's concert was a short speech of apology from the manager. The company were billed for 6pm and turned up 25 minutes late. The manager bustled in and said: 'I'm exceedingly sorry to think that you have been kept waiting. The most detestable feature in man to me is the fellow who has no respect for his own appointments. This, I assure you, is absolutely no fault of ours; we did not know where to find you and have been shockingly misdirected. I am downright sorry men.'

These few words were naturally greeted with loud cheers. Seldom does it fall to a soldier's lot to hear an apology. If only our inspecting officers could have heard this speech, it might have done them a whole lot of good. It may possibly lead them to appreciate the fact that a soldier is human after all. These inspecting officers sometimes keep whole battalions waiting for a whole day. In Egypt, I remember lying out in the hot sun from 9am to

1.15pm and then no inspection took place. This set a bad example to men who are still flesh and blood and have a sort of mind and conscience left them. They hate this sheer pompousness, and men brought up in a business and commercial world, or bushmen who are in the habit of taking a man's word for his bond, lose faith in their officers generally, particularly when each and every man of them knows the value of punctuality and find the men who preach it most failing them at every turn.

June 22: There are a lot of English Yeomanry around our district at present; the bulk of their horses I have not seen. They look likely fellows, but still if they are to follow up an attack, then why on earth don't they give us Australian horsemen? They would harass the Germans more in 20 minutes than any bunch of Englishmen would in 24 hours. The Australians would blow up and burn down buildings that the English would take three days in attempting to starve them out. It's war and I believe that the Englishman even now has not learned the lesson. It's go your damnedest, play your enemy at his own game, show no quarter. It's war, that's all, just war! Hard, cold and cruel. The Australian is the adaptable man possessed of coarse, animal instinct and bush resource. The Englishman lacks both dash and resource. He has never been allowed to think and shift for himself. We want the Australians to lead the infantry attacks also. I fear the English will b— about, dig himself in when he has the enemy only half routed, as they lost Helles and Suvla Bay.

June 23: Last night there was a period of very heavy bombarding. At midday it started again and continued until a heavy thunderstorm broke out at 4.30pm. It was the heaviest shower of rain with lightning and thunder that I have yet seen in France. At 5.30 it cleared up and the bombardment continues again; some of the explosions fairly shake the ground around here and we must be six or seven miles back. The rumble is most continuous. It makes me shudder to think of what is really happening and yet as a fellow just casually remarked: 'those damn fools will be killing someone yet,' referring to the roar of cannons and trench mortars. I am not so much sorry for the killed or wounded as I am over the fact that they don't get a sporting chance for their lives at all.

June 24: With all the rain of yesterday, the football field behind the transport lines was in real good order for a scratch match. A and B teams played a hard, rough and tumble game. There was a lot of minor injuries but nevertheless it was a good natured game and enjoyed by all. The referee's watch stopped, or he did not carry one at all as we played 52 minutes in the first half and 45 in the second. This meant that everybody was played right out. I had a lot to do at fullback and could hardly stand up at the finish of the game. Three of our officers played and were handled with a little more dispatch than the others.

June 27: The army is a mass of corruption and robbery. Yet I wish I could run a more genial disposition and not be so doubtful about everything.

Chapter 12

TOWARDS THE FRONT, 1916

July 4: Pulling down tents at 5.30am—this came especially hard on last night's drunks and imaginary drunks. It was a bustling morning right enough and by 2pm we lined up and started out. For the past two hours it had been thundering and cloudy with light flashes of lightning. But as soon as we started it rained fairly heavily and continued right along to our destination eight miles away and across the Belgian frontier. There did not seem to be any roadway or division between the farms, but there surely must have been.

Today brings back memories as we went through recruit drills, stretcher drills and semaphore signalling. I feel very wroth at being pushed and buffeted about at this awful drill stuff; at the same time I agree that something of the kind is absolutely necessary as the fellows are getting lazy and lax. Trouble began when the WO in his opening remarks concerning the necessity for better discipline said that the majority of the fellows are well behaved and clean living but I am going to punish them also for not looking after the others and keeping them in order. A terrible thing I think that the good fellows should be openly penalised, particularly as there were only two men drunk and could not move off. Both of whom the WO knew of yesterday morning—in fact he was drinking beer with one of the defaulters himself. He is a low down scoundrel.

July 6: Cricket and football were played after tea until the German guns dropped pieces of shells around. Just about this time—8.40pm—three of our men while walking along the main road were knocked down by a shell that struck a tree on the roadside killing Stan Bull, taking 'Goldie' Warran's arm off and hitting Ford slightly on the stern. These are the first casualties in France amongst our unit.

July 7: I have just come into the tent after having an eight mile route march in the wet and rain. With Watts and Reynolds I went and had some beer. The beer at 1d a glass was awful. I thought it tasted of cascara. Watts suggested quinine. Reynolds (a knowing bird) said it was soap, and as proof looked at the top where the froth had fallen in filling the jugs and sure enough it did look like soapsuds. The 2d and 3d beer was sold out. We then went next door and got 12 eggs made up into an omelette and coffee in the usual basin. One of the girls had a wonderful grip of English slang. We passed many remarks, not expecting her to hear, but she did easily. Our men are a whole lot more careful in their talk than the Tommies when dealing with the women of France and Belgium.

July 8: It rained this morning but cleared off splendidly in the afternoon when a game of football between A and B sections took place. The rivalry was intense throughout and the barracking terrific as the game has long been talked about and there was wholesale betting going on with A favourites. The game was fast. I was the fullback as usual, but with a bad back and it is jolly bad tonight, worse perhaps than it has been for many attacks now.

July 9: It is 4pm as I write; a cricket match is in progress just outside. The guns are thundering all around. One German 5.9 is dropping shells only a little way off us, and in the air duels are being fought all day long.[1] It is a lovely day, a clear blue sky with big fleecy clouds moving over, in which the aeroplanes disappear from our sight. This has been going on all day now, and the anti-aircraft guns have had a very busy time indeed. We are packed up and ready to move off in half an hour. For where?

1　The German 5.9 was a heavy field howitzer used in World War I and the beginning of World War II.

It's wonderful how well secrets are kept as we or nobody else knows where they are going to. And any who think that they really do know all differ in their 'inside' knowledge. The Somme is the popular feeling but if this is so it looks like splitting the Australians up.

Maybe we are weakening the enemy also by our many retreats and I don't doubt but that the German will be the first to sue for peace. The Turk seems to be holding his end splendidly still. He's a great fighter. I've never heard an Australian who really fought against the Turk condemn him. In fact, we all just love him for his gameness and good sportsmanship.

July 10: There seems to be a good deal of confidence at present about the war terminating this year. I however remain prepared for anything and as far as I can see there's nothing to indicate an early peace. The driving back of the Germans may yet be more costly in human life than either the British or French can afford. I don't know any more than that our task is an enormous one and will be hard to accomplish against clever and stubborn soldiers.

July 25: News from the Somme area not over bright. It seems our Australians did well but got knocked about severely. The truly remarkable thing is how the enemy can hold out under the present pressure. On the Somme terrific fighting has been going on for 26 days now. It was heart breaking to read some of the 8th Brigade being broken up in a fruitless attack on the German trenches up near Armentières. The 4th Division are moving up now towards the front. Jack Hynes says that with the 15th Battalion before Anzac it was a disgrace to fall out of a route. The men used to count a man out and curse him for falling out of the ranks.[2] But now the men fall out like flies and are cheered by the men for doing so.

July 26: It's jolly hard luck again to be loafing back here now, not that I profess to be a lover of shot and shell, I just want to take my part in the game. And hanging about gives a fellow the chance to think rather too freely. I worry a lot about what I am going to do when peace comes again.

---

2 'Counting out' was a way Australian soldiers voiced their disapproval, by counting in unison from one to nine and then, like a boxing referee, shouting, 'ten . . . you're out.'

July 27: I learn from some fellows who have just returned from the battle front that the whole of the 1st Division are out of the trenches and have had a terrible knocking about. Ambulance men and all have been shot about severely. It makes one think that we should be thankful for being well away from it, and then it seems very hard luck to be missing such a remarkable adventure. Our Australian troops gained a whole lot of ground including Pozières from where other troops had been driven back several times. But being driven back does not count for much as it depends upon how the artillery have acted in cutting out barbed wire, upsetting machine gun positions and blowing in 'dugouts'.

July 29: It's been an inferno here at the dressing station (12 miles from the firing line) this morning. Men able to walk and men lying down on stretchers crowd the pathways. Ambulance cars and communication wagons up to the gate. Men with rough dressing and in all stages of mutilation lie and sit around. It's not the sight of these great fighters as much as the story they tell that grieves one so. It seems our artillery has been in amongst our own men and assisted in blowing them to blazes. I don't know whose fault it was, but there was a terrible ado. The 5th Brigade were the chief sufferers. It seems when they made their dash up the enemy's trench, the barbed wire in front had not been broken away and the machine gunner's bombs soon knocked them down while hung up in the barbed wire. These men do not tell a very clear story as the big shells have played up with them.

2pm: I am sitting on the front of an ambulance car which has two wounded men inside; a third is being lifted in on a stretcher. No 2 exclaims: 'What George, where did they get you?' 'On the knee,' said George, 'a few minutes after you left. It tore a bit of a hole out but it's not much.'

An officer now came along with an arm badly broken. Tears welled in his eyes as he enquired how the stretcher bearers were getting along. His Company had practically been lost. They faced ill fortune and death fighting against barbed wire and their own artillery fire. Smashed his units and broken down beyond repair, and nothing done at all. A night of sheer failure and desolate, cruel waste. Nothing seemed to go right at all.

July 30: The stretcher bearers have worked terrifically while the dressing sections and the doctors have been going from daylight to dark for nine days and turned over thousands of cases; many operations were performed, some of them without even ether or other than an injection of morphia. Our men are wonderful beyond belief. Yesterday some of them lay out in the garden from 8 until 5 only to be dressed and sent on to the clearing station from where I hope they go to England, the place so loved by us all. Many a man smiles when he is told he will never be able to fight again or that he won't be right again for some months. It's Blighty for a spell anyhow and probably back to Australia again, he may casually remark. The fellows shake hands with and congratulate their mates and brothers when they find they have a wound that is not likely to be serious, but will most likely keep them away for a few months. Spotswood, one of our cooks, had his top jaw fractured and as he lay in much pain on the ground, his foster father smiled joyfully and remarked: 'Spotty, you are a certainty for "Blighty" and a damned good job. You're a very lucky fellow.' So you can quite see how much our men are prepared to suffer to visit England after so much service and military law as we old hands know.

In looking back over yesterday, it's marvellous what I saw and experienced. It was probably the greatest day of all days as far as war experiences go. In the early morning I had to sew up a corpse in a blanket for burial, a sickly joy. Then I helped the wounded who were pouring in thickly, motorcar loads followed one another as in chains. The congestion became terrible. Two doctors worked in the hot operating theatre, one in each of the big tents and four in the main dressing room. They worked until they could hardly stand up and at 5pm I counted up 31 cases still to be dressed. At 11am though I broke down, I could not see such uncomplaining patients suffering, so without a word to anyone I just pulled out and got into an ambulance car, I went out through Albert to the dressing station known as AD Dump. The drive was something to be remembered: never have I appreciated nature's lavish flower garden more. Rich scarlet poppies and delightful royal blue bloom cornflowers, but there were others (I don't know the name) the very same as I used to pluck and admire on Anzac. It is the first time I have seen it here in France. It gave me many unpleasant memories as it, with the poppies, seems to be a kind of ill omen, and brought back Anzac's dark and cruel recollections.

About 3½ miles from Albert the front line of the German position stands. Watts and I got a car again at 5.30pm and rode to Albert. From there we walked the 3½ miles to the old German front line.

The chief feature of Albert is its immense brick built church with very high tower. Now, however, the whole structure is tottering to a fall. Shells have riddled it through and through and made such inroads into the square tower that it's strange to see it standing up at all. There was a figure of the Virgin and child. A statue standing perhaps 22 feet in height, it now leans right over the side and is drooping into the roadway. Looking at it from underneath it seems that the Virgin is holding out her child so as to save it from harm in the fall. The child has hands uplifted as though ready to jump into the onlookers' arms. It makes a striking picture. The local superstition is that when the statue falls the war will immediately close.

Later we could see in Pozières and for miles around the country was racked and shattered. It was now just dark; we lay down for 1½ hours, to observe the flashes of our own hundreds of guns and the bursting of the German shells. The stars came out and shone but yet it was dark enough for the star shells to light up all around us. The bombardment became terrific about 10pm. Shrapnel burst around and some of these shells were entirely new to me, as when they burst a spray of sparks followed the downward throw of the pellets, making quite a fireworks effect. Big high explosive shells shook the whole surroundings, and machine guns and rifle fire broke out in terrific force. What was coming, we wondered. Was the German counter attacking? We thought not, as his infantry will not stand up to our men. Our fellows tell tales and make big jokes of the German infantry throwing down their arms and crying: 'Comrade Australia.' Our men loathe them and curse them for running away as they do.

The sky is now aglow for miles around with star shells of different colours and a hundred and one explosive devices. The rage quietened down and gave us the impression that it was only a false or frightened attack. So realising that we had seen as much as we were likely to see and taken all the risks it was necessary to take, we would wander back towards home, Warloy 12 miles distant. We got an ambulance wagon at the AD Dump, and arrived back to camp well on for 3am after a great day, a day I am hardly likely to ever forget.

July 31: The 1st Field Ambulance casualties during the four days' battle of the 1st Division was three killed and 15 wounded. Our bearers are in good heart and have earned a rest after the trying spell of hard and heart-breaking work in the frontline. I really have been thankful for the spell also, but now I feel well again and will be anxious to go out when the reserves are called up.

August 2: The fellows were talking of Captain Tozar who was blown up and killed last Sunday night. Strange, out of the three of them, they agreed that an act of Providence must have directed the shell on top of so miserable a man as Tozar seemed to be. They say he never would speak decently to anybody at all, and was a curse to work with.

August 3: With Jack Hynes I had some stout and it was easily the worst drink that it had been my misfortune to pay for. Yet the Australian fellows bought it up eagerly at 5d per glass extra price. Our fellows just must spend their money, that's all.

August 4: The German has lost a whole lot of my respect for his thoroughness, as his helmet, which I have always been led to believe was made from steel, is nothing more than a bit of paper, leather with a glossy surface, a hollow brass spike on the top, the whole thing being no heavier than a straw hat. When I saw these hats weeks ago back along the road, I thought they were not the German infantry man helmet. But now I find they are, and to allow themselves to be pushed from those marvellous first line trenches is a terrible blow to my idea of the Germans' great fighting qualities.

August 5: I went over to the dressing station before breakfast and found the 4th Division had followed up an artillery preparation and gained possession of the crest of the ridge beyond Pozières. Regardless of the Germans' costly counter-attacks, our men gave no ground. It was a far different air the wounded carried from the first attack by the same battalion six days ago. On that occasion everything went wrong, and our men, after struggling with barbed wire while machine guns played amongst them, were forced to return to the trenches without gaining a foot of ground and losing very heavily. Officers broke down and wept when coming through wounded and the men were strangely silent and heavy hearted. Today, however, it is quite different although our men were not smiling. They were just satisfied they had done their duty and triumphed. I am told by one of the wounded they were instructed to take no prisoners, but whether this is correct or not, some prisoners were taken, from 500 to 1000. About 29 German wounded passed through the clearing station during the day; they were not a bad type of man at all. Youngish men with excellent physique and very clean both in dress and body. One of them spoke English as well as any of us. I spoke with him for some time and found he came from South Africa, Port Elizabeth, where he said he kept a hotel. Having come to Germany on a visit to his parents when war broke out, he was compelled to enlist. He did not say much about the war, it was mostly South African talk. But when I did ask him how it was possible for the Tommies to push the Germans from the front line of trench, so powerful and staunch were the positions, he simply said the whole of Germany was crying about the General in charge of this Somme for not digging stronger defences, and under the strain the General shot himself.

August 6: All night long four doctors were kept working without a break, and several amputations were put through, fingers, hands and even an arm. At these operations they were performed without chloroform or anaesthetic of any kind. How these lovely heroes stood it I cannot realise; many of the cases had been lying out in No Man's Land for over a day. One case that hurt me very much was a big fellow with a more or less unimportant wound on his thigh but he must have bled very heavily indeed for he had but very little hope when we got to him. Another arrived dead in the car through his wound opening and bleeding him to death. These cases were an awful blow as either of them could have been saved easily had the men nearby known anything about First Aid work.

All of the wounds were from shell fire and, although the majority of them were slight, some were in a terrible mess, particularly those who were hit by the phosphorus shells. They in appearance were the worst as they had burnt patches all over them, face and hands of course, as the phosphorus would not burn through the clothes. The men who were peppered by dirt and stones looked very bad also, with head and hands buried in cotton wool and bandages, leaving only a space to breathe through. A few of the fellows, after they had had a drink of tea and fowl to eat, spoke up cheerfully, mostly those who were in the counter attack by the Germans.

Our men who jumped out and met the counter attack were proud of themselves after just lying down all day long waiting for a shell to bury them up or blow them out. They dare not dig their trench, for fear the artillery will see their plight and blow them right out of it altogether.

All night long we worked from 8pm until 8am unloading cars and sorting out the bad cases for immediate treatment. The four doctors could not cope with the steady flow and so the patients collected in numbers and had to wait for hours for treatment. When the lightly wounded men were asked to have a drink of tea and some fowl, 'Fowl,' they would exclaim, 'you're pulling my leg, aren't you?' But there was fowl there alright and the poor famished heroes did relish it too.

August 7: The 19th Battalion came into Warloy last evening looking so haggard and drawn. They were dust begrimed and their eyes, in many cases, were like those of hunted animals, glassy like and staring as if their nerves were shattered. They were silent and frightened. Tears of pride rose in my eyes as I saw them in twos and threes sauntering along looking for a place to buy eggs, tinned fruit and bread. Several I spoke to told me they didn't care a jot what happened: they had lost their pals and felt fed up with the whole thing.

Others had French bread under their arms and a tin of fruit in their hands and were going expectantly back to their billets to eat their first bread for 11 days. Others were looking for a barber to get their week or more growth off their thin and colourless faces. It was a glorious pageant for any Australian to gaze upon with pride and triumph. But then, Oh God, underneath all there was a horror beyond description. And the world will never know what they have been through, the lovely devils.

Today I met Sid Riddington, the champion diver—he had been in the trenches for ten days. He showed in his very soul a sort of affection, a keen joy, at seeing me. But there was something in the haggard glassy stare and that slow, halting voice that was sufficient explanation as to the despair of that fine young athletic physical bearing. He told me Lieutenant Dos Wallach was well, also Syd Middleton, but alas Capt 'Chap' Kirke got killed in the attack of August 4.

All the time I was walking about admiring our fighting, silent men, I was thinking of Dos Wallach and then decided I had to see him. I enquired where his billet was and walked right in finding that Dos was having a splash up sort of a bath. I wrung his hand in both of mine and could have cried with joy at seeing him alive even if his large kindly blue eyes were drawn and his cheeks hollow. I went up to his bedroom and how clearly yet awfully sad and cruel did he tell me his story of the ten days' experience in the firing line. He pressed me to have dinner with him. I hesitated, but was so glad to surrender and sit down with Lieut Saddler, another 'sub' and Dos. As dinner progressed on fried eggs, salmon and tinned pineapple, lovely red wine and coffee, the conversation got onto war mostly, and it was very interesting to me. Dos and the others agreed that the 2nd Division did wonderfully well, but that it was downright murder and beyond anyone's common reasoning to keep them in there so long. I remained until 10pm and tired by work and want of sleep I wearily pushed off home.

Chapter 13

COUNTER-ATTACKS AND KINGS, 1916

August 8: The Germans are now counter-attacking and showing a bolder front to stay and fight instead of run away as before. But the German infantry is nothing compared to the artillery. The men don't get a dog's chance with the ground churned up so as to resemble a wild and stormy sea. There is no hope of digging trenches at all and the men cannot be allowed to scatter about in craters as the officer gets out of touch with them. And again those shell craters are oftimes full of poisonous gas. Capt Middleton tells me he lost several men that way; they went into a shell hole to do a job for themselves and could not get out. The men tell me that German steel helmets made good WC pots and are then thrown over the front.

At 9am I called in on Syd Middleton. I was so jolly glad to see him, as I could not help thinking he would soon be bowled over, knowing him to be so daring. Oh, what a wreck he is too, he must be looking ten years older since I saw him last. On being told about it, he said: 'Yes, Cocky, I'm a much older man now; these past ten days have been a terrible strain, yes terrible.' The whole time he spoke to me he sat on a bed and looked down onto the floor and mechanically keeping a cigar alight by short puffs now and again. His voice was low, and, like most of the other men, halting. He mentioned that the responsibility of a man in charge of a company, as he is, was fearful—if any little thing went wrong it might mess up the whole of the line for miles, and the Germans may counter attack at your particular point any moment of the day or night. With most of your non-coms and officers dead there was nobody to rely upon and so it was left to himself to be on the alert the whole time. Then, the whole time there were high explosive shells falling around in all directions. One moment there would be a party of men crouching down against a wall jokingly picking out where the next shell will land and who is the next man to be blown up. Capt Middleton looks on at them, passes a word or two, and moves on. Almost immediately he is told that a man is knocked out; he goes back and there are several of the little party scattered about, the wounded are patched up and after separating the 'brain from the guts' the identification disc and pay book are found and then all hands (although many of the dead man's mates fall back and cannot help) throw the body up over the parapet to strengthen it. Oftimes a shell will throw a body back into the trenches after it has been lying there for some days and is an awful proposition to handle. The miserable part about it, says Syd, is that one can do absolutely nothing to help the man. A trench in front or one just behind might be ever so much safer, but he cannot move his men a yard, his instructions were to come to this point, and to that the officer must cling and wait, wait and wait. An attack might give us 400 yards of ground easily, but no, it cannot be done without orders from behind so the men stick on and on waiting their turn to die. There seems no other alternative at all, but die one must. SAM was practically buried five times in one day, his stars were shot away from his shoulder on one side, the heel of his boot was dinted and his foot wrenched, a piece of shell penetrated his side.

And worst of all was a huge lump of dirt that knocked him down and shattered his mind for a few moments. He thought his time had come to die. Day and night there was no relief; the carnage and toll was more than man could ever realise. Dante and his inferno is a huge joke. It is the real Hell.

There have been terrific periods of bombardments at intervals today and as I write 9.30pm it's an awful din the guns are making and I weep for the poor fellows dying without a fighting chance, merely sheep at Flemington,

Sydney, waiting their turn.[1] This military work is all wait, wait and more waiting, but at Gallipoli it was the proper business and we were all satisfied.

August 9: I have been through one of the most trying days of my life. It has been a day of utter misery. A day that exposes a man's absolute weakness and uselessness. Capt Middleton told me only yesterday of his sense of weakness when his men were being blown out of their trenches and the others just sitting around waiting their turn to come and he could not do a single thing to help them. It came home during a rush of wounded this afternoon. I went into the shed where the wounded are placed during a rush, also the men waiting for evacuation. The shed is very hot inside, so I eased the blankets off a number of the men until I came to one chap— GA Webb, 14th Battalion. He had a compound fracture of the right leg, and by his colour had evidently lost a lot of blood; he was in great pain, and although his chest was hot and his face perspiring freely, his hands and feet were stone cold. I fanned him, now and again rubbing the palms of his hands, but I could see the chap slowly sinking. I asked a doctor if he could not do something. We then put him into bed and he was alive at 6 o'clock but, God, he would have died in an hour if left in my puny hands. I went outside and there was a ghastly looking case lying by quite conscious. I spoke to him and found he wanted to spit and clear his throat. I lifted his head and turned him on his side; he spat out some blood, and the poor fellow's lungs were penetrated, that was clear.

Mackenzie of the 47th Battalion was his name, a man with very prominent front teeth. I found that my hand was covered in blood. I then turned him again and had a look and to my surprise and horror there was an undressed hole several inches big and every time he breathed the blood just gushed out. Again a doctor was brought, but what use a doctor? He could do nothing; nobody could do anything right from the very start. But then the extraordinary part of it is that this man had been through first the regimental doctor, the dressing station at Becourt and now has been passed through the 13th Field Ambulance and was lying ready for evacuation before so huge and dangerous a wound was even found out and dressed.

---

1   Flemington was the site of Sydney's slaughter yards and abattoir.

They say the King of England is expected to visit our front. I know he won't, but I should love him to have an opportunity of seeing what I see. The paths are swept and flowers are placed about for him.

August 10: At 10am the rain ceased and definite news came along that the King was to visit the hospital in the afternoon; needless to say every available man and woman around the RAMC outfit were busy making things look pretty. Taking carpets on floor, setting up bunches of flowers and polishing the floor. At 2.45pm the streets were lined with Australians on either side. The men were not armed and wore only a belt which surprised me very much. The King drove through the street by the side of General Birdwood at a rapid rate. Sir Douglas Haig and the Prince of Wales wearing three stars on his shoulder were there. There followed a party of lean looking officers of all ranks making in all perhaps twelve men. I was too busy getting pictures to take much notice of the party going by, but I had a good look at the Prince while he and some six others waited outside the hospital. When the King came out after about 20 minutes inside, he looked very thin and troubled like with a beautiful red nose that looked almost suspicious. He was taller than I expected to find him; this probably was due to his company being small. Inside the hospital the King spoke to none of the patients nor did he have a consoling word for those lonely nurses working amongst those awful cases. The impression left by the King was very weak indeed. Inside they were all very disappointed, in fact, hurt. Lieut Col Walsh was not introduced to the King and he was very hurt at the English Surgeon General for doing the whole of the work.

August 11: With the King's visit . . . came the rumour that the 1st Division counted him and Birdwood out (which I of course don't believe). The King with General Birdwood by his side drove at a fast pace through the Australian lined streets of Warloy without any outward show or feeling of pride. Yes, he saluted and that kind of thing, but the whole show was miserably formal and cold. Our men are greatly disappointed, many exceedingly annoyed. It is the first time they have seen a King and they wanted to see him stand up and wave his cap and his hands to show them he is sorry for all the suffering they have been through and that he appreciates their efforts in the interests of the Empire. In the hospital he walked about without a word of cheer to the patients or to the nurses. Better by far had he not called at all. He might suit English ideas but he won't do our democratic Australians. He was too reserved and sober.

August 13: After the service, General Birdwood in company with General Forsyth gave out some 11 war decorations. I thought he should have pinned them onto their chests, but he only put them in their hands and in shaking hands said a few kind words to each of them. They were mostly officers. The ceremony finished, General Birdwood commenced an address—in plain words that seemed to carry right to the furthest edge of the square, in soft tones and without any exertion at all. He started off saying that the King was worried that he did not see more of the Australian troops. He particularly wished to see the 1st Division after the good work they had done, but time would not permit. He then went on to describe the position on the Somme front. He said the French had been doing splendid work on the right of the British front. Although many men present might wonder why the Australians were not allowed to advance more rapidly it was simply because it would be of no advantage at the moment.

'And although your losses have been heavy, every possible precaution has been taken to make the losses as light as possible and nothing has been left undone in your interests.'

He continued, every man of you has done remarkably well, especially the stretcher bearers and the runners. If 2000 Victoria Crosses were handed to [him] for distribution, not one man could he give one to that had not thoroughly earned it, times over and again.

'I might as well tell you,' he went on, 'that there is a whole lot of work to be done yet; we must keep at those enemies of ours all day and all night and every day and every night; there must be no letting up; we must fight on and continuous; there is to be no rest for you boys.'

The 2nd Division did very well indeed during their rather long stay in the front line. The artillery let them down by failing to cut the wire which was covered by long grass. (I think Birdwood was just excuse-making here as a line of long grass denotes barbed wire itself.) Anyhow the infantry had to return, went on General Birdwood. There was another very remarkable happening, says he, just at the moment of a portion of the 4th Division taking over from the 2nd Division: the Germans made a very determined counter-attack and had it not been for one of the 2nd Division machine gun officers who refused to leave, or be relieved, the position may have been lost. So you can see very clearly my men that there is still room for individual initiative.

'Now my boys, I want to thank you very deeply, for the splendid work you have already accomplished, and although we will have a whole lot of work yet to do, hard work too, I fear, the German is no longer a menace to us. He will not stand and fight a hand to hand fight. Against the 2nd Division the German infantry were ordered to charge but on approaching our trenches they threw away their rifles and holding their hands high above their heads came running up to our trenches; our men withheld their fire and waited until they got near them, and at once threw every available bomb into their midst; they turned and fled towards their own trenches, but their own artillery fired onto them and naturally they were in a very bad way. It seems a rather cold and cruel way of doing things but we've been caught before by taking prisoners and then have our positions rushed from in front and the prisoners turn around on us so they only have themselves to blame, we won't now take their surrenders. You boys must be careful and not get caught. Fight him all the time!

'I know that you have hearts of gold, pure gold, and I know you will achieve more success.' 'I thank you boys very much indeed,' was his concluding remark.

General Birdwood displayed excellent tact in his little heart to heart talk. It could not be called a speech, just a quiet and confidential chat. General Birdwood brought a round of cheers when he mentioned the good work of the stretcher bearers. Also a round of good laughter when in referring to the poor fighting qualities of the German infantry he said that our boys had them so quiet now that it was only necessary to look up over the trench and whistle, at the same time beckon with the finger calling them in and they come right up at the double and sit down at your feet.

August 18: I have just heard that Andy Elliott, one of my original stretcher bearers on Gallipoli, has been blown to pieces. He was in a dug out with seven other fellows and four of them were killed outright. This brings our casualty list up to a fairly long one. One case, Fitzgerald, was most pathetic: he was suffering from shell shock and was quite insane, and with his two hands held up, eyes wide open and staring, he cried all the time, howling loudly with each gun report or flash of a gun. These shell shock cases are awful and very plentiful. The fellows are quite mad, or sometimes their reason is alright but their hands shake: it's impossible to hold anything or to find their own mouths. The legs also tremble and shake so that they at times cannot walk without assistance.

August 22: At 11am we left the trenches and the dressing station and are now camped on the 'Brickfields' on the safety side of Albert, but by no means out of gunfire. I am very pleased indeed to see the last of the Pozières front, not so much for myself as for the good men we have out there dying every few minutes.

The 2nd Division are now in front amidst the heavy shell fire and death. My heart goes out to them. I will not be at all content until the whole of the Australian forces are withdrawn from the Somme front. Of course things may be just as bad wherever we go. Be that as it may, the Somme front and its murder is so well brought home and lies so heavily upon hearts and minds that a change, even if it be no better, will still be a change. It's a wonder that I had not previously mentioned the matter of rats about these places. At Becourt you could see them running across the roads at all hours of the night. There were thousands of them.

One mile from Albert with some 20 men I had one of the most enjoyable swims I yet have had in a large lake off the River Ancre. The water was clear and deep and the men enjoyed it more than men ever enjoyed a swim and a wash.

August 24: We marched out of Warloy by 9.30am and turned northwards in the direction of Doullens. Now it is quite clear as to our intended direction. We've heard a whole lot about going up to Flanders again, but it seemed so good that after our punishments of late I thought the news much too good. Now my heart is easy, but it will not be clear until after the 2nd and 4th Divisions of Australians are withdrawn from that murderous failure on the Somme.

August 25: Two years ago today since I signed on in the Army. I don't feel at all enthusiastic about it either, as it has been 24 months of isolation and bondage. Not that I regret it for a moment, the opposite, in fact; I'm mighty pleased to know that I've done as much for my country as the gods running the 'show' will permit of me. I've just battled quietly along doing as instructed mechanically. One side of my mental being has become machine-like and very hardened. Yet through it all I believe I've not altered in habit or in manner.

Six privates have gone from our unit to the 1st Brigade as one-star men, five to the 1st Battalion. Captain Lee said he would send my name in for a commission, but I don't think it fair for an ambulance man to run over the top of the hard-done-by infantryman, and again our men will need a lot of training before they will be of much use. The infantrymen from other battalions should be given the positions.

September 2: I went on to the Picture Show. There are three of them in town, and I enjoyed the show right enough although there was a love contest so thrillingly and sobbingly contested that I was displeased, more by jealousy than anything else possibly. The piano and a violin follow the films pleasingly along. The place, however, was very close, no ventilation whatever, and the fellows would smoke until the air was putrid. It was a treat to breathe the fresh air at the conclusion of the performance.

September 6: Today has been a great day, so delightfully soft and sun shining so innocently that one would hardly think it ever rained, or was disagreeable in Flanders. There is a cricket match going on. I had no particular reason for going down in the direction of Mont de Cats although the French girl down that way who allowed herself to be kissed last Sunday may have been an inducement.

September 11: It has been a dusty, misty kind of day but a cricket match between B and C sections passed the day splendidly. It is my first cricket match. B batted first and totalled 53 on a rather bad wicket. C looked promising at three down for 30. I went in at four down and was still in at eight down for 35 runs. The game seemed lost but the unexpected happened: the bowler sent along a lovely ball for me and, as the side's only chance rested in my hands, I opened out and hit him for four. This was repeated four times and the game was saved midst great jubilation. It certainly was a remarkable finish. My score was 22 bowled. Our officers all take a very keen interest in both football and cricket, and everything runs along splendidly. It is in a position like the present that one notices the even temperament of a man who is a follower of sport. Absolutely the pick of the unit are the fellows who take a lively interest in sporting matters.

September 12: I have just finished reading 'Canadian Born'. This brings back to me the fact Australia has never yet turned out a decent good reading book that in any way portrayed Australian life and characters. Steele Rudd[2] is positive nonsense and must do a young country a whole lot of harm if read in other lands, but I am pleased to think that few people would ever attempt to waste time on such poor stuff in other lands when better reading is at hand. Most other Australian writers work in raging bushfires, terrible droughts, floods, vice and a raid by blood-thirsty blacks or robberies by bush-rangers. Anyhow I sometimes think that the Australian mind is of a morbid and melancholy temperament, or an upright clean and pleasant theme would stand out in their writings. It is high time that the Australian knew Australia better too. It is literature like 'Canadian Born' that puts the Hall Mark of confidence into an outward people concerning the future. The good and the patriotism of the settlers have a great influence on intending settlers far away.

September 15: Tomorrow is our big Sports Day. The men are all very keen on the races and great doings are expected. There are a number of jumping events for the horses and although they are a poor lot of animals, the galloping and schooling they have been getting the past few weeks has done a surprising amount of good. I went into Poperinghe tonight to get some prizes for the events. There was very little to choose from so we finished up with some different sizes in electric torches and a handful of cigarette cases.

September 16: After a big day's work our sports program was carried through very successfully. Excitement ran at fever heat during many of the events whilst every contest was keenly fought out. First the Australians beat the Canadians [in the tug-of-war], then the Scotch pulled the English team over. The final pull between Scotland and Australia was a great go: first one

---

2   Steele Rudd, an Australian writer, was best known for the book *On Our Selection*. Rudd was the pseudonym of Arthur Hoey Davis.

side and then the other held the advantage. Cheering on the respective sides stirred interest to a great pitch. For minutes neither side wavered, then the greater endurance and determination of the Colonials became manifest and ended in a glorious win for our team of stalwarts and the crowd going wild with glee, throwing up caps and hats with tremendous shouting.

The Victoria Cross, Gretna Green and Point to Point races on horseback were very good events and put everybody in splendid humour. The tug-of-war on horseback was good, also the cock-fighting. In the latter there were no rules; one rider had to be clearly thrown or it was fight on. Most of the bouts were most vigorously contested and caused much merriment. Bert Boardman and I ran out the winners. I took no part in the foot races which were strongly contested and went very much in 'C' section's favour, Higgens winning 100 and 440. The high jump was a keenly fought out event— Boardman, Jacobs and myself cleared at 4 ft 7 in. Jacobs was the only one to clear the next rise. I threw myself over the last jump landing right on my side to the consternation of the spectators.

September 17: I went out at 7.30am in the wagon for six miles and enjoyed the crisp morning air as well as taking a whole lot of interest in the folk coming and going from Church. There are a few nicely developed girls about here; most of them are heavily built, thick ankles, oversized shoulders and big necked, due to their annual labours. But many of the girls are fond of strongly contrasting stockings, perhaps a dark skirt, blue shoes and yellow stockings. They certainly catch the eye and after all I expect that is always the wearer's chief mission in such stockings.

September 22: I am being bothered by the fellows around to put in an application for a commission. But to me it is not honourable or fair to apply for a position of honour; these positions to my mind should be given to selected men, or men actually asked by Headquarters to fill out a form. For a person to boast himself into a position of that kind is intolerable. I may yet do so but it will be hurtful to me to lower myself.

September 27: Had I seen Ypres without the war raging through and around it there would have been an entirely different effect with the surroundings. No civilian remains in Ypres; this in itself speaks plainly of the danger. But

I did see a notice saying the YMCA was just down a lane. Here no doubt was the only store in Ypres. The town nevertheless was by no means deserted as there were hundreds of both English and Australian troops about. There was no house fit to billet in, but as far as I could see the men made use of cellars and used large numbers of sandbags for protection. There was one strange scene, one which I did not take very much notice of at the time but now it comes back and puzzles me. At the military barracks there did not seem to be quite so much wreckage lying about. In front was a guard lined up of 300 men while the square inside the fence and the street about was crowds of men. The puzzle is, how is it that military barracks shelter so many soldiers and are not shelled? Possibly the cheek of so doing puts the German off his guard, as it really seems an impossible matter; on the other hand it may be a kind of mutual understanding. You don't shell our camp and we won't shell yours, like Armentières and Lille.

Chapter 14

BLIGHTY, 1916

—⟶⊰•⊱⟵—

September 30: I got several different fellows to call me this morning to make sure that I would not sleep in. The train left the siding at 6.25am and away I went to Hazebrouck, feeling a doubtful kind of a sensation as to whether it could really be true: my going to England after living so long away from civilisation and looking forward so keenly to a few days of freedom and peace. England is only for eight days, but what a change and how much it really does mean to a mentally starved and grooved individual roving the hills of Anzac, the desert of Egypt and the terrors of the Somme.

October 1: A little wait on the wharf and we were loaded onto the vessel *Queen Mary*—a regular channel boat. At Folkestone we were soon aboard the train bound for London. I nearly cried for joy as the people, children as well as men and women of all ages, came to their comfortable cottage doors and waved their white handkerchiefs or threw kisses. It was all so wholesome and so pretty to be welcomed in such a quiet, but effective way.

Nearing London without a stop I began to think it was the same dear old sleepy England that I knew four years ago. Hardly a romantic country but a solid country, slow to move but very effective.

At Victoria Station, 5 o'clock, there was a large crowd of people waiting; we Australians marched by in six lines of four men without any cheering, but much appreciation and joy was showing in the eyes of all. I was watching the crowd never expecting to be recognised or waited for, but to my astonishment two old friends of mine—Mabel and Gertie Williams—stepped from the crowd and greeted me. I fell out of the lines and could hardly talk to them I was so embarrassed. Anyway I told them I was going up to the Headquarters at Horseferry Road and away I went. At Headquarters my pack was taken charge of and I drew 8 pounds on my pay book. In a taxi car I tried to find the girls but failing to do so I ordered to run over to the Imperial Hotel, Russell Square. Oh what an inspiring drive it was, along Victoria Street, and behold there stood before me my old friend and guiding point—Westminster Abbey.

Along Southampton Row the car raced with ease and grace right to the door of the Imperial Hotel. I thought I saw the hall porter's face colour a little with disappointment as I stumbled out of the carriage, poorly clad and with my worldly possessions, a small haversack and a rainproof cape on my arm. A bell boy about ten years of age showed me up to my room and ordered a bath to be ready. The maid came and told me that it was alright. I sallied forth and found a plunge bath filled with warm water, a bath mat spread on the floor, a clean towel over the back of the chair with soap and brushes laid out.

I got busy on the finest bath I've had for a very long time, the water being so soft and clean. A cold shower and I was a new man again. With that bath I believe I washed off all traces of the roughness and laxity of my two years of camp life; my mind was awake and thrown right back to the days when I was a free man and familiar with big Hotel life and the ways and manners of the city. I dressed, but alas in the same old military clothes frayed and creased. Oh how I longed for a suit of civilian clothes so that I could be a man again and care nothing and not be reminded by my own reflection that I am still merely a soldier. I went downstairs, had my boots cleaned and then took a taxi out to Clapham to try and find Mrs Perry and Gertie Williams whom I missed at the appointed place when the train came in.

Ten minutes later I noticed the hotels were open by the dull light showing through the posted doors. I asked the driver to put up at a decent house as I wanted a drink. I am back in civilisation again where there are no restrictions upon what kind of liquor a man can have. Oh no, the hotel was free for me to choose anything from the shelves and rows of bottles. Like a flash it came to me: my old favourite appetiser, the delight of many a before dinner drink after a good ramble and fight with the surf in dear old Manly. The drink that softens one's palate, loosens the tongue and brightens the eye.

I called again on the driver to stop as I was frantic for a reminder of old and good times, a drink that revives and recalls moments of happiness and cheer. The car stopped; I asked the driver in to have a drink. He consented but at the door told me that no treating was allowed and that I would have to give him the money and then we would both have to pay for our own. Inside there was a comfortable bar room nicely lit and a fine healthy woman behind the bar—a fair picture to gaze upon in my dull senses of woman's brighter qualities. The driver had a pint of half and half. I stood erect and called quietly but firmly in a proud and confident air for a gin and vermouth, and lo it was delicious, it cooled my throat and quickened my pulse. I was tempted to ask for another but no, I could not spoil the effect, the thrill of that one short but life-giving glass. We drove on and with a whole lot of guiding and enquiring for directions we arrived at the house to find nobody was at home.

I returned to the Imperial Hotel, paid the driver nine shillings and went in to dinner. The room was nearly full with a fashionable crowd. I moved unconcernedly down the room to a vacant seat and standing beside it for a minute waiting for the head waitress to consent to my sitting there. As no notice was taken of me I sat down with a good but somewhat poorly cooked meal. I had a bottle of Bass and got along fairly well.

At the office I was told there was a letter for me and to my disgust the Perrys had been and now gone home to await my coming to the house at Clapham where I had already been. This time I took the tube and went out to them. We sat around talking unsettled and unenthusiastically as things were not running in harmony. At 11.50pm we went out, the four of us, and watched the searchlights in dozens hovering criss-cross wise through the sky. Away in the distance we saw a sheet of flame and the girls were sure it was a Zeppelin down. A little later the cheers that filled the streets and travelled from one house and another showed the girls that their guess was right and another zeppelin was brought down in London. To bed at 1am and slept soundly until morning.

October 2: At the Bank of England I met G Williams and we went away down to Piccadilly for lunch at Slaters where I was disappointed but as it was nearly 2pm perhaps it was our fault that the grub was not so pleasing. After lunch we went down to the Hippodrome to the Revue 'Flying Colours'. The show was not the kind of thing I most care for. The girls, some hundred or more of them, were not up to expectations. Either their features or their figures failed them right along.

October 8: At Charing Cross I got a taxi to the Anzac Buffet, where I met Drummond, Wilby and Yeadon, and we had tea and cake. When I put my hand into my pocket for money I got blown up; the lady said prettily: 'Oh you men! You are at home now; just let us treat you for once. This is your home free for you to come and to go with gladness and freedom.'

On the Strand later I saw dozens and dozens of night girls wandering about.

October 9: Lunch at Frascates, Oxford Street. Lunch 4/6 Wine SA 2/- Coffee 6d waiter 1 shilling. Total 8/-

I walked into the place with the air and confidence of an old habitué. The cleanliness and glitter of the place nearly overcame me, but on I went looking around at the elaborate ground floor with all its pomp and exclusiveness and up the stairs to the balcony, more exclusive. Nobody took much notice of me outside of the people sitting around at the tables and they gazed at me in curious wonderment as I strolled along, head erect, hat in hand, proud and reserved even if threadbare and torn. At last a waiter offered me a seat in one of the two large recesses at a table with two seats. I gave my hat and coat (a long light cape that looked like a bullfighter's cloak). I sat down under the idle gaze of many, and to assure them that I was right and invited no interruption I got up and turned the opposite empty chair about.

I chose 'Table d'Hôte' menu and away we went, starting with fresh oysters. On looking over the wine card I saw South Australian Port, and at once ordered a small bottle. As 'South Australia' was written in big letters I kept turning the label around so that any who wished could read the class of wine I chose out of more than 110 different brands. It was a great meal, the memory of which will keep good and long.

October 10: Booked two seats at a Music Hall near Victoria Station. The show was decidedly poor. I slept close to the station so as to catch the early train without trouble, and went to bed feeling very gloomy indeed, as there were many things I wanted to do but had no time to do them and it might be a very long time before I see England again.

October 12: Last night our train reached Hazebrouck at 1 o'clock. Most of the men went into billets for the night, but I got a 'wink' and slept in a railway carriage fairly comfortable until 8am. I went into the village for breakfast, the usual omelette and bread and butter. A walk around and back to the station to catch the 10 o'clock train to Poperinghe. At noon I strolled back into camp to be asked and pestered with anxious questions regarding my trip and doings. I was in a poor mood to talk, as in coming back to camp I felt as though I was losing something very dear to me, and had little to look forward to. The homecoming was hard to swallow and I felt that I wanted to be left alone.

October 17: The great event of a restful day was the voting on conscription for Australia. There is, however, very little difference of opinion about the matter, and but few voted other than 'yes'. I voted 'yes' not out of any jealous feeling for the chaps at home, but because I firmly believe every country should be able to call up its manhood in defence of its birthright, not perhaps against the will of the person but simply to ensure the most advantageous working of the country's welfare while the war is going on. The volunteer system to my mind is a ghastly failure because men come away who would be of more value sitting at home.

We have made a great mistake in not choosing and picking our fighting forces right from the very start: there would be an easy going systematic flow of men from all ranks and classes thoroughly balanced and ready for the worst. Conscription such as France and Germany has tolerated for years I would decry with all my strength in Australia, but conscription in the time of war is absolutely essential.

The extreme Labor men with ideas that all industry, in fact everything, should be nationalised and run by the Government is the chief objector to conscription, and after all does not nationalisation and conscription mean actually the same thing? I would not vote for conscription if I thought that it meant sending more of our men over to die. I believe even our politicians would not foolishly throw away our little bit of population recklessly and foolishly.

October 18: The evidence shows clearly that the Somme is to be our destination. Nobody is upset or worried about it, although we know it will be certain death or injury to 50 per cent or more of our forces. Our battalions are not yet up to strength and a survey of the situation seems to disclose a scheme of wanton destruction to send our ragged men back there again.

While having tea some 12th Infantry chaps came along and in their own manner cried down conscription as well as expressing a hope that no more Australians would ever be brought into a hole and be hacked about like they have been. 'Oh no, very few votes in our company will favour conscription,' one of them said. I am very sorry indeed that I did not find out how long these men have been on active service. I fancy they are only new arrivals. New men mostly squeak.

October 19: In the river stream nearby, our men have been using bombs to blow up fish. I don't know if they had any luck or not, but the men who would go into the water today deserve fish of the best and finest quality. This afternoon, I heard cheers. I thought there must be some unusual happenings going on over there. At the risk of losing my tea, I slopped across the low lying field to the rustic bridge spanning the narrow river. Here the cause of so much hilarity and hearty vents of enthusiasm was easily found to be encasing a football match.

The teams were from the 12th Battalion A Company versus the Bombers. The surroundings were almost Australian in their appearance. The playing field was roomy and the grass delightful both in its softness and colour. A rough hedge of hawthorn and fruit bearing blackberry bushes protected one side and end, a row of tall majestic trees towered close to the other side and the watercress banks of the river framed off the end. Some cows browsing in the field continually called, and added a bush effect that must have been an unconscious undercurrent to urge on these valiant athletes to fight relent-lessly for the honour, the prestige of each particular section.

Tomorrow they will be en route for the Somme and the greatest Hell ever thought of, greater even than man's imagination is capable of conceiving. But what care they for the morrow, let's first find out who are the best football-ers while there is still time in hand. So along the field the ball travelled with speed and precision, first up one side and down the other, across the field and back again, each piece of good play being awarded its due recompense from the keen supporters. The kicking, fielding and marking was surpris-ingly good. Goals came very slowly, so keen and buoyed up was the defence. No player dared make a mistake: in his mess he would obtain no peace for weeks should he fail to keep up his end.

No international match was more keenly fought out, and as the defeated side came off the field their friends went over and sympathised in the manner of true sportsmen and noble soldiers. They had played a good game. At the bloody Somme any day now both conqueror and vanquished will fight a differ-ent fight where rules do not govern the struggle and God alone is the referee.

October 30: The only difference between this and the past few days on the Somme is that we have had more rain and wind than usual. How awful it will be up over those horse tracks with this rain soaking into the stiff ruts and feet tracks to a depth of over two feet in places. The poor infantry man can get but little to eat as the wagons cannot possibly get up to him. The pack horses and mules break their legs and get bogged so tightly that they are often shot.

October 31: Coming in with patients is the most trying task of the whole realm of war. A man can hit out on his own in most branches without a thought or a care but when it comes to having some two or four badly wounded men under your care over a log road, or what we call a corduroy road, a man feels the pain of every jolt from the whole of the groaning men. It is awful. I would not, if I had my own way in the matter, travel one hundred yards over that awful road with a body injury for pounds and pounds. Yet here was I today doing four trips and each time I had a bad case and a journey of two miles to do. Tears filled my eyes as those men were being bounced six inches and more up from their stretchers as well as being buffeted by the side roll and banged upon the axle. It was cruel, and all I could do was to hold onto the fellows and try to steady the bouncing a little. Be an infantry man, be anything at all, but run an ambulance wagon over these roads and feel the pain of all the occupants combined. It so disheartens a man like myself who has taken the war over serious right from the very commencement.

November 3: 'Trench feet' are reported to be received and treated as self-inflicted wounds, but seeing that the fellows have no possible chance of keeping their feet dry, this seems impossible. Our men came down here from Belgium with holes in the uppers of their boots and the soles worn out and no new boots obtainable and now they talk of 'trench feet' being due to neglect on the part of the men. I agree if the men took their boots off and dried and rubbed their feet there would be less trouble with the feet, but it is nonsense to speak of them as being self-inflicted. Our men are suffering very badly too, as those 'trench feet' are most painful. The appearance is very much the same as after a person has had their hands in water for an excessive length of time; when they take their boots off they can't get them on again.

November 13: The dishonesty and love for thieving in the Army is striking, but with the transport sections, particularly of Australian units, it's a horror. It seems no man can be reasonably trusted with his mate's rations. Every man for himself seems to be the motto.

November 14: I have just returned from the prisoners' cage where I found 19 young and well built Germans enclosed. There is something strikingly interesting about these Germans, and numbers of English and Australian troops stand around looking at them and eager to get a few words of conversation with them. Two of the party speak English a little. In reply to one of our officers, a German said: 'Well, I thought we were winning the war up to yesterday.'

There is something to admire about these Germans: they move about or stand up with a composure that speaks openly for their strong spirit and air of careless independence. They address our men as 'comrade' and butt in for a cigarette or to have one lighted with all the confidence, right to do so and earnestness of a man amongst his most exclusive friends. They stroll about jauntily with one or both hands deep into their side pockets and set up posing attitudes when standing around. They indeed seem unembarrassed by their captivity and all apparently carefree and cool individuals.

Chapter 15

INFANTRYMAN, 1916–17

November 16: Well, great things have happened today. A change has come about that has altered my military career materially. Major Bamsden of our unit has recommended myself amongst four others for a commission in the 1st Battalion. Following upon his appointment I saw the Colonel this morning at 11.30. He asked me a number of questions which seemed to satisfy him and then asked me if I thought I could command and lead a body of men. My reply was: 'On condition that I knew my subject, object and work, which I doubted without first having some training.'

He checked me at once, stating he was there to judge that matter. This afternoon three of us—Woollams, Dingle and myself—were sent for to see the Brigadier. General Smyth, in few words of questioning, said he would accept the Colonel's recommendation and hoped I would be successful and rise to promotion rapidly.

So tonight matters stand greatly altered. Tomorrow I go into Amiens and do some shopping before being called to face the Battalion. I do not rejoice over the matter. It may be honour, credit and all that sort of thing, but then my chance comes only through the number of casualties and the demand there is at present for officers. Anybody really can get one, but I take a whole lot of satisfaction from the fact that I was sent for.

I know the danger of the undertaking full well. Eleven officers were shot out of the 1st Battalion during their few days in the trenches of Longueval, some wounded of course. Out of 36 bombers, only six now answer the roll call. I would not have accepted the position only for the fact that I came away to do the bidding of my country. I came to help in any work that those above me saw fit to give me, and now I graciously accept a position of grave danger, and in doing so I have no fear but that I am doing the right thing, and I hold no presentiments on the matter whatever as my motto stands: 'Whatever is, is best'.

November 18: I half expected the 1st Battalion to send for me today, not that I am over anxious or fretting in the slightest about my new position. It will all work out well I am quite certain. Some of the fellows say I'm a damn fool and all the rest of it, as we all know how officers are cut up, but this I can't help. I've been called upon and willingly I go. Never mind the outcome; if it's only a wound I will get the best possible treatment. Oh but it is a nonsense to talk about getting hit. As I have often said: 'If there's a bullet or a shell with my name and address on it, it's no use dodging it.'

November 25: I have had another day in Amiens. Lunch at the Belfort Hotel was a delightful meal. It was a charmingly cooked and served dinner of full French courses. The total cost was 22 francs—10 for lunch, 10 for wine and two for the girl waiter. There were a whole lot of French and English officers about the room but no notice was taken of one another. There is no saluting going on in the streets to speak of at all. I certainly never saluted one man. The Frenchmen seem to salute their officers in a quiet manner when meeting in the cafes or barber shops where the ranker is just as much at home as the officers.

We have heard a whole lot about the large brothel area that exists in Amiens, but after many miles I could find none at all. A few professional women yes, but nothing to speak of. Amiens has many cobble stone paths and the walking made our feet sore.

I brought back some snails and on warming them over the fire in the shell picked them out and ate them. The effect was indeed disappointing as they were like a piece of gristle. I don't think they are chewed but swallowed like an oyster. These anyhow seemed too dry to swallow with ease or satisfaction.

November 29: I learnt this morning first by the congratulations of the fellows and then by enquiring at the orderly room that my commission has gone through and dates from November 25. But why I have not been called upon to go with the battalion worries me very much. But then it is their own lookout and I expect they will know better than to give me work to do that I don't understand. I hope, however, that the delay means going to a school, which is almost more than I can expect. Some fellows got three months' schooling in England however.

December 6: I saw the parade away this morning and had a few words with the men on shaving each day, having their hair cut and keeping themselves generally tidy. It is my first lecture to them. It seems that we don't go into the line. I am sorry if it is to be as I want to show my frame up over that parapet with the rest of them and let them see that I've got courage. It's remarkable how our Australians stick to their officers when they have proven their gameness. They hold off until they see a man properly tested and then they love him, but if he fails them he is right out wide in their estimation.

December 8: At 3pm a message came through for me to report at Battalion Headquarters, Mametz, at once with 11 men. By 6pm we walked the six kilometres and reported in by 7.35pm. The roads were wet and muddy but the moonlight was splendid although it had the effect of showing up the shell riddled dead and twisted trees like dim and grim skeletons.

December 9: A good night's sleep and I suppose I must be thankful or, rather, feel it is a kind of honour to get a doze down on the floor of Battalion Headquarters. There were bunks for nobody, not even chairs to sit upon. But the half round huts were good and comfortable and there are hundreds of them about. There is deep and nasty mud everywhere to break the comfort of the huts as you can't step outside.

I have to report into the 1st Division Headquarters and go with a party of 21 men and three NCOs up to the line to put down some dugouts. I think they are to be deep and large ones like the Germans'. The weather is wet and cold and slimy and my zone is certain to be under heavy shell fire. An inquiry into men reported missing is being held in the front half of the room, and one man they are calling for evidence about is PT Richards AE [no relation]. On hearing this name naturally I started up.

December 11: I was late in moving off with my party of 24 men and joining up with the 2nd and 4th Battalion parties. The road was very mucky and slushy all the way into Bazentin. We put up at what is called the Sugar Mill but why I don't know as there is nothing about to warrant the name. Anyway, it is, or was, a big building very much battered about and the only building to be seen in Bazentin village. Instead of walking into the shell shattered building and taking possession of the place and the maze of German dugouts that go with it, we found the 11th Battalion in possession. So now the trouble is going to be to get the men out and to install our own men. In our party are three officers, including myself.

The moment one moves towards the firing line the worse the roads become, and the more numerous the road cleaning parties. It would be very humorous if it were not so damnable cruel to see these sun tanned men from the home of bright sunny weather, struggling with scoops and brooms to bale or drain the roads, and coughing bitterly.

December 12: As we bumped along that corduroy road, the biting wind blew straight down the road into our faces, stinging severely. There seemed no way of avoiding punishment, the big flakes would land on the corner of the eye, and blind it. Those snowflakes got right up under the broad brim on my hat and also did their best to fill up the collar. It was only a distance of 1½ miles and took us, perhaps, only 30 minutes to do the journey, but it seemed hours and during which time the whole country became totally clean white and transformed the desolate aspect of this battered country to one of much charm. The gaunt skeletons of trees that stood up boldly in the disfigure- ment of the skyline were now wrapped in a mantle of poor whiteness, and lent attractiveness of a weird and unaccountable nature to the strange scene.

We succeeded today in turning the 11th Battalion out and putting our own men into the underground passages of the connected dugouts and also into the cellars of the building. These 11th Battalion people simply bustled their way into this place. They were not sent here nor had any authority to be here but in typical Australian style saw the chance of a decent place to settle down in and they grabbed it!

December 13: There seems to be an awful feeling of depression concerning the state of the war just now. Men who were confident we were winning easily are now shaking their heads and asking one another 'will we be in the final peace conference at all, or will Germany have it all their own way?'

There is no doubt we have paid heavily for our successes on the Somme and now that the enemy have given us a display of their power in overcoming Romania with such rapidity and apparent ease our chances look very gloomy indeed.

The Australian people have shown clearly they are sick of the whole business and now that the English people are being pinched there is an inclination to squeak right through Great Britain, while France is nearly depleted of man power. There is clearly something lacking over in the Russian area. Yes, we Allies are fast weakening and show signs of almost impossible attempts at organisation. There are gaps right throughout our service. Gaps that make one stop and glare in dazed wonderment. There are days and days wasted waiting for materials. For instance here we are with a party of 80 and three officers and this is the fourth day we have been sitting on the job. Everybody complains of the same thing, and nobody bothers much as it 'belongs to the other department', so we sit around unconcerned and wait, wait, wait. I seem to have been doing nothing else since 1914.

December 15: Tonight the conversation drifted between two officers, 11th and 4th Battalions, on their attacks and the awful mistakes that occur. Whole Battalions get lost out in 'no man's land' and shoot one another. Patrols get into bombing range of one another and kill their own men. One said the 5th Battalion were positively slaughtered at Flanders. Not only were they let down by the Tommies on either side, but they failed to get orders and went on to their death. Some 9000 Australian casualties were reported and nothing gained whereas the charge was a glorious success and would have broken the German line to hell had there been any support for the men. But no, they were the only Division to attack and away they went with great dash only to meet the concentrated fire of the Germans for miles around. They say it is positively the worst mistake since the war started. These mistakes have been many and gigantic.

The stories of these officers would have been humorous were it not for the seriousness and the loss of life entailed. Yet we did laugh, we laughed when the story of the wounded German being buried live was told. A fellow came along and saw the earth moving as it was being thrown out of a trench. The sergeant's attention was drawn to it, and he coolly remarked: 'Yes sir, I know there's a German b— under there, but we didn't bother about him.'

December 17: The ups and downs of one's ideas on military matters is strange and liable to rapid fluctuation. The men who were last week asking themselves whether we would lose the war or not, are today gleefully declaring a victory, taking the German peace terms as a sign of their weakness and a good chance of the damn business being over before long. I still sit stolidly on the fence waiting, ever waiting.

December 18: A fellow officer today tells of how in the rush to dig a trench at Pozières it was necessary to throw a wounded man over the top of the half dug trench to take his chance. It was hard but had to be.

December 19: It is about the coldest night on record, this morning and all day the ground has been frozen hard. It was the first time that I heard the horses' feet ringing as though on the hard streets of London. The poor brutes slipped and skidded about frightfully.

Our building is lousy, the men complain. Today the men were discussing what they should do with the Kaiser when they get him. The punishment and the language therein expressed are unwritable, but the fellow who took my 'eye' came out with these words intermingled with many adjectives: 'When we get the — we should put a chatty (lousy) shirt on him and cut his two arms off.'

December 20: This morning, with last night's fall of snow still upon the hard frozen ground, the sun shone weakly but prettily in the east, and there were signs of a brilliant day. I felt overjoyed at the prospect of a walk out. On coming up from a look around the dugouts there was a sky full of aeroplanes hovering around and fighting one another. Gun-fire could be plainly heard all around and big shells commenced to land nearby with a crunching burst. In a moment I saw the fruits of a bright day and my jaws came together with a hard cynical jamb. To think that man had turned so fine a day into a butchery such as the early Romans, with their lowly forms of civilisation, could never realise. Dugouts and those half round houses were blown up with men and other contents. The body of a traffic officer was thrown up 70 feet in the air.

December 25: At 8pm last night a heavy artillery bombardment started from the German side and our guns replied vigorously for 40 minutes. The result is that the 3rd and 4th Battalion men have been flowing through the Hospital all day long. Fritz seemed to have done very well indeed for a Xmas Eve, only he will never have the satisfaction of knowing whether he has done any damage or not.

Today has had flashes of sunshine running through it but for the most part it was cold, showery and gloomy. There was plum pudding for the men; the issue was 8 lbs to 21 but I spent 60 francs on a whole lot of canteen goods and it brought the pudding up to ½ lb a man.

Around about work went on as usual but I was very reasonable with my men and worked them only a few hours, on a job of enlarging Brigade Headquarters, which I hope will see the next eight days over comfortably as we can keep our feet dry now and sleep, work also, in safety. It was a quiet and a dull Xmas all things considered. I am writing at the moment in my tunnel home reasonably free from shells, with dry feet, eating lollies, nuts, biscuits, drinking cocoa and dreaming of home, parents and good friends far away.

December 29: There seems to be the greatest possible trouble in obtaining socks and boots. For weeks past hundreds of men have had their feet on the ground and still orders come through regarding the care and the attention of the feet. Whale oil must be rubbed in at least twice a day. Platoon commanders are half responsible if this is not done while company commanders will be called to account for all cases of trench feet. The men with 'trench feet' will be held as having 'self inflicted' wounds and tried by court martial for same. And yet we have no boots to wear.

January 3, 1917: The shelling that goes on about here is awful; and to walk over the flat from here to the Chalk Cliffs ¾ miles away is one of the most interesting possible. Huge craters have to be passed that were made only a few hours before, judging by their newness.

It is strange where one's mind does get to in such exposed surroundings, more particularly around the mysterious village of Gueudecourt. Mysterious because the Germans won't allow troops to go near it by keeping an almost continual fire on to it. Day and night high explosives and shrapnel are thrown into it. For what reason nobody seems to know, but there undoubtedly is a reason for the Germans paying it so much attention.

January 5: There is trouble about rations this morning. The QM evidently forgot to include my 20 men on his ration strength and our men took the 2nd Battalion Mining Platoon tucker. This is a terrible mess. The rotten part is that 42 men have to live on half rations when full rations will only just keep a man alive.

January 6: There was very little gun fire going on so I thought it a splendid opportunity to go into Gueudecourt village and have a look around. I strolled up and walked precariously about amongst huge shell holes. The place is so absolutely chopped about that nothing could be recognised. This is the mysterious village which the German is always shelling day and night. Some tell stories of deep dugouts full of ammunition and valuable stores, also that there are several batteries of heavy guns there. Anyhow I saw very little indeed; the place is churned up to a depth of 8 foot.

I passed on down through the village noticing an Australian big hat, a Tommy cap and some coils of wire, shovels, picks, etc. There were no dead, probably blown to bits or covered over by the earth.

While overlooking 'no man's land' with its many dead, Germans as well as our own, I saw two of our Australians waving a white flag. Three minutes later they hopped over, one man carrying a stretcher. They went 30 yards, hurriedly opened the stretcher, put a man on to it and stooping low hurried safely back into the trench. It was a brilliant sight and speaks well of the German's sense of humour, after the awful things we've heard about.

January 8: At 9am all hands moved out with the Mining Platoon in the rear of Battalion. At the Railway Dump we waited an hour before getting aboard the train. We moved off slowly to Meaulte where we got out, dumped the kits and walked into Ribemont where we are billeted.

There is a kind of unconscious feeling that the air is a whole lot lighter and easier to breathe out here away from gun range. Yet there is no jubilation or laughing that one might expect. It seems the men are all wooden now and never smile or show emotion although they must surely feel the security that goes with being once again clear of the firing line.

January 15: In the Mess I heard repeated the story of a spy from Cairo. Blair Swannell took a great liking to an Egyptian fellow and he was allowed to wander anywhere at will. He often wandered alone for hours in the officers' rooms waiting their return. He was aboard the troop ship when the Battalion sailed from Alexandria and was made a big fuss over. Well on the day of the armistice at Gallipoli, a Turkish officer came over and spoke to Major Stevens congratulating him upon his promotion and here sure enough was the Battalion's and Blair Swannell's Cairo friend.

January 18: It has been snowing more or less all day. We went on with the drill as usual. In the afternoon, the men came in at 3pm while the officers played football against the 3rd Battalion officers. This game of football is probably one of the most remarkable games by Australians on account entirely of the elements. A thickly covered ground now stamped into hard ice by the feet, and Australians romping around as if it were a mild winter's day at home.

The 3rd has jerseys and pants while we didn't have anything at all. At full-time, 20 men each way, there was no score, although we had men who've never played rugby before and were tired. We suggested an extra five minutes' play—during which time they scored, through our fullback (soccer player) not knowing that he should have saved by falling on the ball when over the goal line.

January 25: The behaviour of the officers sometimes is rather childish and worries me a whole lot. But then they also are fed up with the war and must act childishly to keep themselves alive. Yet, it's hard to live as one should do or like to do. It's just a matter of adapting oneself to the times.

January 26: We move up to the line in the morning. It is so cold one wonders how the men will live through it. Rumour has it that Australians have already been found frozen at their posts. I feel sure that there is going to be a lot of frozen feet. My experience is that unless I keep moving both feet and hands become hard and powerless.

I badly want to do a turn in the trenches, but somehow I feel satisfied to stay in the rear while the weather is so bad. I doubt at the same time whether this frozen weather is not a whole lot better for our men than the rain and continual wet feet and dull clouds with a dank atmosphere and an environment of depression.

Chapter 16

FRONTLINE, 1917

January 27: We have 'moved up'. Tonight I sit in a low dugout in the side of a trench. My mining platoon is similarly quartered. The accommodation is better than I expected and sleeping close together no doubt the men will keep fairly warm, say ten to the dugout one blanket each.

I have only one other man in with me but two blankets and I fear for a cold night. Food is very scarce. This morning there was only one loaf of bread to five men, so they have gone hungry to bed tonight. I had only the contents of the parcel Ruth sent me, so I opened the tin of plum pudding and ate it with some real dinkum golden syrup, CSR, which however was hard and almost frozen.

It seems an awful shame to see good old Northern Queensland products so absolutely out of their element. Fancy pineapple with the juice turned to ice and the fruit hardened, also golden syrup half frozen.

Our men are taking over a new line of trenches from the Tommys. It seems that the Tommys have on their sector (50th Division Yorks) got so friendly with the Germans that they seldom fire a shot at one another. This was the same when the Australians took over in front of Flers. In fact it is beginning to look as if the Australians are the 'Make War' party all along the sector that we take over. In Flanders the Tommys never fired a shot and it was our men who stirred up the war and made things willing. Now we have more cases of the same thing. It's rather hard on our men as the Germans return our fire and knock nasty holes in our lines. I think we are in this present position now just to stir Fritz up. Our men are too impatient to remain idle; they must be at Fritz the whole time. If we leave him alone he would not interfere at all.

We saw about six of our men looking over the top of the trench (Lewis gun men they were). Lieut Bruton remonstrated with them for exposing themselves so freely. A moment later I could hardly believe my eyes for only 30 to 40 yards away were two Germans waist high over their trench waving a bottle and beckoning to us, at the same time calling out loudly. At first I thought they must be our men having a little joke but no they were Germans, much to my astonishment. I have heard a lot about this kind of thing from time to time but could not believe it. Then again it is said that the Tommys commonly do this sort of thing with the Germans, and in consequence neither side fire at the other.

January 28: On Factory Road I saw some machine gunners working on an emplacement. They told me that they were given the reckon that in a few days' time there will be no looking over at one another: it will be war to the teeth.

February 2: At 5 o'clock I took my party over to Yarra Bank and went on with the dugout work. I did a whole lot of work myself and came home at midnight feeling quite my old self again.

It seems stranger than ever that the German does not fire at our men on this sector. Several nights now I've heard officers say that while going along Fritz has fired a flare pistol straight at them just by way of letting them know he has seen them. None of the officers seem able to account for it. Probably we don't shoot because we have so much the worst of the position, but this is why Fritz should fire. Our Vickers machine guns from concealed positions well behind our line fire away at intervals all night and our artillery keep fairly active.

February 3: Although bad feet are not so common as when we first came into the slop and rain on the Somme in October, there is still a whole lot of fellows about and going to Hospital with nasty looking and swollen feet. It seems that the feet enlarge over-night so that in the morning with the boots frozen hard, the feet have to be forced into the boots which stops the circulation and often breaks the skin. This festers and causes a whole lot of nasty trouble. After all it does not seem quite right to expect Australians to stand up to the rigours of this country. At the same time our men must be doing as well as or perhaps better than the Tommy or we would have been taken away for a spell over the hard months. Our men must be extremely hard old birds.

February 5: I heard yesterday that America had practically declared war on Germany. But then, we hear so many wild stories that I could take little interest in it.

February 7: Last night I went on with the various dugouts as usual, from No 2 job to Yarra Bank which is about 1500 yards across country with only the stars to direct. Last night it was the devil plodding and wandering around amongst the ice bound shell craters every few yards. I got across a new piece of country and found an old wrecked aeroplane. It must have been lying there for quite a long time. Then I stepped onto a frozen corpse. I did not stay to make any examination. I suppose it has been lying there for a very long time.

February 8: I had a rather remarkable experience at 3am. I was at the No 2 job and decided to make across to Yarra Bank. I have done this trip several times without bother although there are only the stars to show the direction across country. I picked up the North Star and set out not going as far to the east as usual. I came into a trench with frozen bottom and a worn path. This bothered me for a moment; I decided to follow it a while. All of the trenches ran at right angles to my path and I was considering when I would get out of it as I must do so sooner or later. Never before had I met or seen a soul on the trip, so I got a big surprise to see two men leaning against the wide open trench looking out over the top. I challenged them and they replied in a whisper that it was all right. I went forward and behold I was in our own front line of trenches with the Germans only 30 yards in front. I felt a bit stupid. I followed the shallow and wide trench along to Yarra Bank.

Once a sentry challenged me with: 'Halt! Who goes there?'

I replied: 'It's all right old fellow, I'm just making along to Yarra Bank.'

He again called: 'What's the password?'

'Oh,' I returned. 'I don't know anything about passwords.'

The sentry spoke to somebody nearby, and then lowered his rifle with bayonet fixed; he said: 'Pass on.'

As I passed about eight men sleeping they told me the password was MAT.

February 9: I have had my eyes opened lately to the unwillingness of our Australians to work on fatigue parties. They have a whole lot to complain about and perhaps are being unfairly treated, but it is awfully annoying to me as I must get the work done and to stand about bullying the men is humiliating work.

This trouble arose on the Yarra Bank job when men who had been on post in the front trenches were sent along to carry sand bags full of dirt up the stairway of the new and deep dugouts until 12 o'clock at night.

Last night, and for some nights past the trouble has been on the No 2 job. Here the men have to do ration fatigue and carry our sand bags from 6pm until 5am. It is a long night's work but yet nothing exceptional. But the men complain they are tired and hungry. They say, why don't they feed us if they want us to work so hard? Sometimes they sit down and it takes them a very long time to get up again and go on with the work. I get onto them, try to bully them. It hurts me very much indeed but there is nothing else for it.

February 19: This morning while at live bomb throwing a really terrible accident happened. Harry Dingle, a splendid man in every respect, came over from the 1st Field Ambulance with me and after a fortnight at a bombing school took charge of the Battalion bombers. He was getting on splendidly with his work and this morning while throwing live bombs from a pit, one bomb burst immediately the lever was released instead of on the five seconds time fuse. This means that the bomb burst about six feet over the head of the thrower, killing the thrower, badly wounding Harry and another man, while 11 others were, more or less, slightly wounded.

February 20: I heard while out on parade in the wet and mud this morning that Harry Dingle has died. I should have expected this but did not think that man with such high ideals and who had lived so clean a life could be taken off this plane without having a fighting chance for his life. The ways of God are indeed strange. Now, I must write to his Mother. He loved his Mother beyond words. She was all to him and my task is a hard one.

February 26: Last night a message came through about Bennett and myself going to a Divisional school for one month.

February 28: Lieut Bennett and I set off from Bazentin to have a look around the newly taken villages of La Barque, Ligny Thilloy and Thilloy. I went on a walk of fully six miles through Factory Corner over our old front line trenches at Yarra Bank onto Bayonet trench to the right of the Maze where our 2nd Australian Division got knocked about some two months ago. There were bodies of Australians lying thickly about on the ground—some of them in most remarkable positions. One was huddled up on his hands and knees as though in the act of crawling away out of the shell hole in which I saw him. Another fellow made a gallant picture lying flat down with his chin resting on the ground looking straight ahead and his rifle with bayonet fixed, still gripped in his left hand and at his side. He died some eight weeks ago, but from the position as I saw him he might have been alive and eager for fight still. Nearby was a sorry sight. This tall and well set up Australian was lying on his back in a large shell hole; his legs were spread apart, his body reclining in a comfortable position with the head resting on the high slope of the hole. He appears to have been placed there by a comrade. Or was he only wounded and crawled away into this hole, made himself comfortable and waited for assistance that never came? The cold weather had preserved the bodies and made the scene all the more weird.

March 5: (Divisional School) A lecture was given on 'Discipline' by Captain Campbell. At dinner Col Stephens had some remarks to make on the mess and its etiquette. He also stated that General Walker had asked him to be strict on discipline and more on saluting than anything as it meant good training and reflected the whole of the work of their units. He mentioned that 'Dreadnought' were on sale at the school, as venereal was prevalent all around here. He stated that in one month there were 170 cases of venereal in the 4th Army and 120 of them were Australians.

March 18: In the American Bar we had a few cocktails and a chat with a couple of airmen. They stated that the enemy had a new trench system waiting to fall back into and that there were many villages in flames this morning. We discovered a whole lot about Amiens by walking about. I met two girls, evidently street girls, and had a bottle of champagne with them and caught the 6.18pm train back home.

April 3: Today I leave to pick up the Battalion, which is supposed to have gone forward to the line. This is after having spent four weeks at School on the Somme River at Tirancourt. It is also exactly one year to the day since the Australian Forces came to France. How well I remember sailing into Marseilles and the train trip up into Flanders and the weather experienced there. The weather is just the same at the present time.

April 8: Just woken up after four hours' sleep in the dismal cold. Last night should have been the big night, but it was postponed and I went out on a log patrol stunt with three men. We went a long way and gathered some good information towards Hermies, but I must not give particulars here as there is a big chance of being shot and this book getting into enemy hands. Half an hour later a terrible bombardment broke forth and with rifle and machine gun fire away to the left and Fritz knocking our position about we had a jolly rough time until 4.30.

It was a birthday greeting for me. Birthdays only remind me that I am one year older nowadays. Just after reading several letters my dugout was blown in. The bed (one special spring mattress taken from the village by the Germans) which I had that moment got up from was buried in broken wood and dirt. Some of my souvenirs are buried now. I got a couple of scratches only out of it.

April 9: Great things have happened in my military career since yesterday. At dawn this morning we set out to find a map reference number in the dark and up against a heavy stream of machine gun fire. It was anxious work, but we did it very well and before daylight broke we were 'dug in' 2000 yards ahead of where we started from. The village of Demicourt was on our program but at the moment we are holding it good and well. The shelling today has been awfully heavy indeed. As we have little artillery support it is a trying business.

I am sitting in a German shelter where the enemy went to sleep last night but woke early and 'beat it' leaving behind everything he possessed so that our men have today eaten his bread which is a dirty brown colour, very sodden and sour like. But with German jam on the bread the boys barged into it. Hermies is in our hands.

April 10: It is nearly 7 o'clock. I am officer on watch and have been on duty since 2am in bitterly cold weather. Every day we have had frost, snow or rain and it's the devil with only our ordinary clothes as neither blankets or overcoats were allowed to go with us. All we have for protection is a ground sheet. This seems to keep the shoulders dry, but it's an awfully cold thing to sleep with in a damp hole dug deep into the ground. Never mind I have had the pleasure of eating German bread and jam, smoked German cigars and drank their coffee as well as slept with one of the enemy overcoats in his own sleeping shelter.

6pm: I have been in the village of Hermies and such destruction one could never dream of. It would not shelter a goat as there is not a portion of a roof or a corner of a building left. It must have taken a whole lot of explosive to complete such a job. I am back in the Company Headquarters shelter and while the wind is blowing a hurricane and the snow is beating down the collar and filling up both eyes and ears, the batman is playing a mouth organ and Blake and the other chaps are singing. There is no shelling today but it is a rotten time for the poor men. We expected to be relieved tonight but I fear it will not be so.

April 12: We have done nothing but assist the men in making their holes comfortable by drawing iron and timber from the village. Howell Price and I built a good shelter in the sunken road and tonight have a stove in it and are very comfortable.

In strolling through Doignies today getting timber to build a dugout, I found 21 boxes of 79 shells each buried near the Church. The Church is beyond recognition; but for the cemetery by the side it might have passed unnoticed. In one of the houses we had quite an interesting time scratching around amongst the debris picking up letters, cards, tin boxes and a whole lot of German military curios. What a wreckage. All for what purpose?

April 18: Today has been wet. The men lying outside in the shallow trenches have had a rough time right enough.

April 20: We were relieved last night by 'C' company. This will be a much needed spell for the fellows as they have been having a jolly rough time of it since the third of the month. This open warfare means a whole lot more work and a keener observation. The strain is much greater on the men added to which the weather makes matters damnably bad. It is wet and cold. We don't so much mind the cold, but it's the wet that counts against our men. To make matters worse there is no place to sleep at all. Last night the darkness was very trying when going from one post to the other, distances often of only 100 yards, but it was very difficult to keep direction. My book [diary] of late has been starved due to the possibility of being taken prisoner and the contents being of use to them. Besides there is little chance of writing as it takes me all day to get enough sleep to carry on the business of war over night. Our position is very safe at daylight but in the night time the Germans are likely to rush in on us.

It is 6pm. I have just had a wash and shave in a quart of water. I cleaned my teeth, picked off a few lice, ruffled the dust off my underclothes and as I sit in my lowly roadside dugout on the Doignies–Demicourt Road I felt quite a new and proud man. It is my second shave in 18 days and about the same number of face and body washes during that time. Our work has been very muddy and trying digging trenches and outposts nearly every night and running around preparing to reinforce one and another front. There is no doubt about the hardship of an infantry man's life. They suffer both from work exposure and under feeding—the latter to a disgusting extent. Any other branch of the service is heaven compared to the infantry life.

April 21: It is a wonder that I have not mentioned before about a piece of shell that cut its way through my leather vest tunic and pants without me being aware of it until seeing the holes. This happened ten or 12 days ago, and it caused me so little concern that I had forgotten until I saw my tunic a moment ago.

Rumour says that Sir Douglas Haig declares the war will be over in another 14 days. This seems impossible to the extreme, but I wish it was so. How happy everybody would be. The German is tired of it and he has been living in luxury compared to the way we have to work and fight. In a six foot by four foot by three foot dugout covered over only by some shrapnel riddled galvanised iron. The villages are always being shelled by Fritz but we do go in prowling about and taking timber, iron, tables, chairs, stoves and anything else of use.

April 23: We took over at 3am. I have been on watch duty all day long in the narrow and shallow trenches. I can see the Hindenburg line plainly.[1] It seems particularly strong in trench systems and wire entanglement. I fear we will require heavy artillery support before we can advance further.

April 24: The eve of the Gallipoli landing and a reminder we have been 12 months in France and 12 months of hard and continuous fighting. There is a Brigade of Lincolns relieving and I find that they have not been in the trenches for five months now. It seems very strange and awfully hard to think that there is no spell for the Colonials after the trying winter and the severe fighting. We are supposed to be going back north to Flanders now. I certainly hope so although I cannot quite believe anything at all. The men are very much worn down—nearly everybody having bad feet.

I have just returned from a stroll around...I saw some 20 German bodies lying about in different positions, mostly in their prepared positions. They all appeared to have been well looted, and if not soon buried will make a terrible smell. I cut off five buttons from a coat of a dead man to keep.

April 27: I saw Syd Middleton and found that the game of football in Paris was still a possibility when we get out of the lines shortly. I saw the trenches in which we go for supports in the big stunt which takes place at any moment. I had a nip of whiskey and a bottle of English beer which was jolly good after having to drink rum to keep out the cold during the past 20 days. My word there is a big battle pending near here, and Fritz will get a hot time. The 2nd Division are training and practising for it now.

May 2: This afternoon orders came for one officer and 50 ranks to be ready to move off in two hours. No order of dress or what the business in hand was

---

1   Established in 1917, the Hindenburg Line was a German defensive position which consisted of three well-defended trench systems.

to be was given. This made it nasty as the men wanted to know and should have known too. Anyhow it turned out to be a walk of 3½ miles to dig a communication trench—500 men engaged at two yards of trench per man. It was 10.20am when we started to dig and by 1pm the trench was completed. A rather good piece of work. At 3.45pm we got back to our camping ground and a little later one of the most intense barrages opened that I have yet seen. It continued for a very long time.

May 3: Near Bullecourt. I am waiting in close supports with the Battalion and ready to go forward at any moment. So what the night will bring forward we are anxious to know.

[Richards did not enter anything in his diary on 4 and 5 May. He then spent the next few days chronicling what had occurred in the heat of battle.]

May 6: I think it is May 6 at this moment of writing and I was right in anticipating there was an anxious time in store for us when I made the above entry on May 3. We have been right into the gaping jaws of Hell and for three whole days engaged the German in bombing attacks and defences, and waited until the Hun artillery, or rather until the devil closed his jaws and crushed us. The devil (in fact) did close his jaws heavy and often some got crushed, mauled and mangled between his teeth; others survived until he opened his mouth again. There were blunders made by the 3rd, 11th and 12th Battalions that were shocking. They got away from the enemy bombing stunts like cattle stampeding. But looking at it from a personal view it was glorious for me, after leading a bombing party and taking 280 yards of main trench out of Fritz's hands with a bombing party as well as 200 yards of communication trench, taking about 18 prisoners. Splendid specimens of men right enough, but they were in a pitiful plight from shock and cried 'Comrade' and would willingly have kissed me but for my demure and impossible countenance.

I built a barricade in the main trench and linked up with the 3rd Battalion. I held the barricade and beat off some heavy attacks from 1pm until 8pm and alas when handing over to Second Lieut Howell-Price a shell smashed his leg to pieces: he has since died.

At 9.30pm word came to Company Headquarters that the 3rd Battalion were retiring. Sure enough I found to my dismay it was a fact. I did not think it possible for a crowd of Australians to throw up the sponge so frightfully.

I got assistance from some 1st Battalion bombers and after a while about 16 of the 3rd were coaxed and bullied to come and build a barrier and make a stand. Right through the night we hung on and at 6am I went into Company Headquarters and the post was relieved by D Company. This morning fully 200 men of the 11th and 12th Battalion came running out before a German bombing attack. I cursed and swore at the top of my voice. Called upon them in the name of Australia to hold out.

May 7: A Devon chap hobbled up to the front of our dugout just now with the heel shot clean off his boot, and other than a little jarring he was uninjured. He cursed his luck at missing so splendid a 'Blighty'. He said that it was like getting his legs kicked out from under him at football.

It has turned 12 o'clock and here I am sitting on my valise in pyjamas, a clean singlet over my dirty skin and no boots or socks on. My feet are dirty and a shame I know but there has not been one spare minute during the 118 hours. There are only a few big guns firing, but the joy and relief of being back in the region of safety again is so great that I don't want to sleep worn and haggard. I have just met Captain Edgely and he fell over me with joy at my release and congratulations at the brilliance shown by A Company.

The Major CO Woodford of the 1st Battalion was very pleased at my bombing expedition the first day in and congratulated me very earnestly, but alas he was wounded a few moments afterwards and is now dead. Oh God when I recall the men that have fallen faithfully by my side it's so pitiful. First there was young Martin my runner, and a fine lad only 19 years of age: he jumped up onto the bank where I was sniping Huns with my revolver, to get a rifle shot in; a moment later he fell back onto me with his head blown in and blood flowing all over me. I could see he was dead and raced on around the corner. A moment later blood poured from a fellow's face; he wanted to stop but I pushed him back out over the trench and shouting at the top of my voice went onwards. Later Mackley fell off the communication trench at my feet, shot through the shoulder and lungs. At this moment four Hun prisoners came running back shouting mercy with their hands over their heads. I felt them for firearms and pushed them on carrying Mackley between them and at once linked up with the 3rd Battalion. After putting in posts I went back and bustled the fellows to build a barricade, hanging on to the position with the Germans' own bombs and a very limited number of rifle grenades. It was lovely sport shooting Germans with both revolver and rifle, as well as bombing them down in their dugout. Out of our double entrance 'dugout' nine prisoners were afterwards taken.

But the horror of it was at 7 o'clock when handing over to young Howell-Price. I stood with my hand on his shoulder pointing out the German line of trenches ahead when a shell came from behind and smashed his leg above the thigh very badly. He rolled down and said: 'Goodbye Tom old fellow I'm done.'

I could not answer but on cutting away his pants and binding up the wound, I felt sure that though he was certain to lose his leg he would do alright. I kissed the boy and tears welled up. We got a stretcher at once and on being carried away he gripped my hand with a firm hold. A grip of love and tenderness. I went down into the deep dugout—A Company Headquarters, taken from Fritz this morning—and had a meal, but a little later news came along that the Germans had broken through the 3rd Battalion and they were retiring. I rushed up and found it was only too true. My heard bled to think that Australians would leave their post and run away from a bombing attack. It took a whole lot of coaxing to get 14 of the 50 or 60 to stay with me and hold out. We held out all night in great style but I did curse and swear at them and then pleaded with them in the name of Australia to stick. Had it not been for a few of the 1st Battalion perhaps we never would have held out. A barrage of Mills bombs turned the tide. I threw bombs with the men and later settled back and rallied the fellows with cheers and shouts, like a mighty barracker at a football match, whenever a German attack was launched. We got them every 40 minutes or so until daylight.

After my batman and myself beat off this attack and the confusion cleared, here was my faithful Lple Byers with his legs broken and battered as well as three other men knocked out.

No sooner was Byers got back into the main trench than a man, shot through the body, fell off the side of the trench and knocked my feet from under me. He died a moment later.

At daylight I was relieved by D Company and went away to rest down in Battalion Headquarters dugout, somewhat the worse for wear and with a bullet graze on my left upper arm, also a shrapnel mark on the forearm and thumb.

At 'stand to' the following morning, I was talking to some of the boys when the word came along that the 11th were retiring. I ran up and after stopping some of the 11th and 12th I found sure enough that they had actually left their trenches and were going back over the open ground. I got up several boxes of Mills bombs on either side of the trench and pushed some of the 11th into the posts. One 'windy' cove cried that he could not throw bombs he was too knocked up. But as he trembled with fear I cursed him, hit him a whack on the jaw and shoved him into the post making him take bomb for bomb with me and throw it, while my cheering and shouting brought several to our assistance. I then ran down and onto the opposite post, got the fellows working there and then went back along the road side bank now lined by 170 or more 11th and 12th Battalion men. I called on them to remember they were Australians. 'What will Australia think when she knows you deserted your posts and let your brother soldiers down?'

That shifted some back as they passed. I gave them the boxes of bombs lying about and cheered long and loudly as they filed back to their trench. I saw Lieutenant Bruton on the end with his revolver drawn and preventing the men from going further back. This they eventually did, but it was an anxious half hour for us.

While this rallying was going on Corporal Snowy Howell raced away at the head of a bombing party and was pushing the German back at a gallop with the 11th Battalion getting back in their places in good style. In fact in 30 minutes they had recovered the whole of their lost ground and were safe and sound. To every three or four men as they passed I gave a box of 12 bombs assuring him that each of them was guaranteed to drive Fritz back ten yards and that each bomb was worth five quid.

Every man about was examined for injuries and each man that came out of the trench was often sent back to his business at the double with many curses following him. Some of the wounded were ridiculous, their injuries being merely scratches. On the other hand some of the wounds were very bad, but they took their bombs and were back like heroes. Corporal Howell came back badly blown about. Ted Spark came back with a bullet hole through the upper arm and in pain. It was a very exciting hour, I can tell you, and I would have enjoyed it were it men other than Australians. But as it was there was a whole lot of joy and self-satisfaction in getting the 11th and 12th Battalions back in the trenches so successfully.[2]

I have been in command of A Coy since Lt Yates fell back with his brain protruding in my arms. The Coy strength was about 186 and now I could gather together only 43 men to lead out.

---

2   Tom Richards received the Military Cross for his actions. His citation read: 'For conspicuous gallantry and devotion to duty. He was in charge of a bombing party, and despite strenuous opposition succeeded in extending the line 250 yards and holding a strong post. He set a splendid example throughout.'
    Snowy Howell, a builder from the Sydney suburb of Enfield, was awarded the Victoria Cross. Howell had decided that the only way to push the Germans back was going straight for their face. All around Howell egg and stick-bombs were raining down, and on both sides machine guns were cutting any Australian who pushed too close, while right in front of him 80 Germans, led by two officers, were holding firm. Suddenly Howell leapt out, scrambling onto the top of an open parapet and then running along it, hurling bombs down at the enemy, who immediately fled. Richards was close behind, supporting him with a Lewis gun, following along the trench and firing bursts. Howell ran out of bombs but that did not deter him. He chased after the enemy, jabbing down at them with his bayonet, until he crashed into the trench himself when wounded. Richards helped get Howell back to safety. It was later discovered that Howell had suffered at least 28 different wounds, including being hit in both legs by machine gun fire.

Chapter 17

MIXED FORTUNES, 1917–18

May 8, 1917: Breakfast after a refreshing sleep at 10.30am. My heart goes out in sympathy to the lads holding onto that few hundred yards of Hindenburg line. The ground is so churned up to many yards in depth that it will be impossible for anyone to walk over. The few remaining trench walls are so shattered and crumbling that they will run away like water, then the men will have no protection from either the water or shell fire. It's going to be bad when the monster closes its jaws and turns the artillery loose.

It is 9pm; thousands of guns are blazing away all around us. It is a terrific bombardment. I am anxious to know whether it is the enemy or ourselves that are attacking, but the gun fire is attacking.

I have been over to the Dressing Station this afternoon and had a piece of shell taken out of my forearm, and my knee and upper left arm cleaned and iodined. Also an injection. It has been a day of complete rest for us. The only thing I've done was to report on young Howell-Price's injury. He died on his way on to the D Station and is buried near the station.

May 10: We are told for certain we are going back to the front at once. I am fretting, or am nervous or something of the kind as I cannot remember anything clearly. My head is dull and heavy. I take long sighs and broken breaths as a love sick youth.

May 12: It is certain now we are to have a long and much needed rest. I find I am going to a bombing school tomorrow. Capt Edgely is pushing me away for a spell as much as anything; on my return there should be a spell of ten days in England awaiting me.

May 14: The first day at School. The mess seems to be a very good one here and with a bar running at which beer, whiskey etc is retailed. We should be in for a very pleasant 14 days as the bombing squad contains a jolly good lot of fellows too.

May 15: At the first parade Lt Col Fitzgerald put the officers through the correct and only approved form of salute. I must get into conversation with the Colonel as he is the leader in the Australia–France football movement.

We went onto throwing dummy bombs and the practice of bombing down a trench. It was an old trench, one from which the Bosch were driven in the 'big push' of last year. The bag of dummy bombs was placed on the parapet and the 12 bombing officers gathered around talking. The instructor decided to put the bombs into the bag and try another movement before lunch. As the bombs were being thrown into the sandbag I heard a sticker pin go off and someone shout out: 'Look out.' Everybody scrambled up and ran, the bomb exploded and although I was ten or 15 yards away I felt myself hit on the back in several places. By my side was an officer shot in the stomach. I loosened his belt, and then went back to the Hut.

I have a nasty piece of bomb in each of my shoulders. Had the one on the left gone in a little deeper it would have penetrated the lung so I am lucky indeed; as it is I am very sore and cannot move my shoulders at all, but should be alright before very long.

May 16: I went under gas today and had a piece of metal extracted from my shoulder. The whole operation occupied only a few moments. I expected some little sensation when going off to 'sleep' but this I did not feel at all. I 'came to' also with ease, and was surprised at the quickness of the whole job. It is raining today and right into the night which makes me grieve for the troops holding onto Bullecourt midst mud and shells.

May 17: It is an infernally difficult matter to sleep the whole night through in the one position lying half on the back and on the right side. Yes, I will get used to that I expect. We were later quartered at the No 2 British Red Cross Hospital at Rouen.

May 18: The Sisters are hard to beat, not quite what one would call good lookers, but yet real 'dinkums'.[1]

May 23: I was rather disappointed to find a train in waiting instead of a boat to take us down the beautiful River Seine to Havre. At Havre waited aboard the *Esscribo* and stood by until just on dark when we pulled out accompanied by an escort. This hospital ship and all of them are now alike with no distinguishing marks. Once all hospital ships were painted white and had a huge red cross on the side. At night they carried a band of green lights; but since the Germans declared war on Hospital ships they are painted the same as troopships and wait until nightfall to slip across the Channel. This is just what we are doing tonight.

May 24: We slipped into Southampton about daylight this morning and went ashore onto the train for London, arriving at Paddington Station where I was pushed into a lovely big motor car and ran for many miles over to 3rd London General Hospital Wandsworth.

It was Empire Day and the weather most delightful; thousands of children graced the greens and were having a great time of it.

May 31: My head is still bad and I am not allowed out of bed. The lead swinging that goes on is appalling.[2] There is an English officer on each side of me with a wounded hand each. One is a bomb instructor at a school in France and throws with his left hand; his right hand is injured, but he cleans his belt and boots each morning jolly hard with the complaining member but when it's time to go into the City the sister has to tie it up most carefully and put the whole arm into a huge sling. The other chap is an artillery man (one star) and openly tells me he's going to work it as long as possible.

---

1   It was decided to transfer Richards to London for further treatment.
2   Lead swinging was a term used to describe a person who schemed to avoid duty; a malingerer.

A Scottish Captain has a marked arm and he also pays it minute attention when he is about to go out to the City and moves off looking a suffering hero. It's perhaps not so bad making the 'very best' of a wound, but I think it's over the mark to make such a big noise about it.

June 13: A very quiet day, nice and warm, but I have not been far away, only a run around the wards. The air raid is the topic at the moment. Some 15 Hun planes dropped bombs into the heart of London during the middle of the day. This puts the 'wind up' the Londoners right enough.

June 24: Went out and had lunch at the 'Crighton' Clapham Junction. We played billiards for a time, had supper and enjoyed the girlie on the piano very much. We missed going first for one train and another until 10.30pm, arriving back at the hospital about 11pm which is too late to come through the gate without trouble. So we climbed the wall and on the inside were caught by a 'picket' and will be tried in the morning.

June 25: A day of much uncertainty and 'wind up'. Captain Rowley, Captain Oswald and myself appeared before the Colonel this morning and in a few brief words he told us that our conduct as officers in climbing the wall last night was extremely bad and he could do nothing but send us before the General Commanding Officer. This was notified to us by letter with a command to attend the 'Horse Guards' tomorrow.

June 26: At 10.30am the three of us were driven in an ambulance car to the Horse Guards where we were told to take off our belts and proceed before the General, Sir Francis Lloyd. We saluted and he overhauled us one after the other, then on asking if we were under arrest, were told that we were. He wanted to know where the escort was. We had none so he ordered the orderly officer to take us away. So where we stand I don't know. We came back in the ambulance car and have been kept inside the Hospital grounds all day. It is a nasty position to be in after such long and good service.

June 27: At 11.15am a message came that Capt Rowley, Oswald and myself were to be in the main hall in 20 minutes' time. We were there and at once driven up to the Horse Guards where we were presented to General Sir Francis Lloyd who, after a little consideration, gave us a pretty strong blowing up and let us go away. So we are now free. On returning to the Hospital I saw the Colonel, Bruce Porter, who was very agreeable indeed. I told him I thought it extremely hard for a man with nearly three years' service and never a question asked about his conduct to find through a mere misunderstanding that both his conduct is seriously questioned, and his honour held to the stake. He said he was sorry for the whole thing and ended up by shaking hands with me and allowing me to leave the hospital at once.

June 29: In the morning I met Lady Durnley wandering around the building [Wandsworth Hospital]. I was looking for books. She took compassion on me and asked me to come along this afternoon to her own library and make the most of it. In the afternoon Lady Durnley showed me all over the house which is a very remarkable old place full of the finest old family paintings. The mantelpieces are of carved marble and beautifully done. In statues small or large was a tendency to show love scenes and nude works of the best possible workmanship. The building dates to 1559.

On our way round we met Lord Durnley (Ivo Bligh).[3] He showed me the original urn of 'ashes' brought from Australia in 1883. In fact it is easily the most treasured sporting memento he has. I stayed in his library for an hour looking around amongst his books, but alas, they were all printed in old English, Latin or Greek, and though of great value, intensely novel and interesting, it was impossible for me to read them. Shakespeare works were splendidly printed and bound, but in very old English. I did not see Lady Durnley to thank her, but I must do later.

July 2: I obtained leave to spend 24 hours in London and arrived at 11 o'clock at Victoria Station, where in accordance with arrangements I met my good Sister Hickey. This gladdened my heart a whole lot as this is about the gentlest, and most kindly, sympathetic woman I've ever met. She stood out like an angel amongst the Sisters at the Hospital and I could not take my eyes from her as she so cleverly and quickly yet tenderly went about her work. We drove away to my tailor's where I fitted on my new suit and then away to the Zoo for lunch and a look around the birds and beasts.

---

3   Ivo Bligh captained England in the first Test cricket series against Australia with the Ashes at stake in 1882–83. The Ashes urn was presented to Bligh during the Australian tour.

As Sister had to be home by 8pm we spent an hour in a picture show, then by train to Clapham Junction and in a few minutes I was alone. It was a fine day and my good 'Sister' is both good looking and charming, though married.

July 4: I went to Gravesend and met the 10.45 train from London and took my treasured Sister back to Cobham amongst the ferns and bushes. We played happily along, watching the time passing quickly by. But alas before my Sister left me at Sole Street station there were happenings and consequences that will live forever in my mind and remain at all times an inward and heavy secret. Whether we will meet again I can't say just now.

July 6: Lord Roberts flag day today. It seems to me every day is a flag day here in London. I wrote to my good 'Sister' to meet me this afternoon and go shopping with me. I wonder if she will do so? It is no fault of mine if she does or doesn't. Somehow or other I think she will be at Victoria Station as she is extremely sorry for what has taken place and I feel sure we will meet again.

Later: . . . We had tea and onto St Paul's to the whispering gallery and a look over the City. To the Cock Tavern for dinner and the Scala picture show later.

July 26: Went before the Medical Board who passed me for general duty.

August 9: I met my Sister and we lunched at Princes in Piccadilly. It is laid down that men in uniform cannot spend more than 3/6 on lunch, excluding drinks, cigars etc, but as long as there is a person with you not in uniform it can be said they are entertaining and any price can be reached. We had the 3/6 lunch but when I ordered fruit salad and cream it cost me 3 shillings each extra.

August 10: I hope to be in France shortly. I can see this camp life will be the death of me. I am so incompetent and easily worried.

August 21: Left camp at 11.45am and arrived at Southampton by 3pm. Southampton is the usual sort of shipping town. I became bold and picked up a girl, went to tea with her and she turned out an awful 'boob'—knew nothing and had no manners. I slipped away.

August 22: We went aboard at 6pm last night, had tea, slept on the smoke room floor and went ashore at 7.30 at Havre. There was bunk accommodation for 30 officers and as we had 130 on board we had to sleep anywhere at all. Of course the old hands took to it like they take whiskey—never a murmur or a quiver—but complaints and grumbles come from the new fellows. We had breakfast at Havre and left the town by tram at 10am reporting to camp six miles out. I met and strolled into a nearby village with Bob Adamson and recalled many pleasant moments of our American tour.[4]

August 24: I am on board the train making back to the Battalion with 86 2nd Division men. I got warning this morning I would have to report to Headquarters and take a draft away in the evening. I will soon be back again, not to the Battalion, and right glad too, as I don't like camp life. There is nothing settled about it and a whole lot of bothering and messing about.

August 25: It is three years ago today since I joined up, and it seems almost a lifetime.

August 26: We arrived at Hazebrouck only to find the station we should have disembarked at seven miles back along the line. So we have to return tomorrow. Hazebrouck, when I was here some 10 months ago, was a fine little place with any amount of civilian life about, particularly on Sunday afternoon when everybody came out walking, but today there are very few people about at all. Hazebrouck, 14 miles behind the line, has been so bombed and shelled that the people have deserted it. Many buildings are destroyed and thousands of windows broken. It is so sad to see the place deserted and lonely.

September 5: We played two games today against the 3rd Battalion. The men won theirs comfortably but the officers were 11–6 after a hard, gruelling game. Our Colonel is very keen on all hands learning rugby and playing it; but at the same time I wish he would give the players some consideration and play the games during parade hours.

---

4   Bob Adamson was a teammate of Richards's on the Wallabies tour of the United States and Canada in 1912. It was a rip-roaring visit, with the players almost losing the one-off Test against America after days of drinking and gallivanting with the locals.

September 7: I was out coaching the Battalion team, and taught them quite a lot of things. All Australian Battalions are giving a number of men to the farmers around to help in getting their various crops in and ploughing up fresh ground. The hop patches are ready to pull; potatoes are being dug up and oats, wheat collected.

September 15: The Colonel tells me I am attached to Battalion Staff as 'liaison officer' and that my duty will be to keep the flanks of the Battalion in touch with one another and not allow any 'strong points' to split in between our advance. And at the same time organise counter attacks should the enemy push our first line back. It seems a very difficult mission to undertake but a very proud one to have allotted me.

September 17: Our lines were very quiet last night other than a little shelling. I find my mission is a decidedly tough one. I have to be prepared for any emergency. While looking, a piece of shell struck my forearm.

September 18: They operated on my arm last night; the ether did not give me any trouble. I feel very well indeed considering 750 grams of anti-tetanus and an operation. At 5pm a Hospital train called, and I came onto the 24th General Hospital, Etaples. A dose of anti-tetanus is always given to prevent lockjaw in wounds. It makes one very sick at times.

September 19: I arrived here around 4am and have been comfortably put up, though the place is miserably English. One of the Nurses was Australian and she just cried when we talked of Australia and our boys. The Doctor says I will have to go to England. The operation made two big gashes four inches apart to get the metal out.

September 20: It has been decided I go to England tonight. I don't feel at all pleased, as I have no money in my pay book and I should be with the Battalion after my last big spell.

September 24: A nurse with a stretcher on wheels called for me this morning and away we went to the operating room [at London General Hospital Wandsworth]. I then experienced my second dose of ether. The going into unconsciousness is alright only for the nasty heavy smell of the dope and the drumming effect upon the head. I could feel the Doctor cutting for some time before I went off; I could feel him again as I was regaining consciousness.

December 4: I am sitting in a Doctor's waiting room reading the 'Daily Telegraph'—the leader of which annoys me considerably. For three years our Ministers have been taking victory for granted and no one but a fool could dream of the 'Central Powers' having a chance at all; now they have the cheek to preach. Lloyd George says our problem is to organise victory, and not take it for granted. And there are 50,000 aircraft and munitions workers on strike at Coventry. The railway men were on the verge of downing tools and coal miners have actually left their work. This is a disgusting state of affairs, and to think that in puny Australia they are fighting the conscription issue as though it were life and death. Conscript Australia to help England to achieve in a war while she herself looks helplessly on while the factories scarcely work.

January 16, 1918: I have just come in from a concert given by Australian soldiers. It was very good but I return tonight a little homesick as the stage had as a background a picture of Sydney Heads from Middle Head. A Manly ferry boat filled the foreground with several small sailing boats. It was splendid but it gave me many reminders of home and peace. Over the top of the stage was painted a large waratah with a bunch of Xmas bells, flannel flowers and wattle, with two laughing jack-asses on one side, a native bear and a cockatoo on the other. I can remember my last glimpse of Sydney Heads 3½ years ago and oh!!!!

January 17: I have written to several of my girlfriends telling them of my war weariness and homesickness. This, however (be it a fact or not), I have to fight down, live right over the top of it to fulfil my position as a soldier.

January 25: I have been warned for France and leave Southampton on February 2. I am quite wooden as far as feelings go and don't mind France a little bit. I can go just as readily as I can remain here.

January 27: The number of 'absent without leave' prisoners about are most remarkable. There are three or four court martials sitting every day on AWL cases. I was told there are as many as 10,000 Australians running loose in

England. It's a sad business. Some men have been 15 months in England and never been to the front; they are in jail or AWL all the time.

February 3: We arrived uneventfully at Havre, reporting into Camp about noon. In the afternoon we went into Havre. There is an awful brothel quarter and the people promenading the streets were not attractive.

February 8: Morley and I reported at the Battalion this morning and I am now with B. Coy and billeted at a decent place, in a good room with a comfortable bed. It's a pleasure to be back with the 'Boys' again and pleased to receive a merry greeting from all.

February 9: I have a room upstairs at a shop in the Village. There are several girls about and a number of officers gather each night to play with them and sing songs—some of which are vulgar and coarse. It is most certain that these officers are hard up for amusement. It is just a sign of the times, I suppose.

February 28: We moved into position. A wet, muddy, rough and dark walk it was too. Never could such a black shell holed track be imagined. And the guide that led us in was in a terrible hurry to get us there and complete the leave so that he could get away out of it. Relief was complete by 12pm and the 5th Division had moved off.

March 1: First day in a pill box after a long and restless night's watch. A position like this one makes a fellow think a lot, as we are underneath the Hun and he could strafe the whole lot of us day or night. The nights are cold, and the walking about in the dark bog into shell holes is trying. The pill box is about 12 foot long, six foot wide and four foot high, walls are 3–4 feet thick of concrete. Two ventilation holes and a doorway facing the enemy, and water on the floor.[5]

March 24: I've had a hacking cough for ten days. On reaching camp my voice was gone. I saw the Doc and went to bed. There is no doubt that my trouble like dozens of others in the Battalion is caused by gas, delayed action.

---

5   During this period Richards's diary entries were succinct as he waited for action and direction.

March 26: I am remaining in bed again today. News of the war is a little more pleasing today. We have an excellent chance of winning this war at last, by cutting in behind him and throwing our forces against his flanks. If we have neither the grit nor the ability to do this, well it's a sorry look out, and we are going to be well beaten and the best men will win. Good luck to them.

My cough is mighty bad. It shakes and rattles me to bits, and the Doctor can do nothing at all for me. There are a whole lot of officers and men about who have lost their voices and are badly shaken by gas. This is probably why the 1st Division has not already gone south.

March 27: The only relief from coughing was got from whiskey, of which I have drunk some bottle and a half a day.

March 30: Phosgene gas is sent across in liquid form contained in shells, which upon exploding splashed about and slowly became gas. It lay in dug outs out of the wind, for many hours, men took particles into dugouts on their boots, but it was sufficient to kill them in agony; thousands will die in after years from its effect.

April 16: It seems that Strazeele is the key to Hazebrouck and that the 1st Australian Division has sworn to defend it to the very last. It is awfully dark laying down barbed wire and a little discouraging when the Hun puts down his barrage at intervals. We got back to bed at 2.30am, but were disturbed by gas until 'stand to' at 4am. At 2pm we moved 400 yards away into a field, and at 5.15pm, after the boys have made their sleeping position good, we have withdrawn their coat and blanket, rolled them in bundles, given out two bombs and three bandoliers of ammunition to each man, 280 rounds altogether, and are ready to move into action at five minutes' notice.

The church tower at Vieux-Berquin is a good observation point for the enemy. We heard our artillery were going to knock it down this afternoon, and sure enough the tower disappeared at 4pm.

We moved out at 6.30, a Battalion in artillery formation, over the fields with the intention of attacking on the flank of a French Division that was taking Méteren. We came under heavy shell fire and lost men but reached some reserve trenches and lay down there in the cold until nearly 4am, wondering what was going to happen to us, and we as cold as it is possible to be. We were roused up just before daylight and rushed up to a system of outposts where we relieved the Scottish Rifles, and at daylight we were sniping at Huns wandering about in large numbers. I don't know what happened to the French attack, but nothing eventuated at all last night.[6]

April 17: It was a cold night of anxious waiting, but we have had some good sport shooting Huns today, as they seem to be hopping about aplenty. The enemy planes have been especially active: they came down low and fired upon our posts. They also brought down two of our machines and have been fighting and hovering about all day. McGill shot through the head 1.10pm. My batman Lucas also killed at my side. Clarkson shot through the helmet, slightly wounded. We have had some tough sniping set tos, but I reckon we killed a number of Huns. I think I got four for certain with my own rifle. I only have a Lewis gun and nine riflemen as a platoon now. A number of Germans extended out in front, the SOS went up from the adjoining posts on either side, and this move provided us with more shooting. It seems the enemy is attacking strongly on our front. At nightfall we had the Hun as tame as a caged canary, and afraid to look 'over the top' at all. It has been damp with light rain all day and it is cold tonight with frost. The enemy seems to be working in front ... I can see numbers of them; we are also digging in so, alas, I cannot fire on them.

April 18: I buried McGill and Lucas just outside the post. Two good lads.

April 23: We are well back now, and it was a treat to have a few hours' sleep away from the shocks of shell fire.

It is a bit rough when a man has to hold a platoon post with 12 men all told, including Lewis gun post, and then receive orders that there must be no retiring. Fight on and on. When asked had I an SOS signal in my post, I replied: 'No we deal in 303 [rifle ammunition] only.' And although both posts on my right and left did put up the SOS for artillery support, our platoon laughed and went on killing Huns, who seemed to be preparing for attack.

6   The French attack did not begin because the English captured the French runner who had the complete operation order and held him for two hours, believing he was a spy.

Some awful stories of the English troops funking and running away are being told on every hand. Both the French soldiers and civilians on the Somme and here at Méteren say they (the English) were demoralised and broke. Something damned bad must have happened, or the enemy could never have got outside of the artillery range and I fear that the English reputation of being 'bulldogs' is entirely lost. Both here and on the Somme, a few Australians restored the line the moment they got in position and had the finest sport of their lives. Without artillery no troops can possibly push back the opposition if they will fight. It is hard to believe but it seems quite clear the English refused to fight and ran away.

April 24: It seems doubly hard to have to give good lives to regain a high vantage point like Méteren when the Tommy ran away and left it without firing a shot. It is disheartening to us.

April 25: Told to pack up and form the frame work of a new Battalion should it be wiped out in the line. We walked for an hour amidst shell fire and bomb droppings. We had a very rough sleep in a thin wooden hut.

April 30: I had a look at the line we have to man in case of the enemy breaking through. It is well back and no German army can break it down if the 'Tommy' will stand his ground and fight. A 'Tommy' is reputed to have said: 'Here we are trying to end the war and the damn Australians come along and spoil the whole thing by holding the Hun back.' Certainly it is not a general idea, but even if a few have this kind of thing in mind, there is nothing but dcfcat and disaster staring at us. Some of the articles in the papers (those cursed London dailies) have an awfully depressing effect on anybody who reads them. I read a leading article booming the Russian type of aeroplane and then saying that all Russian aerodromes and factories were in German hands and they were turning them out rapidly, so rapidly in fact that America has now disappointed us in the small number she is producing and we have no hope of holding the enemy in the air. We think we are going well and it is a curse for newspapers to break their soldiers' hearts like this.

May 2: I got blown away with a section of a trench some days ago, but although my back has been stiff and sore, I didn't expect it to develop into trouble.

May 5: The doctor has marked me down for England. 'Osteo-arthritis of the lumbar vertebrae.' Just what that means I don't quite know, but it only requires rest and treatment they say.

May 6: I am going across to 'Blighty' today. Arrived at Charing Cross and motored out to 3rd LGH.

May 8: There is a rumpus in the House of Commons over General Maurice's letter stating that Lloyd George told lies concerning the strength of the British Army in France and other military facts. Now there is going to be days wasted in the House discussing a 'no confidence' motion and the countries' honour at stake on the battle field can go to pot until they have settled the political dispute and discouraged millions of people. It's an awful scandal, and if General Maurice is not punished for his treachery it will be a greater scandal. I expect nothing to be the outcome. These Englishmen beat the world for sham and waste. If they win the war it is a thousand times more than they deserve.

May 30: I do not feel inclined to go far away from the Hospital today as my back is not well. I underwent a new form of massage treatment today. Electric bath, electricity and rubbing.

May 31: General Charlie Ryan sent me for a Board examination on Monday and talks of Australia for me. That will do alright providing I can get off at South Africa for a few days.

EPILOGUE

Tom Richards never got over the war. It plagued his body, poisoned his thoughts. Eventually, it killed him.

He was scarred, but not as bad as some. Another serving Wallaby, 1908 tourist Darb Hickey, was so disillusioned about what he had endured that on returning from the front he hurled his war medals into Sydney Harbour. Most soldiers, on being too badly injured or unwell to return to the battle-field, took the quickest route home. Richards, however, took six months, travelling via Cape Town, Johannesburg, Victoria Falls, Stellenbosch and Bloemfontein. When peace was declared, in November 1918, he was in Pretoria.

Three months later, he was striding down the Corso at Manly, having been coaxed into coaching the local football side. He also became head of the employment section at the New South Wales Repatriation Department. He attempted to put some sanity back into his life, which included trying to revive old love affairs. However, he struggled to stand up straight, due to his back complaint, and was morose, serious and standoffish after his war experiences. He had aged appreciably. But in those moments when he overcame his dark moods and allowed himself to blossom, he remained a striking figure, still regarded as one of the most handsome gentlemen in the Manly area.

Never short of female company, Richards became particularly attracted to a striking blonde, seductive woman, Lillian Sandow, who caught the same ferry as he did every weekday morning, from Manly Pier to Sydney's Circular Quay. She was impossible to ignore. She was also everything that Richards wasn't: outgoing, boisterous, vivacious. After numerous ferry rides during which they cast quick glances at each other, Richards built up the courage to speak to her. She responded straight away: yes, of course she knew exactly who he was, and of course she would like to go to the theatre with him, and even maybe walk around Manly with him.

Richards was smitten, but he didn't know what he was becoming involved with. Lil was outrageous, revelling in the Sydney high life. She played cards for money, went to the races and was constantly heading off to a party. He was a loner. She was gregarious. He was fastidious and methodical. She just went with the breeze. He was moralistic, often a pain in the neck with his stern, rigid views of life. She didn't give a damn. She constantly astounded him. He constantly forgave her, calling her his 'Snow White'. She was a reminder of everything that was marvellous about life, and a marked change from the turmoil he had just experienced. Lil revitalised Richards, and he enjoyed her uncontrollable nature and the vibrancy she brought to his too ordered life. And she certainly knew how to shock him, particularly late in 1920, when she declared she would not be able to see him for awhile. She was actually engaged to someone else, Cornelius (Alec) Haley, a local barrister. Haley, who was 23 years older than Lil, had used the wealth from his deceased father's estate to court the impressionable young woman. If the news of this engagement was not a big enough shock, the following week Lil informed Richards that she had secretly married Haley and that they were now living together. An official wedding was later organised so that members of Haley's family could attend, but just before the marriage took place the groom became ill at a private hotel in Manly. Three days later he was dead.

Richards, overwhelmed by this bewildering series of events, fled. Deeply depressed, he resigned from the Repatriation Department and went walkabout, heading for far-flung parts of New South Wales in a bid to forget everything. For a time, he occupied himself by working in an axe factory in Newcastle. Then he found work on a fishing trawler off Eden, followed by a stint at the Christmas Gift goldmine at Cootamundra. Three months later, a shortage of funds took him back to Manly.

Lil, now a free woman, was waiting for him. In 1922 they married, and they had two children: Jim, born in 1923, and Joan, born two years later. But the marriage soon degenerated into a volatile partnership. They were destined to clash. Joan later said:

> Daddy was very earnest, and always wanted to better himself, whereas Mother was looking for the gay, bright lights. She wanted to go to the races, gamble, play cards, go to parties, and have a good time. He didn't like that. They obviously weren't really going to get on.
>
> But he thought she was wonderful, divine, and gorgeous. And she was. Daddy was gorgeous too . . . everyone thought that. Women were always swooping, hovering around him, talking to him, and fussing over him, and Mother hated that. She liked being the kingpin.

Adding to the tension was constant financial pressure. Lil would spend money as soon as she had it, and Richards could not police it, because, finding the only occupation that satisfied his wandering nature was as a travelling salesman, he was often away for weeks on end. Soon their marriage was a marriage in name only.

Richards's war experiences, especially those in France, began to haunt him. His back ached constantly, not helped by long trips negotiating the primitive, bumpy back roads of country New South Wales. In the mid 1920s his rasping cough returned, forcing him to spend three weeks in the Royal Prince Alfred Hospital. Later tests revealed that he had tuberculosis and that, as he put it, 'the gas I swallowed during the war is beating me down steadily'.

Then Lil left him, taking the children with her to Melbourne. Richards was bereft and had, in his words, a 'complete breakdown'. Unable to trace his family and worried that 'the gas will beat me', he decided to occupy himself with 'reading and writing'. His chief exercise was in writing a series of lucid, entertaining and colourful articles about his football career for *The Sydney Mail*. The series enabled him to pay some bills, but he was never far from broke. He didn't even have enough money to attend his battalion officers' reunion in 1931—a situation which deeply embarrassed him.

A trip to New Guinea to write a series for *The Sydney Mail* about a 'land of gold, stone age customs and daring flying men' didn't help: he contracted malaria. While recovering in the Lady Davidson Hospital in Turramurra, on Sydney's North Shore, he was told he had six months to live. Alone, living on a meagre pension and wasting away, he somehow summoned the strength and courage to travel to Melbourne, to throw himself on the mercy of his estranged wife.

Lil was aghast at what she saw on her doorstep. This once proud, stout, statuesque figure was doubled over, gasping for air, desperately hanging on to the side verandah railing to keep his balance. His clothes were too big for him, his eyes cloudy, his hair patchy, his demeanour sad. He had aged twenty years. Richards pleaded: 'I know you hate the sight of me. But I would appreciate if for the final months of my life, my wife and children are with me. Then I will never trouble you again. I do not want to die alone.'

That night, when the children returned from school, they were staggered to see their father sitting in the living room. Lil announced: 'We're going . . . We're packing up and going with Daddy.'

The family moved to the Blue Mountains near Sydney in the hope that the rarefied air would help Richards's breathing. It worked: within months, he had improved. 'Mummy brought him back to life,' Joan said. It was believed that the warmer Queensland climate would be still more advantageous, so, after ten months in the mountains, in April 1935 the family crammed in to their second-hand Hupmobile for the five-day drive north to Brisbane. They moved into a bungalow in Ascot, and for some weeks Richards continued to brighten. However, by July, he was too weak to stay at home. He recorded that his doctors had told him that 'my case is now well advanced and the odds of living very long seem short, but I will fight to the finish'. He was admitted to Rosemount Hospital, his constant companion now an oxygen mask.

Richards died on September 25, 1935, content that his family were around him. To his final day he kept writing, trying to put his emotions into words. Knowing that death was imminent, he sent off letters to an assortment of friends. One read: 'Don't be sorry or sympathetic. I have no requests or regrets, and have well fortified myself so that I can still smile and play to the whistle.' At last he was at peace with himself.